# Liberty and Love

Peter Malekin has been a lecturer in English at the University of Durham since 1965. Before that, he taught at the universities of Tübingen, Baghdad and Uppsala. He has experience of broadcasting, has worked as a translator, and has done a great deal of public speaking in England and Ireland. His interests include mysticism, approached non-denominationally as a phenomenon of the human mind. His wife is Swedish and they have a large family.

# Liberty and Love
English Literature and Society 1640–88

## Peter Malekin
*Lecturer in English, University of Durham*

Hutchinson

London Melbourne Sydney Auckland Johannesburg

Hutchinson & Co. (Publishers) Ltd
An imprint of the Hutchinson Publishing Group
24 Highbury Crescent, London N5 1RX

Hutchinson Group (Australia) Pty Ltd
30–32 Cremorne Street, Richmond South, Victoria 3121
PO Box 151, Broadway, New South Wales 2007

Hutchinson Group (NZ) Ltd
32–34 View Road, PO Box 40–086, Glenfield, Auckland 10

Hutchinson Group (SA) (Pty) Ltd
PO Box 337, Bergvlei 2012, South Africa

First published 1981

Set in English Times by T. J. Press (Padstow) Ltd

Printed in Great Britain by The Anchor Press Ltd
and bound by Wm Brendon & Son Ltd
both of Tiptree, Essex

**British Library Cataloguing in Publication Data**

Malekin, Peter
  Liberty and love.
  1. Constitutions in literature
  2. English literature—17th century—History and criticism
  3. Women in literature
  I. Title
  820'.9'355      PR439.C6

ISBN 0 09 143040 2 cased
     0 09 143041 0 paper

# Contents

*To Mid*

Der Leser soll wissen, dass in Jah und Nein alle Dinge bestehen, es sey Göttlich, Teuflisch, Irdisch, oder was genant mag werden. Das Eine, als das Jah ist eitel Kraft und Leben . . . [doch] wäre in sich [selbst] unerkentlich, und wäre darinnen keine Freude oder Erheblichkeit, noch Empfindlichkeit ohne das Nein . . . Und können doch nicht sagen, dass das Jah vom Nein abgesondert, und zwey Dinge neben einander sind, sondern sie sind nur Ein Ding.

(The reader should know, that in Yes and No all things consist, be they divine, devilish, earthly, or whatever may be named. The One, that is the Yes, is pure power and life . . . yet [it] would be unknowable in [itself], and there would be in it neither joy nor exaltation nor feeling without the No . . . And yet we cannot say that the Yes is divided off from the No and that they are two things next to each other, but instead they are only one thing.)

JACOB BOEHME

# Preface

The seventeenth century was the period in which our modern world struggled into birth, and it is therefore inherently of interest to us: I hope I may have avoided killing out the life in an interesting subject. The book is aimed at the energetic and intelligent general rather than specialist reader, though I have relied heavily on specialists in writing it. I would like to acknowledge my debt to the historians and social historians who have been producing so much work of excellence on the period, and to the numerous literary critics and scholars, for it is not always practical to acknowledge or even possible to remember the source of every detailed insight originally suggested by others.

I have tried to prune the notes as far as possible, giving titles of relevant works in a list of further reading. References to poems have usually been by title and line numbers only, immediately after the quotation; this seemed a sensible arrangement, since the work of many poets occurs in more than one respectable edition. Similarly, short prose works have been referred to by title only. Citations from long works would, however, be difficult to locate, and in this case I have succumbed to a note with fuller information. In quotations from plays speech headings have been standardized and stage directions within completed square brackets are additions (all those with only the opening bracket are in the original).

I would like to express my thanks to Raymond Williams for his help in having my manuscript read by two specialists at Cambridge; many of their comments were extremely shrewd and helpful. I would also like to thank Claire L'Enfant of Hutchinson for coaxing the work to the press; the University of Durham for granting a sabbatical term for the completion of the book; the library staff at Durham, to whom I have frequently turned for help; Laura and Lee for the typing of an illegible manuscript; and Clare Robinson for preparing the index.

Finally I would like to express my gratitude to my wife for her support and care during the writing of the book, and to my family for putting up with an author in the house.

# Introduction

> *Johnson.* We must consider how very little history there is; I mean real authentick history. That certain Kings reigned, and certain battles were fought, we can depend upon as true; but all the colouring, all the philosophy, of history is conjecture.
>
> *Boswell.* Then, Sir, you would reduce all history to no better than an almanack, a mere chronological series of remarkable events.
>
> BOSWELL, Life of Johnson ('Tuesday, 18 April 1775')

History, by itself, is a gloomy subject. It recalls Gibbon's remark on Antoninus: 'His reign is marked by the rare advantage of furnishing very few materials for history; which is, indeed, little more than the register of the crimes, follies, and misfortunes of mankind.'[1]• A modern historian would doubtless disagree, feeling that history has taken giant strides since Gibbon's day, though a glance at the history in which we ourselves happen to be living makes Gibbon's observation appear uncomfortably accurate. Why then link literature with history? An obvious answer is that history is not something that we can escape – we are ourselves part of it whether we will or no – while literature, also a part of history, has equally a history of its own that helps to make it what it is. If you are trapped in a net it is best to try to understand what a net is, how it functions, and what part of you remains outside it so that you can feel 'trapped'; in other words you need both a theory of nets and a theory of yourself – one implies the other and one without the other is as useless as a table with two legs. A philosophy of history is half of a theory of nets, mere conjecture Johnson would have us believe, but mere conjecture is better than none. (Johnson indeed had his own theory of history, implicit in his religious and moral beliefs, and he may even have feared an explicitness in history that might have forced him to justify the beliefs he preferred to take for granted.) To relate literature to history is valuable, because it is to relate it to human nature and to human

---

*Superior figures refer to the Notes and references on pages 201 – 8.

life. But history must then be taken in its widest sense and not com-partmentalized. The older kind of history – kings, battles and Acts of Parliament – is now out of fashion, though it had its own validity, and attention has been largely shifted to economic and technological change, demography and social conditions. For a man who meddles with literature this is no bad thing, for it opens up new access to the quality of life in the past. It is the environment of a writer that gives him a form and an audience, or permits him to develop a form and anticipate an audience. The quality of life is also the material on which his sensibility operates: the greater the understanding we can have of it, the greater our understanding of the literature. Nevertheless the development and use of new types of history does not obviate either the need for or the limitations of a philosophy of history. Certain parts of the methodology of history have become 'scientific' in the sense that limited hypotheses can be tested against empirical data by statistical investigation, but there is no overall theory of historical causation that can be established by this kind of investigation, and in the broadest sense there is no scientific history. This is a point which may seem obvious to some, but has particular relevance to the use of history made by critics of literature.

Critics of literature have tended to take their own fundamental presuppositions for granted. The older, moralistic school of critics in England, stemming largely from Leavis, usually did so, and moralistic criticism has generally tended to assume confidently a consensus on right and wrong. Most of the literature of the later seventeenth century deliberately set out to subvert and question this kind of consensus, and to approach this literature with a modern normative social paradigm in mind is to produce such intelligent absurdities as Holland's analysis of Wycherley in pursuit of a right-way/wrong-way dichotomy in marriage (one of Wycherley's subor-dinate points is that there is no single 'right way' in such matters) and Paul C. Davies's unlikely hypothesis that the Earl of Rochester is the spokesman of restraint and decorum.[2] In this respect older criticism, such as C. S. Lewis on *Paradise Lost*, at least had the ad-vantage of stating its premises, even though it might try to bludgeon the reader into accepting them by an assumption of establishment superiority. It is to the honour of the Marxist critics that they have insisted that all criticism must imply an ideology – in the sense of emotional attitudes and evaluative assumptions that imply a view of life, however incoherent – and that an ideology must involve an evaluation of history. However, they seem keener on questioning the ideologies of others than on having their own subjected to scrutiny. Their assumption that all ideologies but their own stem from class allegiance is unproven and they tend to take their own ideology very much for granted.

The relationship between criticism, underlying ideology, and the interpretation of history is particularly relevant to seventeenth-century English literature, because of the historical change in that century of crisis, and because the nature of the change has made it a focus of Marxist interest. Marxist historians, through their very sympathy with revolutionary movements, have contributed invaluable insights into the state of England in the seventeenth century; but they have failed to demonstrate the presence of a class war or of the Marxist dialectic in the history of the period. Marxism's theory of history and economics is in fact fraught with difficulties. Marx forecast the millennium of the withering away of the state and the common ownership of the earth's resources, with a consequent limitation of personal property, as a result of an inevitable historical process; but the process began in an a-historical 'state of nature' marked by precisely such common ownership of the earth's resources. The argument concerning the nature of history builds in the conclusion *a priori*; a state of common ownership may be desirable, but cannot be assumed as 'natural'. In the more immediate area of historical observation the maintenance of the fictions of natural common ownership and the 'objectivity' of the process of historical necessity involves the creation of Marx's implausible objective theory of value, which denies value to natural things in themselves and attributes it only to manufactured artifacts on the basis of labour-time in their production, computed according to the technological norms of the period (this softens the obvious difficulties of the common ownership theory and attempts to eliminate subjectivity and associated market fluctuations from estimates of value). Even the valuable theory of alienation is questionable in its assumption that the root of alienation is solely in the productive system; alienation, or something very like it, seems to have occurred repeatedly in many cultures with many productive systems. The detailed strains and implausibilities of Marxist theory all ultimately arise from its view of the relationship of mind and matter. Within the historical process,

The basic position of Marx and Engels is . . . that the authority of delusions over human minds is not a result of mental distortion that can be cured by working upon the consciousness, but is rooted in social conditions and is only the intellectual expression of social servitude.[3]

Behind this lies the assumption that mind is entirely the product of matter, that there is no base for mind independent of the physical world. It is noticeable that even a Marxist-trained critic of Marxism like Leszek Kolakowski repeatedly returns to this basic point;

What can be said with truth is that in Marx's view personality is not a mere matter of self-experience on the lines of the *cogito ergo sum*, since there is no such thing as pure self-knowledge apart from consciousness of the social life in which the individual has his being.[4]

And again, when treating Marx's critique of Hegel:

The assumption of pure self-awareness as a starting-point rests on the fiction of a subject capable of apprehending itself altogether independently of its being in nature and society.[5]

However, this kind of self-awareness, which is fundamental to the philosophy of Plato and Plotinus (it is in fact very accurately described by Plotinus), is most certainly no fiction, and its existence is acknowledged in most of the major religious and philosophical traditions of the world. Here, for instance, is Arthur Waley in his introduction to the *Tao Tê Ching*, discussing its role in two of the thought systems of ancient China. The first is what he called the 'Quietists':

The process of Quietism, then, consisted in travelling back through the successive layers of consciousness to the point when one arrived at Pure Consciousness, where one no longer saw 'things perceived', but 'that whereby we perceive'. For never to have known 'that whereby we know' is to cast away a treasure that is ours. Soon on the 'way back' one comes to the point where language, created to meet the demands of ordinary, upper consciousness, no longer applies.[6]

The second is the system of Mencius, the author of the great Chinese classic on the nature of the mind:

Mencius's 'stilling of the mind' . . . led him to make a distinction between two kinds of knowledge, the one the result of mental activity, the other passive and as we should say 'intuitive'; and it is the second kind that he calls 'good knowledge'. Indeed, the whole of education consists, Mencius says, in recapturing intuitive faculties that in the stress of life have been allowed to go astray. With him these faculties are moral.[7]

While all this may at first seem a far cry from English literature, the presence of a similar strand in the major English tradition is apparent from the Wordsworthian ring of the second quotation, and awareness of this aspect and power of mind in the Western tradition goes back to Plotinus and Plato. Now the existence of such a condition of mind is one thing, and the interpretations that may be placed upon it are another, for it may be regarded as anything from a cognition of Reality – the position of Plotinus, and also Wordsworth in his great decade – to a neurologically induced illusion; but the mere fact that it exists reduces the basic assumption behind Marxism to its proper status as an assumption.[8] The fundamental question of the relationship between mind and matter is an open one. The Marxist version of history is no more 'scientific' and no less 'subjective' than anybody else's. Even in limited contexts it has no precise and testable predictive power; acceptance of its efficacy is nearer to the religious believer's acceptance of the efficacy of petitionary prayer: if the prayer is 'answered', this is taken to indicate its efficacy, and if it is not answered this is taken to indicate that it was not really desirable for the petitioner to get what he wanted. This does not, of course, prove that either petitionary prayer or Marxist theory is invalid; it merely points out that neither can claim to have been scientifically established. The true status of Marxist theory has been neatly summarized by Professor Kolakowski:

The idea that half a million years of man's life on earth and five thousand years of written history will suddenly culminate in a 'happy ending' is an expression of hope. Those who cherish this hope are not in a better intellectual position than others. Marx's faith in the 'end of prehistory' is not a scientist's theory but the exhortation of a prophet.[9]

Inevitably, therefore, any literary criticism based upon a Marxist interpretation of history is open to fundamental objection – and sometimes rejection.

The degree of attention demanded by Marxist theory in particular arises because Marxism is currently the only coherent worldview to be presented in literary criticism with much conviction, and its adherents, or those influenced by it, have produced lively, interesting and incisive work. Nevertheless, the Marxist dialectic of history is often slipped into such work as irrefutable fact. The Marxist position can both stimulate and arbitrarily limit powerful literary insight.

In Marxist criticism the view of history usually controls the single act of literary judgement; but no apparently isolated and independent judgement can escape the implication of a view of history and an interpretation of the nature of the human mind. These factors in their turn imply at least a rudimentary theory of aesthetics and a scale of literary values, and give meaning to the terminology of criticism. In aesthetics and literary judgement the nature of the human mind would seem indisputably the fundamental factor – a quality transcending time can, for instance, hardly be ascribed to art unless the human mind itself has the possibility of access to timelessness, and if the mind is thought of as confined entirely to time and place, then language too will be thought of as utterly limited by temporal and spatial context and meaning. It is not the main concern in the present work to elucidate such implications, but neither can they be entirely shirked.

In this consideration of the life and literature of the central seventeenth century a balance has been attempted, allowing historical context to illuminate literary work and vice versa. But this has necessitated concern with the basic questions of critical and historical ideology, and has meant ranging considerably beyond the central focus of the book – the two themes of the political constitution and woman's role in the family and the two dates mentioned in the title, 1640 and 1688. These themes are intended as a focus, not a boundary. The political philosophy of the seventeenth century was rooted in immediate practical concerns which cannot be understood without a historical grasp of changes that started long before. Its effect on the minor and major literature of the period and the relevance of both literature and philosophy to ourselves means connecting seventeenth-century experience with our own, which has in fact grown from it. Political philosophy and the organization of the family are linked not only by the explicit parallels drawn between the two at the time, but because a philosopher's first training in politics takes place as a child in a family, and a family involves questions of economics and, in the seventeenth century, religion. Beyond marking roughly the central period of crisis in the century the dates are arbitrary. 1640 is a suitable round number suggesting the lull between the Bishops' War and the opening of the Civil War proper, when political issues were coming to a military head. 1688, the year of the Glorious Revolution, conveniently marks the close of the most intensive period of political crisis.

These same years of revolution and its aftermath also mark the period of most open challenge to the older patterns of family and sexual life. While the extreme revolutionary tendencies were scotched in state and family alike, both institutions changed direction in this period and our mode of life was made possible by the new direction that was taken. There was in both the very hesitant beginning of an attempt to modify coercion by consent (and this was accompanied by an even more hesitant tendency to reassess ideas concerning the law of nature and man's relationship to it, with implications for the conceptualization of the authority of God), and by developments in the understanding of the human mind.

Just as the historical origins of state and family organization have been sketched in, and some of the consequences of the revolutionary years touched upon, so the literature also has been treated with chronological freedom. Estate poems by Jonson and Carew have been briefly discussed to provide a context for the political development of topographical poetry by Denham and the linking of this development to the emotional life and practical conditions of the time; the amorous poetry of Carew and Suckling has been discussed in the context of attitudes to sex and marriage in Caroline court circles, and Restoration comedy has been traced down to the beginning of the eighteenth century to show how the social rebelliousness and generation gap that mark the plays of Etherege and Wycherley was superceded by an acceptance of social hypocrisy as inevitable, and by the final snuffing out of any rebellious criticism of the pretences of official morality. An attempt has also been made to indicate in passing an undertow in seventeenth-century society, a muzzled but unextinguished opposition to establishment values, which found no direct expression in literature, but did exert some influence indirectly through the urbane irony of the high Augustans and was to re-emerge much later in a period of romanticism and revolutionary instinct, finding supreme expression in the work of Wordsworth and Blake.

References to Wordsworth and Blake have also been used to clarify features of the mind and sensibility of the seventeenth century which will become increasingly relevant to our own age. The central critical question of the coming decade or so will, in my judgement, be the nature of the human mind and the effect of literature upon it, not through the modification of ideas, but through the direct modification of the perceiving mind itself, through the alteration of the subjective mode of awareness. Moves in this direction are already taking place, for instance in the emphasis on creative response in the criticism of Wolfgang Iser, but they will go much further.[10] This is part of a general shift in many fields towards a belated recognition of the importance of the human mind as a shaping factor in the processes of human life.

Noam Chomsky's ideas have opened up argument on this area in linguistics, and an economic historian like Peter Mathias can begin to acknowledge the importance of psychological factors in industrial and economic history (dare one hope for the eventual emergence of an ecological science of psycho-economics which will measure GNP in terms of the production of human happiness instead of manufactured artifacts?).[11] Eventually Western psychology will also have to broaden its concept of the human mind, as well as revise its assessment of the possible modes of communication between mind and mind. By that time a new synthesis of knowledge should be possible, with some general consensus about the nature, role and value of literature. Until the 'objectivity' of a shared subjective interpretation is reattained, literary criticism must content itself with being overtly and personally subjective.

In the last resort people are the most interesting – and infuriating – facts. It is hoped that the subjective element in this book may add to rather than detract from its interest. It contains a number of new glances at old faces; at Milton's less conventional aspects; at Dryden, who has always risked becoming a dead classic; at Restoration comedy, which has had such a rough press for all the wrong reasons since its own day – although it has never proved incapable of provoking prejudice, which, if I am right about its nature, would have pleased its creators. The major works discussed are central to the development of English literature, the minor ones relate to the two selected themes. Major works like *The Pilgrim's Progress* which did not relate to these themes have not been discussed. Pepys has also been omitted, perhaps wrongly, but he did not constitute part of the public literature of the seventeenth century itself, and his comments on marriage and life in the period have been absorbed as part of the source material of social history. In the discussion of marriage the relationship between the parents has received greater emphasis than the treatment of children, partly because changes in the latter stemmed from changes in the former, partly because relationships of marriage and love figure far more prominently in a literature written by adults and designed for an adult audience. The themes of the family and state have been placed side by side, or one after the other, without the parallels between the two being laboured. The similarity of the changes in the attitudes to monarchical authority in the one and paternal and husbandly authority in the other is obvious, but there was no simple cause-and-effect relationship between the two. While the two are so intimately linked, to have attempted to place them both in a single field of causation would have meant the flooding of light into those dark areas of common human ignorance that have been discussed in this introduction. The aim of this book is to ask and imply questions and to keep issues open, not to provide answers where none are as yet to be found. To leave the links tentative and call upon the constructive and inductive powers of the reader seemed both more stimulating and truer to that state of ignorance which we are pleased to call the present state of knowledge. My own implied values and views have been left latent in the body of the book, though they are there to see for those who choose to look. In holding them it is my conviction that I have the tide of history on my side; whether I am right, time alone will tell.

# Abbreviations

| | |
|---|---|
| *BSDWE* | *The Dramatic Works of Sir George Etherege,* ed. H. F. B. Brett-Smith (2 vols., Oxford: Blackwell 1927) |
| *CP* | *The Clarke Papers,* ed. C. H. Firth (Camden Society 1891), vol. 1 |
| *DCPC* | *The Complete Plays of William Congreve,* ed. Hubert Davis (University of Chicago Press 1967) |
| *ECK* | Alan Everitt, *The Community of Kent and the Great Rebellion, 1640-60* (Leicester University Press 1966) |
| *ELH* | *Journal of English Literary History* |
| *GLLEC* | M. Dorothy George, *London Life in the Eighteenth Century* (Penguin 1966; first published 1925) |
| *HCC* | Christopher Hill, *Change and Continuity in Seventeenth Century England* (Weidenfeld and Nicolson 1974) |
| *HLQ* | *Huntingdon Library Quarterly* |
| *HMER* | Christopher Hill, *Milton and the English Revolution* (Faber 1977) |
| *HWTUD* | Christopher Hill, *The World Turned Upside Down: Radical Ideas During the English Revolution* (Penguin 1975; first published 1972) |
| *LFLIL* | Peter Laslett, *Family Life and Illicit Love in Earlier Generations* (Cambridge University Press 1977) |
| *LWWL* | Peter Laslett, *The World We Have Lost,* 2nd ed. (Methuen 1971) |
| *POAS* | *Poems on Affairs of State,* vol.1: *1660-1678,* ed. G. de Forest Lord (Yale University Press 1963); vol.2: *1678 – 1681,* ed. E. F. Mengel, Jr. (1965); vol.3: *1682 – 1685,* ed. H. H. Schless (1968) |
| *SFSM* | Lawrence Stone, *The Family, Sex and Marriage in England, 1500-1800* (Weidenfeld and Nicolson 1977) |
| *SPF* | Levin L. Schücking, *The Puritan Family: A Social Study from the Literary Sources* (Routledge & |

|        | Kegan Paul 1969; original German ed. 1929, rev. ed. 1964) |
|--------|-----------|
| *SWS*  | *The Complete Works of Thomas Shadwell*, ed. M. Summers (5 vols., Fortune Press 1927) |
| *TRDM* | Keith Thomas, *Religion and the Decline of Magic* (Weidenfeld and Nicolson 1971) |
| *WPH*  | E. A. Wrigley, *Population and History* (Weidenfeld and Nicolson 1969) |
| *WPW*  | *The Complete Plays of William Wycherley*, ed. G. Weales (University of London Press 1967) |

# Part One
# Sweet Land of Liberty

The tree of liberty must be refreshed from time to time with the blood of patriots and tyrants. It is its natural manure.

THOMAS JEFFERSON

# 1 Prologue: Jacobean and Caroline political trends

Heraclitus remarked: 'You cannot put your foot in the same stream twice'; a disciple is said to have answered, 'You cannot put your foot in the same stream once.' The stream of seventeenth-century English history is now a figure on a map; for those alive at the time it was moving in spate, carrying them along helpless, sometimes bewildered, often alarmed. The modern historian looks back and analyses past events according to notions of historical causation current now. In imposing his own frame of reference he claims greater accuracy, fullness, objectivity and understanding than the seventeenth century itself possessed. Perhaps he is right; but he certainly alters, possibly falsifies, the experience of the period in the process, and if he is not right, he may turn out to have written a history of the twentieth century thinly disguised.

With the wisdom of our own unsolved problems we are aware of the inflation, bureaucratic control and social malaise of England in the earlier seventeenth century. In the Tudor period prices in England had risen fivefold, and they went on rising until about 1650. Rents, which had provided most of the income of the landed aristocracy, did not rise proportionately, and supplementary income was sought from investment in trade, piracy, manufacture or the more time-honoured road of court preferment. The courtier, angling for preferment, required the gambling spirit of an entrepreneur, poising the costs of maintaining a figure at court against uncertain hopes of future gain. Office once obtained, its tenure remained precarious and some quick profit was to be looked for by a prudent man, whether from the fees of office, the sale of influence, the disposal of subordinate positions or perhaps the sale of his own position to the next comer. These accepted practices were hardly discouraged by a royal master, who not only sold knighthoods himself, but on occasion paid bills by delegating to the creditor the right to sell a knighthood on his behalf, as well as the trouble of finding a buyer. Power lies partly in the opinion of others that we have it, and those in the ascendant in King James I's reign bought land, a durable investment, and laid out lavish sums on the erection or renovation of imposing houses around London, houses where the king himself, the fount of preferment, might deign to stay. At the opposite end of the social order many of the 'masterless men' had been dispossessed of their ancient homes in forest clearing or marshland by the remorseless progress of deforestation, land enclosure and fen drainage. The pressures of growing population and prolonged inflation were increased by the failure of agricultural output to rise correspondingly. Sturdy beggars and landless poor became features of the Jacobean landscape, physical, political and imaginative.[1]

As the economy of the country had become unbalanced, so had religious dissension inexorably increased. During the sixteenth century waves of Protestant refugees had fled from Catholic persecution on the Continent and settled in the eastern counties that were to become the strongholds of Parliamentary support in the Civil War. They brought with them their trades and their Bibles, and they made their way by dint of industry in an alien land. The soil of England was a refuge from which they won a home by their own efforts; they owed nothing to the traditional hierarchies of the land, or to the hierarchies of the half-reformed Church of England, for they sought direct commerce with God by consulting His written word and their own hearts, no spiritual middleman between. King James, called upon to rule this heterogeneous people, was himself a foreigner, who had arrived on the throne of England late in life, ignorant of English ways and drunk with the heady ideals of Renaissance kingship. Aware of accountability to God, he was not equally aware of his practical responsibility to, as well as for, his people. He chose to discontinue the royal progresses which had formed part of Queen Elizabeth's publicity operations. His remark 'No bishop, no king' evidences his awareness of the tremors threatening the traditional order of things: however, his pursuit of national unity was un-singleminded enough for him to die in his bed.

James's son, Charles, inherited some of his father's predispositions. A shy withdrawn youth, he unexpectedly became heir to the throne on the death of his successful and greatly admired elder brother. Idealistic, introverted, genuinely religious, he remained isolated from many of his own courtiers as well as from the people at large. While generally intransigent, he would give way to weakness and vacillation when in a tight corner. As he attempted to govern with the full prerogatives of the Crown and to use his God-given authority to impose religious uniformity upon the rebellious consciences of his subjects, he succeeded only in alienating the court from the city and much of the country. His high Anglican religion, redolent of popery, his Catholic wife, his reserve, his autocratic leanings and tendency to seek the comforting support of some special favourite all worked against him in his lifetime. His artistic taste, which led him to form the great collection of paintings that Cromwell later sold, found an outlet in the royal emblazonry of the court masques, whose transient splendour carried a message of regal glory to some of his courtiers and of extravagant waste to others. Combined with his religious sense, his artistic and dramatic instincts eventually led to his noble behaviour on the scaffold, outside the windows of his own banqueting hall, and this in turn, taken together with his private virtues as a father and a husband, led to the surprisingly powerful symbol of Charles, the royal martyr.

The cult of the royal martyr made most sense when society had settled again, however uneasily, later in the century. In Charles's lifetime the forefront of awareness was occupied by the shockingly successful onslaughts on all that had previously been taken for granted. Nowadays there is a tendency to regard the religious and political conflicts of the seventeenth century as basically economic. In the seventeenth century there was a tendency to see economics, and to some extent politics, as basically religious. The onslaught on the king's power and the abandonment of traditional constitutional norms during the interregnum led to a questioning of the nature of kingship, the basis of political power, the foundations of the social order, the validity of religious institutions and the nature of man himself. As opinion divides against opinion on all these issues, there is a fragmentation of vision, and yet underlying it all there is some unity. The nature of man decides his relationship with cosmos and Creator, of which relationship religion is an expression and economics are an effect, while the events of history spell out the relationship upon the page of time. It is the combination of questioning and wholeness that makes the peculiar excitement of the seventeenth century, and it enabled many who were not solely or primarily writers to produce works from passing occasions that rise to the dignity of literature. The works that are the subject of Part One of this book concentrate upon the central political issue of the seventeenth century, the nature of the constitution, not viewed as a practical question empirically considered for practical ends, but rather felt as an expression of all the groping intuitions of men about their own nature and their relationship with time and to eternity.

# 2 Denham's 'Cooper's Hill' and the constitution: a royalist viewpoint

Apart from being cuckolded by the Duke of York later in life, Denham has no great claim to historical renown. As a writer, however, he is now decidedly underrated, for he has the unfashionable virtues of lucidity and charm. Morally and politically he was a moderate traditionalist, and he conceived of virtue in both public and private life as an Aristotelian golden mean between vicious extremes. It was in these terms that he praised Sir George Croke, a judge of the King's bench, who had resisted pressure by the king (the 'highest Mover') and found for John Hampden against the Crown on the question of the legality of ship money, while at the same time remaining a faithful royalist:

Who saw him on the Bench would think the name
Of Friendship or Affection never came
Within his thoughts: who saw him thence might know
He never had nor could deserve a Foe;
Only assuming Rigor with his Gown,
And with his Purple laid his Rigor down.
Him nor Respect nor Disrespect could move;
He Knew no Anger, nor his Place no Love.
So mixd the Stream of all his Actions ran,
So much a Judge so much a Gentleman;
Who durst be just when justice was a crime,
Yet durst no more even in too just a Time;
Not hurried by the highest Movers force
Against his proper and resolved course;
But when our World did turn, so kept his Ground
He seemed the Axe on which the Wheel went round.
Whose Zeal was warm when all to Ice did turn,
Yet was but warm when all the World did burn.
No ague in Religion eer inclin'd
To this or that Extream his fixed Mind.
    ['Elegy on the Death of Judge Croke', ll. 17 – 36]

Typically, Denham seeks proof of Sir George's fixed integrity of mind in the moving 'stream' of his actions, a stream he calls 'mixt', while making the point that the judge and private man were kept unmixed, separate, a series of contradictions that he finally synthesizes in the image of the moving wheel, the circle of perfection, turning upon the still axle at its centre. What is lacking to the passage and the images, is a sense of a dimension transcending the logical dichotomies, of unity underlying duality; instead opposites are counterpoised and stasis is achieved within duality by an act of will. This gives a prosaic and unresonant quality to the lines, though within their limitations they remain admirable.

To hold the middle ground by an act of will is a traditional Aristotelian conception, virtue being defined in the *Nicomachean Ethics* as a disposition of the will. The view of individual virtue as the golden mean went with a political attitude that sought a middle ground between the tyranny of absolute monarchy and the anarchy of government by the people, or rather by Parliament, which represented only a small part of the people. The middle ground in a time of shifting and violent conflict was, however, difficult to find and to maintain; in consequence moderates in opposing parties often had more sympathy with each other than with the extremists of their own sides. Indeed, the moderates not infrequently changed sides in an uneasy search for something approximating to their own position (the Earls of Strafford and Shaftesbury as well as the poet Marvell were among the many men, since famous, who changed sides, sometimes repeatedly). To many at its outset the Civil War seemed a limited rebellion, an attempt at readjustment within the accepted social order. It became, however, a revolution, leading to the abolition of the House of Lords, the abolition of bishops, the appointment of Puritan clergy under the auspices of the Commons, and eventually the trial and execution of the king himself. As the process gathered momentum, the old order, once taken for granted, was increasingly in need of defence or justification. Adherence to the traditional constitution represented more than an abstract intellectual position; it represented a whole way of life, a system of values, a way of feeling. Denham's 'Cooper's Hill' attempts to catch the value of this way of life and, in the earlier version of the poem begun about 1642, to bolster the passing order before it is irrevocably destroyed. The basic text was revised a number of times, and to some extent recast after the death of the king. It is with the final version of the poem, the B text in Professor

O'Hehir's edition of the work, that we will be primarily concerned here.[1]

'Cooper's Hill' is a topographical poem, ostensibly a description of a stretch of the Thames, with Cooper's Hill, Windsor Castle, the ruins of Chertsey Abbey and the meadows of Runnymede beside it. As descriptive topography it has classical precedents in the *Mosella* of Decimus Magnus Ausonius (AD 371) on the valley of the Moselle, the *De reditu suo* of Rutilius Claudius Namatianus (*c.* AD 417) on a voyage from Rome to Gaul, and various other extant poems.[2] It also has, as Professor O'Hehir points out, affiliations with Georgic poetry in its linking of politics with rural concerns, but in its immediate context it is an extension of the genre of poetry on country houses instanced by Jonson's 'To Penshurst' and Carew's '*To my Friend* G. N. *from* Wrest'. A building is nowadays defined by its function; a house is accordingly a box to live in, and looks it. The seventeenth century had inherited from the Middle Ages a sense that the symbolic significance should relate the building and its occupants to the whole order of creation. It had therefore been easy for Jonson to see in Penshurst a symbol for social and natural harmony:

The painted partrich lyes in every field,
And, for thy messe, is willing to be kill'd . . .
The blushing apricot, and woolly peach
Hang on thy walls, that every child may reach.
And though thy walls be of the countrey stone,
They're rear'd with no mans ruine, no mans grone,
There's none, that dwell about them, wish them downe;
But all come in, the farmer, and the clowne:
And no one empty-handed, to salute
Thy lord, and lady, though they have no sute.
     [ll. 29 – 50]

This is, of course, playful pastoral make-believe, but it does epitomize Jonson's sense of what things should be like, of the relationship that should exist between the different orders of English society. The poem specifically mentions and attempts to harmonize all the strata of English society, from King James to the peasantry, and Penshurst, built in native stone, can serve as an admonition to more modern aristocratic builders, whose mansions of luxurious imported stones could symbolize an individual and heartless success.[3] Carew's '*To my friend* G. N. *from* Wrest' echoed Jonson's poem in many details. It was probably written in 1639, after the agreement on peace terms with the Scottish Covenanters at Berwick. This campaign against the Covenanters proved to be the opening skirmish in the Civil War and was, in fact, the culmination of a series of blunders. Charles had already misconducted a war with Spain and slithered into a war with France, in which his favourite, the Duke of Buckingham, had signally failed to be of practical assistance to the Protestant Huguenots, and the king had, moreover, aroused grave misgivings at home by giving leading ecclesiastical positions to high churchmen of suspected Papist leanings and by treating the Roman Catholics with humanity. All this he had capped by his attempt to thrust the Anglican prayer book on the Kirk, thus sparking off the rising of the Covenanters. Faced with this, Carew is less confident of the social implications of Wrest. The house is praised in contrast to the rigours of the northern climate in the opening sequence, and G. N.'s hunting is contrasted with war in the closing remarks. Wrest itself is praised for its 'useful comeliness' and its owners' preference for hospitality rather than architectural ostentation:

> *Amalthea's* Horne
> Of plentie is not in Effigie worne
> Without the gate, but she within the dore
> Empties her free and unexhausted store.
> Nor, croun'd with wheaten wreathes, doth *Ceres* stand
> In stone, with a crook'd sickle in her hand:
> Nor, croun'd with wheaten wreathes, doth *Ceres* stand
> With grapes, is curl'd uncizard *Bacchus* rear'd.
> We offer not in Emblemes to the eyes,
> But to the taste those useful Deities.
> Wee presse the juicie God, and quaffe his blood,
> And grinde the Yeallow Goddesse into food.
>     [ll. 57 – 68]

The emphasis on hospitality and on the combination of usefulness and beauty in the layout of the estate is almost eighteenth-century in feel, but the poem celebrates the private way of life of the estate owner, without confidently treating his relationship with society as a whole as Jonson had done. The estate is not regarded as simply a retreat from the world; on the other hand, the political precariousness of the envisaged way of life is firmly ignored.

Carew at the end of his life (he died in 1640) could afford to ignore ugly political issues. Denham, starting 'Cooper's Hill' in 1642, could not. It was no longer possible to do what Jonson had done (treat one building or estate, taking its proper symbolic relationship with the social landscape for granted), and the violent hurry of decisive action rendered untimely the poetry of rural retreat. Yet a traditionalist's sense of the constitution of England as a natural growth would find congenial expression in the relationship, especially the harmonious relationship, between old-established buildings and landscape. It was a stroke of inventive genius on Denham's part to pick upon the Thames valley, its natural features adorned by man, as the setting of his poem. The great buildings visible from Cooper's Hill were associated by history and purpose with the constitution and social ordering of England, and the link between the landscape and human edifices expressed a fundamental link between the divine ordering of nature and the sound ordering of society that was not lost sight of until the nineteenth century. When the Victorians saw nature, red in tooth and claw, as the savage competition of Darwinian evolution, they saw it in terms of the ruthless economic competition of their own society, in which technological industry had gained importance at the expense of landowning and the more traditional forms of commerce. This Victorian view stands between us and Denham's poem, for modern attitudes, whether capitalist or Marxist, are dominated by the Victorian experience. To the seventeenth and eighteenth centuries the main characteristic of nature was balance, the wise, intelligent ordering of the whole, a view that has partially returned in the conceptions of modern ecology, though the balance earlier perceived was static, whereas now it is dynamic. The landscape of 'Cooper's Hill' is aesthetically balanced, while the relationship between the Thames and the agriculture on its banks is economically balanced; moreover, the main features of the landscape mirror the main elements which should be balanced in the state, Windsor being associated with the king, Chertsey with the afflicted Church of England, Runnymede with Magna Charta and the guaranteed liberty of the subject, and the Thames with trade and the financial power of the City.

In the later drafts of the poem (the B text and the final version of the A text) Denham proceeds directly from a very brief introduction to commentary on St Paul's Cathedral. This was a particularly suitable start. The old spired St Paul's, later destroyed in the Great Fire, was a traditional religious building in the midst of a city already associated with Puritanism, finance and Parliamentarian opposition. The building had, in addition, fallen into decay and been repaired on the orders of the king, and the event had been celebrated by Waller, whose name was later to be repeatedly linked with Denham's in celebrations of the twin 'reformers of English numbers', for the two men shared aesthetic as well as political ideals. Contrasted with the harmonious height of St Paul's, the City is reduced to a mere scurry of money-getting, a place which

Seems at this distance but a darker cloud:
And is to him who rightly things esteems,
No other in effect than what it seems:
Where, with like hast, though several ways, they run
Some to undo, and some to be undone;
While luxury, and wealth, like war and peace,
Are each the others ruine, and increase.
                    [ll. 28 – 34]

Here extravagant waste and hoarded wealth alternate in mutual destruction, just as man preys upon man destructively. St Paul's,

Aspiring mountain, or descending cloud
                    [l. 18]

had brought the ways of Heaven and Earth harmoniously together, and been the care of the king, the head of a temporal state by divine right. To the king, the reconciler of opposites, the poem now returns with the description of Windsor:

*Windsor* the next (where *Mars* with *Venus* dwells.
Beauty with strength) above the Valley swells
Into my eye, and doth itself present
With such an easie and unforc't ascent,
That no stupendious precipice denies
Access, no horror turns away our eyes:
But such a Rise, as doth at once invite
A pleasure, and a reverence from the sight.
Thy mighty Masters Embleme, in whose face
Sate meekness, heightned with Majestic Grace
Such seems thy gentle height, made only proud
To be the basis of that pompous load,
Than which, a nobler weight no Mountain bears,
But *Atlas* only that supports the Sphears.
                    [ll. 39 – 52]

The verb 'swells' has overtones of fertile sexuality (all the versions of the A text of 'Cooper's Hill' actually contain an explicit simile of pregnancy at this point but, quite apart from this, the word usually has such overtones in seventeenth-century poetry, as in Donne's phrase 'A Pregnant bank swel'd up' in 'The Extasie', or Milton's 'half her swelling Brest/Naked met his' in *Paradise Lost*, Book IV). Atlas establishes the microcosmic-macrocosmic link cherished by royalist thought and makes the king the main support for the world in little of human society. Mars and Venus, beauty and strength, refer to the beauty and strength of the fortification but extend well beyond that obvious meaning. They were a common renaissance symbol for a perfect sexual relationship, and the qualities of both deities were also combined in a perfect human being (they occur in these senses throughout *Antony and Cleopatra*, for instance, and the masculine and feminine principles recur as 'sweetness' and 'strength' rolled into the perfect sphere in 'To his Coy Mistress'). There is a good deal of royalist wishful thinking here, for Charles was no Mars and many of the royalist factions deeply distrusted the French and Catholic Queen, but the relationship had become one of the few royal marriages of love in Europe, and Henrietta Maria had exerted a softening influence on the life of the court which was of some value to the nation as a whole. Nevertheless, the link between Windsor and Charles, and the lines on the providential siting of Windsor, work on the political level to imply a combination of providence and intelligent self-interest in an acceptance of the monarchical constitution:

When Natures hand this ground did thus advance,
'Twas guided by a wiser power than Chance;
Mark't out for such a use, as if 'twere meant
T'invite the builder, and his choice prevent.
Nor can we call it choice, when what we chuse,
Folly, or blindness only could refuse.
    [ll. 53 – 8]

The traditional constitution is thus given sanction as an outgrowth of nature. The following excursus through medieval English history leads back to 'the royal pair', the descendants of the glorious dead and heirs to their greatness, and briefly glances at Charles's building up of the British navy so that it became for a while the foremost in Western Europe and therefore the world (ironically Charles's achievement was part of his undoing; it was the use of the navy against the Dutch that sparked off the revolt against ship money, and after the revolution the navy became a useful Parliamentarian weapon against the royalists). Britain's relationship with the sea will be picked up again by Denham in the later passages on seaborne trade. Meanwhile, the passing references to the Order of the Garter gained additional force when Charles, like St George, the patron saint of the Order, was martyred. The sacrilegious execution of the king came in the B text to form a natural transition to the sacrilegious destruction of Chertsey Abbey.

As the ruins of the chapel of Chertsey Abbey attract the poet's eye, religion – in Henry VIII's time the passive prey to the royal predator – is seen now to have become a raging and destructive force cloaked in the name of zeal, paralleling the destructive relationship of opposites found earlier in the City. As the poem has already established a sense that the traditional balance within the constitution is part of the order of nature, which is in turn the handwork of God, religion is here felt to have turned into its opposite, irreligion, in threatening the traditional order. With a shudder the poet turns away from Chertsey:

Parting from thence 'twixt anger, shame, & fear,
Those for whats past, & this for whats too near.
   [ll. 157 – 8]

Denham now turns to the central feature of the landscape, the Thames itself:

*Thames*, the most lov'd of all the Oceans sons,
By his old Sire to his embraces runs,
Hasting to pay his tribute to the Sea,
Like mortal life to meet Eternity.
Though with those streams he no resemblance hold,
Whose foam is Amber, and their Gravel Gold;
His genuine, and less guilty wealth t'explore,
Search not his bottom, but survey his shore;
Ore which he kindly spreads his spacious wing,
And hatches plenty for th'ensuing Spring.
Nor then destroys it with too fond a stay,
Like Mothers which their Infants overlay.
Nor with a sudden and impetuous wave,
Like profuse Kings, resumes the wealth he gave.
No unexpected inundations spoyl
The mowers hopes, nor mock the plowmans toyl:
But God-like his unwearied Bounty flows;
First loves to do, then loves the Good he does.
Nor are his Blessings to his banks confin'd,
But free, and common, as the Sea or Wind;

When he to boast, or to disperse his stores
Full of the tributes of his grateful shores,
Visits the world, and in his flying towers
Brings home to us, and makes both *Indies* ours;
Finds wealth where 'tis, bestows it where it wants
Cities in deserts, woods in Cities plants.
So that to us no thing, no place is strange,
While his fair bosom is the worlds exchange.
O could I flow like thee, and make thy stream
My great example, as it is my theme!
Though deep, yet clear, though gentle, yet not dull,
Strong without rage, without ore-flowing full.
        [ll. 161 – 92]

This passage is the finest in the poem, and the last four lines
became deservedly famous. The fundamental reason is that the
poem here temporarily transcends its own logical limitations; the
Thames becomes a symbol that is instinctively felt rather than
logically defined. The river of mortal life seeking the sea of eternity
is indeed an archetypal image, occurring, for instance, in Buddhist
contexts quite alien to Denham's doctrinal tradition and rational
concepts. Water flowing to water carries an emotional sense of
fulfilment, of individual life at one with and fulfilled in the life of
the universe. Thus the Thames represents more than a delicate
poise between extremes; it represents the harmonizing power of life
within the landscape, within nature, within man, as well as the flow
of inspiration within the poem. The passage can therefore shift
easily from pride in the familiar English landscape, enhanced by
classical associations, to the practical usefulness of the Thames in
supporting the two sources of national wealth, agriculture and
trade, and from these to the inspiration of the poem harmonizing
and combining opposite or contrasting aesthetic qualities. A particularly neat contrast is that formed by agriculture and trade, for
the major items of English export at the time were agricultural, and
the practice of agriculture on the river bank depended on the
cyclical flooding and ebbing of the Thames, directed by man-built
dams and barriers. That trade combines the benefits of east and
west, of town and country, seems therefore no more than an extension of the co-operation of man and nature in the universal order.
Like harmonious contrast in aesthetic qualities, a moderate cyclical
alteration of opposites is seen as beneficial and is distinguished
from violent alternation in the line

Like profuse Kings, resumes the wealth he gave
    [1. 174]

which glances back to Henry VIII's despoiling of Chertsey and to the present threat of religious irruption. Throughout this passage the Thames thus symbolizes the intelligence of life reconciling all contrasts and oppositions, maintaining diversity in unity.

In the passage that follows, the intuition of fundamental unity is lost; the Thames itself becomes one of a pair of opposites, an extreme of gentle calmness counterpoised by the shaggy roughness of Cooper's Hill. Denham lapses into a cruder view of opposites as mechanistically separate entities, and the poetry grows laxer, more prosaic. The intellectual vision is of an opposition of harmonious strife nevertheless:

Wisely she [Nature] knew, the harmony of things,
As well as that of sounds, from discords springs.
Such was the discord, which did first disperse
Form, order, beauty through the Universe;
While driness moysture, coldness heat resists
All that we have, all that we are, subsists.
While the steep horrid roughness of the Wood
Strives with the gentle calmness of the flood.
Such huge extreams when Nature doth unite,
Wonder from thence results, from thence delight.
    [ll. 203 – 12]

The thought was commonplace enough in the seventeenth century; compare Milton's lines:

Eldest *Night*
And *Chaos,* Ancestors of Nature, hold
Eternal Anarchie, amidst the noise
Of endless warrs, and by confusion stand.
For hot, cold, moist, and dry, four Champions fierce
Strive here for Maistrie, and to Battel bring
Thir embryon Atoms.
    [*Paradise Lost*, Book II, pp. 894 – 900]

It is, however, in this form ultimately inadequate, for nothing that fails to combine diversity with the complete simplicity of unity will permanently satisfy the human mind. Denham is providing a superficial treatment of a profound idea.

The return to the Thames as only one element in the external scene also brings the poem back to politics, tritely implying the wisdom of accepting difference, the unwisdom of egalitarianism and of political and religious strife. Nurtured by the flood and sheltered by the hill, the plain is graced by the references to Faunus and Sylvanus, to woodland deities and sylvan poetry, and is made the setting of the hunt, the peacetime alternative to war. There are two versions of the hunt. Professor O'Hehir sees the stag in the A version as an allegory of Strafford, abandoned by the king and hunted by his enemies, while in the B version, written after the execution of Charles, the stag becomes the king himself; however, both interpretations are open to obvious and acknowledged objections, since Charles hardly hunted Strafford, and if Charles becomes the stag in the B version, then the hunting king has to become someone other than Charles. The main point of the hunt is rather to stand as the wise alternative to civil war, and it leads up to praise of the balance between king and subject briefly achieved by Magna Charta, a document actually signed in the meadows of Runnymede:

This a more Innocent, and happy chase,
Than when of old, but in the self-same place,
Fair liberty pursu'd, and meant a Prey
To lawless power, here turn'd, and stood at bay.
When in that remedy all hope was plac't
Which was, or should have been at least, the last.
Here was that Charter seal'd, wherein the Crown
All marks of Arbitrary power lays down:
Tyrant and slave, those names of hate and fear,
The happier stile of King and Subject bear:
Happy, when both to the same Center move,
When Kings give liberty, and Subjects love.
      [ll. 323 – 34]

The gentle interchange of liberty and love has, however, given way before oppression and rebellion:

Thus Kings, by grasping more than they could hold,
First made their Subjects by oppression bold:
And popular sway, by forcing Kings to give
More than was fit for Subjects to receive,
Ran to the same extreams; and one excess
Made both, by striving to be greater, less.
      [ll. 343 – 8]

If mutual interdependence, the very lesson of the landscape, is ignored, then interchange becomes interception, violent collision.

At this point the river recurs as allegorical feature:

When a calm River rais'd with sudden rains,
Or Snows dissolv'd, oreflows th'adjoyning Plains,
The Husbandmen with high-rais'd banks secure
Their greedy hopes, and this he can endure.
But if with Bays and Dams they strive to force
His channel to a new, or narrow course;
No longer then within his banks he dwells,
First to a Torrent, then a Deluge swells:
Stronger, and fiercer by restraint he roars,
And knows no bound, but makes his power his shores.
      [ll. 349 – 58]

In the A text the river had been specifically equated with royal power. After the execution of the king a threat of royal inundation became untenable. In the B text, rather than specific identifications for the husbandmen or river, it is the relationship between the two that becomes important, the alternatives of violent conflict or moderate mutual restraint. The earlier text had implied at least some explanation for the arbitrary actions of the king, such as the invasion of the Commons for the arrest of the five members, though it had been careful not to sanction such arbitrary action in its balanced ending:

Therefore their boundlesse power let Princes draw
Within the Channell, and the shores of Law,
And may that Law, which teaches Kings to sway
Their Scepters, teach their Subjects to obey.
      [A text, draft III, ll. 351 – 4]

This emphasis on the final authority of the law embodied in the traditional constitution is a typically moderate, conservative position, limiting but accepting royal power. The B text is less detailed in contemporary application, but the outlook remains the same. Liberty is guaranteed by the acceptance of its limitations: the alternative is violence.

While 'Cooper's Hill' openly handles political issues, it is hardly polemical, for it implies no before and after of debate. As a statement of belief, however, the A text did one great polemical service to the king's party; it tried to distinguish between lawful and unlawful rebellion, admitting that the king's power was not absolute and that the subject was justified in defending his liberty (the relevant passages were made less explicit in the B text, after the execution of the king). It thus struck at the weak point in the Parliamentarian cause, for the followers of Parliament knew what they were against rather than what they were for; they started with grievances, not a blueprint for a new society, and many boggled at the thought of a new order. After all, Wentworth, Earl of Strafford, whose blood was shed to appease the Commons, had started by being a leader of the parliamentary opposition to the throne, and he was merely one of the first of those who went over to the king or grew dissatisfied with the revolutionary government. It was the opinion of the wearied moderates from either party that eventually gave a basis for the Restoration settlement, but in the short term moderate opinion failed to allow for two decisive factors, the determined fighting power of the unpropertied masses, who had no stake whatever in the existing political order, and the military genius of Oliver Cromwell. In the longer run, however, it was the more moderate men of property who foreshadowed the order of the eighteenth century, and it was in the late seventeenth and eighteenth centuries that 'Cooper's Hill' became an accepted, if minor, classic.

The politics of 'Cooper's Hill' were undoubtedly congenial to the succeeding age, with its advocacy of a balance of conflicting interests within a framework of traditional law, its emphasis on real but limited royal power, and its recognition of the importance of trade, together with its comforting sense that the English constitution was an outgrowth of nature. It was not the political ideas as such, however, that gave the poem its fame. This was due rather to the success of 'Cooper's Hill' in embodying a whole world view, a mode of sensibility, that was later to become dominant. The way in which 'Cooper's Hill' orders its reader's perception of the universe was recognized and valued by the Augustans, and this ordering is expressed just as much – perhaps more – in the structure of Denham's couplets than in his relatively commonplace ideas. What exactly he did can be seen if we look both back to Jonson and forward to Pope.

The couplet as used by Jonson had been rhetorical. His habit of ending the syntactical units within the line had meant that rhymes and line endings had been passed over relatively lightly and the long cadences of the speaking voice dominated the flow of the verse. Jonson's verse also had a characteristic difficulty not unconnected with Donne's; not only were the sentences often long, but the reader had little guidance at the beginning as to how they were to end, being required to wait for several lines before the pattern was revealed. Denham instead end-stops his couplets and tends to work within them. He uses an abundance of main clauses and he often places subordinate clauses and phrases in parallel, or balances them within the balanced lines of the couplet. This produces a lucidity and ease of reading which Jonson neither had nor sought. Denham also emphasizes the rhyme words and uses them to point the meaning. The meaning itself he packs, using as few words as are compatible with clarity and the reader's ease. He thus combines lucidity and ease with forcefulness, developing the strong lines of Jonson and Donne into a form acceptable to the following age, so that he received the accolade of Dr Johnson's acknowledgement, 'The critical decision has given the praise of strength to Denham, and of sweetness to Waller.' It was the combination of forcefulness, ease and lucidity within an exquisitely elaborate order of balances that gave such fame to the couplets

O could I flow like thee, and make thy stream
My great example, as it is my theme!
Though deep, yet clear, though gentle, yet not dull,
Strong without rage, without ore-flowing full.
        [ll. 189 – 92]⁴

The music of the verse, the music of the heroic couplet, is new; its intricate balances and resolved conflicts soothe the ear and mark Denham's view not only of politics but of life itself. In this way the verse, the man and the matter are of a piece. It is this unity that gives such strength to the flow of the lines; and since the perception of a Denhamesque kind of order constituted the mainspring of eighteenth-century English poetry, 'Cooper's Hill' exerted a fascination on the poets and critics of the following century. Dr Johnson expressed the then accepted view when he wrote:

Denham is deservedly considered as one of the fathers of English poetry. 'Denham and Waller,' says Prior, 'improved our versification, and Dryden perfected it'. . . . He is one of the writers that improved our taste, and advanced our language.
        [*Life of Denham*]

The stylistic debt of Dryden and Pope to 'Cooper's Hill' is obvious. The poem also had many successors in the minor genre of English topographical poetry, though most of these are poems of description interspersed with moralizing. Only Pope's 'Windsor Forest' stands out as a topographical poem with a political message. The reasons are not far to seek. As a form of political verse the topographical poem is most useful for defending a *status quo* that is under threat. The descriptive form is a hindrance in open controversy. Pope, writing in the reign of the last of the Stuarts, found himself in a position similar to Denham's and could use the same form. In a more settled situation, or one of more violent conflict, the form is useless, and the political poetry of the years immediately following 'Cooper's Hill' was mostly written in quite different genres, though the more limited topographical description of a particular estate continued to carry a limited political meaning, usually through a contrast between an orderly estate and the world without its walls.[5]

Pope emulated and surpassed Denham, both in the use of the couplet and in the development of the topographical poem. He also refined Denham's mode of sensibility, while at the same time broadening its range. Denham had paralleled the broad features of a landscape and a social order. Pope could parallel the order of nature with detail of the rituals of social life. A couplet like

From silver Spouts the grateful Liquors glide,
While *China*'s Earth receives the smoking Tyde
    [*The Rape of the Lock*, III, ll. 109–10]

has a poignancy because the parallel is at once absurd and completely fitting. The couplet thus compounds opposite qualities, each of which might be expected to annihilate the other. Is it too fanciful to think that the sensibility here, and the parallel between social trivia and vast geographical phenomena, may perhaps owe something to Pope's experience of 'Cooper's Hill'?

# 3 Marvell and the constitution: a Parliamentarian viewpoint

'Cooper's Hill' is the statement of a moderate royalist. Marvell was also a moderate and probably started as a royalist, though he crossed to the opposing lines, and he too wrote poetry on the constitutional issues of the Civil War, focusing his attention upon the fundamental questions raised by Cromwell's success. The king's trial had been implemented by the few unpurged extremists remaining in the Rump Parliament and the proceedings sustained by the indomitable will of Cromwell. The consensus of legality had broken down: the court was a revolutionary court, and the standards by which it judged were those of revolution. The execution of the king was commonly greeted by reactions that ranged from outraged horror to stunned incredulity. The horrified royalist reaction was voiced in a poem dubiously attributed to Cleveland:

[This] crime hath widdowed our whole Nation,
Voided all Forms, left but privation
In *Church* and *State*; inverting ev'ry right;
Brought in Hells State of fire without light . . .
Let *Christians* then use otherwise this blood,
Detest the Act, yet turn it to their good;
Thinking how like a *King of death* He dies;
We easily may the world and death despise:
Death had no sting for him, and its sharp arm,
Onely of all the troop, meant him no harm.
And so he look'd upon the *Axe*, as one
Weapon yet left, to guard Him to His Throne;
In His great Name, then may His Subjects cry,
*Death thou art swallowed up in Victory.*
    ['An Elegie upon King Charles the First, murthered
    publikely by His Subjects']

The martyrizing of Charles, upon which he had counted, was already taking place. For the more moderate, however, the event was less easy to pigeonhole. Charles's actions and policies had themselves been extreme, and his attempts to play off Scots against

English, Presbyterians against Independents, had given him an unsavoury reputation for double-dealing and unreliability, which lent
force to Cromwell's view of the king as a man of blood, the cause
of avoidable slaughter. The most common view of history at the
time was providential; history recorded man's virtuous and sinful
actions and God's reactions to the deeds of men. In this view there
was always room for extraordinary interventions and judgements
of God. If Cromwell were chosen for some special purpose and
were, as he himself claimed, carrying out the will of God, then it
would be not only pointless but wrong to oppose him. The only
tests that could be applied to decide the question were the degree
of righteousness in Cromwell's actions and the degree of success
that was granted to them by the Almighty. On the first point
opinions differed, but as to Cromwell's success, there was little
doubt. When the Scots had broken the Solemn League and Covenant on the instigation of the king and had invaded England in
1648, Cromwell had put down a Welsh rebellion, defeated the invading Scots, beheaded the king and, having seen the establishment
of the oligarchic Council of State, proceeded to put down various
Leveller mutinies in the army, crush a royalist rebellion in Ireland
and then defeat Charles II and yet another invading Scots army at
the battle of Worcester in 1651, while the Parliamentarian fleet, led
by Admiral Blake, decisively defeated a royalist fleet, gathered and
led by Prince Rupert. It was nothing if not a success story, and
most of the successes were due to Cromwell personally. Even the
staunchest royalists were daunted; the anger of God at the murder
of the king seemed slow in manifesting itself. For the moderates
there was not only the sense that evidence of the Almighty's disapproval was lacking; there was also awareness that Cromwell was a
rock of order in the seething cross-currents of religion and politics,
and for the propertied and educated classes there was an awareness
that he had at least defended them from democracy, mob rule
and the destruction of private property. In their view, without
Cromwell anarchy threatened. Moderate opinion, therefore, in
varying degrees reconciled itself to Cromwell as a fact of nature.
The process can be seen happening in Marvell's political poetry,
starting with '*An* Horatian *Ode upon* Cromwel's *Return from*
Ireland'.

The 'Horatian *Ode*' has been accorded a great deal of discussion,
its lines being wrenched this way and that in attempts to force from
them a neat, overall political meaning. However, within the poem

itself ideas and feelings are divided: Marvell is in the act of reconciling himself to Cromwell's actions. Modern political thinking
tends to assume tacitly that mind is merely the product of matter:
from this standpoint Marvell's lines

'Tis Madness to resist or blame
The force of angry Heavens flame
    [ll. 25 – 6]

have a shocking naivety and must therefore be interpreted as ironic,
a condemnation of a fanatical religious understanding of politics;
however, in the seventeenth century the surface sentiment was as
commonplace as Marxist millenarianism today. The interpretation
of these lines affects the interpretation of the passage that
immediately follows:

And, if we would speak true,
  Much to the Man is due.
Who, from his private Gardens, where
He liv'd reserved and austere,
  As if his highest plot
  To plant the Bergamot,
Could by industrious Valour climbe
To ruine the great Work of Time,
  And cast the Kingdome old
  Into another Mold.
Though Justice against Fate complain,
And plead the antient Rights in vain:
  But those do hold or break
  As Men are strong or weak.
Nature that hateth emptiness,
Allows of penetration less:
  And therefore must make room
  Where greater Spirits come.
    [ll. 27 – 44]

According to the 'antient Rights' and the common idea of justice at
the time, there was no doubt whatever that the king had been
wrongfully executed. The lines could therefore possibly be interpreted as a Machiavellian recognition of brute force as triumphing
over right, or rather as right residing with brute force, a view found
in most centuries. Alternatively, if phrases like 'greater Spirits' are
taken ironically, the passage could be interpreted as defending the
justice of the ancient rights against the sordid Machiavellianism of
Cromwell. If, however, the passage is taken to mean what it says,

then it recognizes that justice and ancient rights lay with the king, but it also recognizes the demise of the old justice through the weakness (not only military but in character) of Charles, and the great spirit of Cromwell, who is obeying the ordinance of heaven by forcing a way for a new order of things: such an attitude is by no means inconsistent with a moderately traditionalist and conservative outlook; it is even a principle of English law, hardly a radical institution, that the possession of property or governmental power, however illegally it may have been gained, becomes legal when sanctioned by the passing of sufficient time. The wrongs of yesterday become the rights of today. The trouble with Cromwell was that he had not been around for long and he put people into positions in which they had to make up their minds quickly. Marvell's judgement and feelings pull in different directions. The lines

And, if we would speak true,
Much to the Man is due,

are hardly enthusiastic, while an element of almost hypocritical calculation creeps in with 'As if', to be maintained by 'plot' (an emotive word in seventeenth-century usage), and to culminate in 'industrious Valour', where the spontaneous quality of 'Valour' is played off against the busy, calculating quality of 'industrious', just as the cumulative achievement associated with industriousness sets off the following verse,

To ruine the great Work of Time.

('Ruine' here suggests wastage rather than any later association with the romantic beauty of decay.) On the other hand, Cromwell has an irresistible quality, earlier suggested by 'Heavens flame' (lightning, with associations of inspired genius) and here conveyed by 'Fate' (not a very cheerful word, by contrast with 'destiny'). Irresistibility becomes explicit in the succeeding references to the laws of physics and the truths they convey about the spiritual levels of creation, which they reflect. There is also a positive recognition that destruction clears the way for creation, for the recasting of the 'Kingdome old'. There is, therefore, a process of acceptance in the passage. Marvell is coming to terms with things.

The description of the execution of the king, which follows soon after, poses problems of a slightly different sort. Today the playing of social roles is often considered to impose from without a sense of identity on the actor. Traditionally, much more emphasis was laid on the integrity of a man or woman in him- or herself; the role played was, at least in theory, secondary to the excellence of the playing, which reflected the inner integrity. This attitude recurred in a long strand of European civilization, from Augustus's remark as he lay dying, 'Haven't I acted my part well in this farce?', to the lines of Pope in the eighteenth century:

Honour and shame from no Condition rise;
Act well your part, there all the honour lies.
Fortune in Men has some small diff'rence made,
One flaunts in rags, one flutters in brocade,
The cobler apron'd, and the parson gown'd,
The friar hooded, and the monarch crown'd.
'What differ more (you cry) than crown and cowl?'
I'll tell you, friend! a Wise man and a Fool.
You'll find, if once the monarch acts the monk,
Or, cobler-like, the parson will be drunk,
Worth makes the man, and want of it, the fellow;
The rest is all but leather or prunella.
        ['An Essay on Man', Epistle IV, ll. 193 – 204]

Here the attitude is typically combined with a conservative emphasis on the need for clarity in divisions between social roles for the sake of the well-being of society as a whole, and with a disinclination to disturb the social order; at the same time from the modern point of view the passage is disconcertingly democratic in its refusal to confuse the worth of the man with the social prestige of a role. The existence of this kind of attitude makes it possible to see how Marvell can use the image of acting in connection with Charles I's death without irony. It was, in fact, universally admitted that the king had acted with impressive dignity on the scaffold, with a full awareness of how a king should act on such an occasion. In so far as any act of dignity enhances the dignity of mankind, he had served humanity by doing so. The recognition of this might well go with a sense that the execution was inevitable and that the old order had passed, as it seemed to many at the time, for good. Indeed, the old order had passed for good, in that kingship in this country could never again be the same after the advent of Oliver Cromwell. The sense of transition is marked by Marvell:

This was that memorable Hour
Which first assur'd the forced Pow'r.
    So when they did design
    The *Capitols* first Line,
A bleeding Head where they begun,
Did fright the Architects to run;

And yet in that the *State*
Foresaw it's happy Fate.
　　[ll. 65 – 72]

From a contemporary English viewpoint, Marvell was saying no more than the truth. Cromwell's power was very obviously 'forced', and his advent had been happy in that it had turned English swords against foreign enemies and had led to victory at somebody else's expense. After civil war this was a change for the better. Thus the 'Ode' expresses a shocked hard-headedness, a careful conservatism tempered by pragmatism, a tendency to co-operate whenever possible with the inevitable, and a groping after a pattern of meaning behind the brute facts of history. It was a poem sufficiently pro-Cromwellian to be cancelled from virtually all the copies of the 1681 folio.

The subsequent shifts in Marvell's position are consistent with this interpretation and were not uncommon at the time. 'The First Anniversary *of the Government under* O.C.' praises Cromwell's attempts to frame a constitution and rule as Lord Protector with Parliament:

The crossest Spirits here do take their part,
Fast'ning the Contignation which they thwart;
And they, whose Nature leads them to divide,
Uphold, this one, and that the other Side;
But the most Equal still sustein the Height,
And they as Pillars keep the Work upright;
While the resistance of opposed Minds,
The Fabrick as with Arches stronger binds,
Which on the Basis of a Senate free,
Knit by the Roofs Protecting weight agree.
　　[ll. 89 – 98]

The couplets are not as smooth or as elegant as Denham's, but the sentiments, though Cromwellian, have a striking similarity. Cromwell is praised for creating stability and unity on the basis of diversity and opposites, exactly the virtue of the traditional constitutional arrangement according to 'Cooper's Hill'. As moderates the two men are thinking alike: the overriding appeal of Cromwell's government for Marvell at this juncture is that it appears to be working. Whereas the surrounding and ineffective monarchs

No more contribute to the state of Things,
Then wooden Heads unto the Viols strings
　　[ll. 43 – 4]

Cromwell indefatigably

                                    hyes,
And cuts his way still nearer to the Skyes,
Learning a Musique in the Region clear,
To tune this lower to that higher Sphere.
        [ll. 45 – 8]

Even the appeal to the relationship between the macrocosm and the microcosmic state, here figured by the harmony of the constitution chiming with the harmony of the spheres, is found in Denham. The poem then turns to Cromwell's relations with foreign princes and casts Cromwell in the apocalyptic role of ushering in the millennium, remarking that if only the kings of Europe could recognize Cromwell for what he was,

How might they under such a Captain raise
The great Designes kept for the latter Dayes!
        [ll. 109 – 10]

Marvell's attitude at this time was no more unreasonable than the twentieth-century hope of building an age of gold on the manipulation of political and social systems. Nevertheless, in the midst of his enthusiasm Marvell retains his vein of sceptical pragmatism; the millennium will come, but it may not be yet:

'Tis the most which we determine can,
If these the Times, then this must be the Man.
        [ll. 143 – 4]

The poem then returns to Cromwell's private virtues, his necessity to the state as defender of true freedom, the middle way between tyranny and licence, and his status abroad as lord of the victorious fleets of England.

   Cromwell, of course, did not inaugurate the millennium. Nevertheless, the '*Poem upon the Death of* O.C.' still celebrates Cromwell's providential character:

O *Cromwell, Heavens Favorite*! To none
Have such high honours from above been shown.
        [ll. 157 – 8]

At the time of writing this poem, however, Marvell was still anticipating the succession of Richard in his father's stead. When General Monck marched on London and engineered the restoration of the monarchy, it looked as if the nation had returned to its original state, and certainly the battle between the throne and

Parliament reopened, though at first this was not generally apparent.

Charles II's very circumspect attempts to assert royal power inevitably entailed a strained relationship with Parliament as a result of the old issues of religion and money. Charles's desire for financial independence led him to seek the assistance of Louis XIV, the only person likely to subsidize him. Louis was, in fact, at loggerheads with the Pope, but he did have the ambition of founding a great Christian (that is, Roman Catholic) empire, and from this side of the Channel he was something of a bogeyman threatening the religion of the Church of England and the freedom of the country. A close relationship with Louis entailed a pro-Catholic policy which was in any case congenial to Charles, and the only practical way to pursue a pro-Catholic policy was to work for religious toleration of the Puritan and Nonconformist sects as well as the Catholics. The Church of England had recently suffered from the one and greatly feared the other, so that its supporters felt themselves hemmed in by insidious enemies and tended to come out strongly against toleration. At the same time the large latitudinarian grouping within the Church of England sought to broaden the basis of the Church by insisting only on a few essential articles of faith and tolerating the operation of private conscience on all other matters: it was the latitudinarian party that eventually gained the ascendancy in the eighteenth century after many high churchmen had become non-jurors (had refused to forswear allegiance to the Stuarts and had been ejected from the main corpus of the Church of England in the reign of William and Mary or, later, under the Hanoverians). There were, therefore, areas of opinion in the Church of England under Charles that were broadly tolerant in outlook, though it by no means followed that they would consider it wise to give the Protestant sects or the Church of Rome official political recognition. Marvell's own position, after his experience of the disastrous consequences of religious dissension, was firmly for toleration, and for once he saw eye to eye with Charles's official policy. His devastating attack on Samuel Parker in *The Rehearsal Transpros'd* is both a blow in support of the king's policy and an attempt to make the policy as explicit as possible, so that it could not later be twisted in a purely pro-Catholic direction. It was in the course of this work that Marvell made his last pronouncement on the constitutional issue and the Civil War:

Whether it were a War of Religion, or of Liberty, is not worth the labour to enquire. Which-soever was at the top, the other was at the bottom; but upon considering all, I think the Cause was too good to have been fought for. Men ought to have trusted God; they ought and might have trusted the King with the whole matter. The *Arms of the Church are Prayers and Tears*, the Arms of the Subjects are Patience and Petitions. The King himself being of so accurate and piercing a judgment, would soon have felt where it stuck. For men may spare their pains where Nature is at work, and the world will not go the faster for our driving. Even as his present Majesties happy Restauration did it self, so all things else happen in their best and proper time, without any need of our officiousness.[1]

In retrospect, so much bloodshed seemed to have achieved so little! Logically, if providence were responsible for the rise of Cromwell, it was also responsible for the return of the king, a point that occurred to royalist and Roundhead alike (Milton took some trouble to explain it away on the basis of the unworthiness of the people to receive a better fate). Millenarian attitudes in politics gave way for a time to a much more sceptical and cautious approach to the specific issue of the moment, but they flowed on underground through the English eighteenth century to re-emerge at the time of the French Revolution. Even so, Charles II's reign gave rise to many issues of the moment that were both stormy and important, and on most of these Marvell and the country at large were against the king.

In a more restricted form the constitutional question did once re-emerge in Charles II's reign, during the Exclusion Crisis of the 1680s, by which time Marvell himself was dead. To that crisis we must return later, but first we should consider the wider spectrum of positions adopted during the Civil War.

# 4 Liberty and order: the wider spectrum

## Filmer

Marvell's poems were published by his widow, probably in an attempt to consolidate her claim to his estate, in 1681; before that time nearly all would have circulated in manuscript. A similar fate befell *Patriarcha*, the major work of Sir Robert Filmer, written between 1635 and 1642, and only printed in 1680, twenty-seven years after Filmer's death. During his own lifetime he published a few short pamphlets, including the brief *Observations on Mr Hobbes's Leviathan* and *Observations on Mr Milton Against Salmasius*. In the latter part of the century, because of the Exclusion Crisis, Filmer's work assumed polemical importance: in the earlier part of the century it attracted little notice. Its importance to us is that it represents one extreme of the seventeenth-century political spectrum. Sir Robert Filmer was a Kentish country gentleman writing to ease the scruples of his friends and embodying in his *Patriarcha* the assumptions of his kind and generation, assumptions that could no longer be taken absolutely for granted. Like so much of the political writing of the century, including the work of Hobbes and Locke, it was written for direct application to the contemporary situation and, as its name suggests, it was based upon the conventions of patriarchalism. As Peter Laslett has pointed out,[1] patriarchalism was the dominant archetype in the life of seventeenth-century Englishmen, as it still is in Britain today, though greatly weakened (it remains embedded in many traditional institutions: the religious would, for instance, find it surprising to hear God spoken of as 'she'). This appeal to the way society was known to function and the way people were brought up to feel gave the work much of its power; for those comfortably ensconced and conventionally nurtured it was an appeal almost irresistible; for the dispossessed and landless living in less authoritarian family units on the rebellious fringes of society its appeal would have been slight indeed; and for the thrusting mercantilist and the intellectual advocates of change its appeal was at best but partial.

Despite its limitations, however, *Patriarcha* does have solid virtues that are even now not always recognized. First, compared with most works of its type, it reads well. As with most seventeenth- and eighteenth-century works of controversy, too much of it is taken up in hagglings over minutiae in the texts of opponents, and in the process the opponents' arguments are not always represented with scrupulous honesty, but the same could be said of political speeches and television debates today. Also over-much ground is beaten in a search for authorities. Nevertheless, opponents are treated with a courtesy rare for the period, which makes the tone of the work agreeable; the sentences have a graceful flow to them; and there is a certain pungency of understatement, often reserved for the end of sentences, where it humorously undercuts what has gone before:

This tenet [that men are born free] was first hatched in the Schools for good Divinity, and hath been fostered by succeeding Papists. The Divines of the Reformed Churches have entertained it, and the common people everywhere tenderly embrace it as being most plausible to flesh and blood, for that it prodigally distributes a portion of liberty to the meanest of the multitude, who magnify liberty as if the height of human felicity were only to be found in it, never remembering that the desire of liberty was the cause of the fall of Adam. . . . The rebellious consequence which follows this prime article of the natural freedom of mankind may be my sufficient warrant for a modest examination of the original truth of it; much hath been said, and by many, for the affirmative; equity requires that an ear be reserved a little for the negative.
[I, pp. 53 – 4]

The slightly waspish suavity is well suited to a defence of the *status quo*, and it *is* the *status quo* that Filmer has in mind. He is quick to point out that he is not minded to curtail liberties already enjoyed:

I am not to question or quarrel at the rights or liberties of this or any other nation; my task is chiefly to inquire from whom these came, not to dispute what or how many they are, but whether they are derived from the laws of natural liberty or from the grace and bounty of Princes.
[I, p. 55]

He genuinely feels that monarchy best serves the interests of the people, that 'the new coined distinction into Royalists and Patriots is most unnatural, since the relation between King and people is so great that their well-being is reciprocal'. Nevertheless, his arguments could be used to support any monarchy, however tyrannous.

In his search for the justification of monarchy Filmer naturally turns to history and especially to the Scriptures, since these include the only absolutely reliable section of human history, the Old Testament account of the Jews, springing from God Himself, and since scriptural history instances with peculiar clarity the workings of God's providence and the nature of God's will in the affairs of men. Filmer's thesis is simple. The 'only right and natural authority' is paternal. From this stem the two human institutions of political power and the right to property. Political power descends from Adam:

For as Adam was lord of his children, so his children under him had a command over their own children, but still with subordination to the first parent, who is lord paramount over his children's children to all generations, as being the grandfather of his people.
[III, p. 57]

Adam had this right of God, being created first and alone by God, and after the Flood 'the three sons of Noah had the whole world divided amongst them by their Father', thus originating plurality of kingship, a process taken further when the confusion of tongues after Babel led to greater differentiation between the families of men. Nevertheless, all political power remains in its basis paternal, and the state is an aggregate of paternalistic families owing allegiance to the head of the royal family originally and ideally in the direct line of descent from Noah's sons (Filmer allowed such practical compromises as the election of a king by the heads of the leading families of a state if the royal line failed utterly). This was the supreme form of government:

The best order, the greatest strength, the most stability and easiest government are to be found in monarchy, and in no other form of government.
[XV, p. 86]

As for democracy,

No democracy can extend further than to one city. It is impossible to govern a kingdom, much less many kingdoms, by the whole people, or by the greatest part of them.
[XVI, p. 87]

In this he was clearly right. Even today, with modern communications, we have so-called representative democracy, not full democracy, and we have very little say in the decisions of government. Filmer also held, less reasonably, that democracy inevitably led to bloodshed, taking Rome as an example:

Often contrary factions fell to blows, sometimes with stones, and sometimes swords. The blood hath been sucked up in the market-places with sponges: the river Tiber hath been filled with the dead bodies of citizens, and the common privies stuffed full with them.

If any man think these disorders in popular states were but casual or such as may happen under any kind of government, he must know that such mischiefs are unavoidable and of necessity do follow all democratical regiments.
[XVIII, p. 89]

In fairness to Filmer, it should be remembered that in his diatribes against democracy he probably had the violence of the London mob in mind, a violence accepted as regrettable but inevitable, and not regarded as an aberration like the crowd violence of today. Given this order of things, it necessarily follows that a king's duty is the fatherly care of his people:

If we compare the natural duties of a Father with those of a King, we find them to be all one, without any difference at all but only in the latitude or extent of them. As the Father over one family, so the King, as Father over many families, extends his care to preserve, feed, clothe, instruct and defend the whole commonwealth. His wars, his peace, his courts of justice, and all his acts of sovereignty, tend only to preserve and distribute to every subordinate and inferior Father, and to their children, their rights and privileges, so that all the duties of a King are summed up in an universal fatherly care of his people.
[VII, p. 63]

This order of government, being based on the will of God at the creation of the world, is an embodiment of the law of nature (a term not defined, and presumably taken as synonymous with the order imposed by God at the creation). The system therefore has an inherent tendency to work well, for 'It is the multitude of people and the abundance of their riches which are the strength and glory of every Prince.' As for the right to property, that also stems from the delegated rights of Adam, for 'the natural and private dominion of Adam' is 'the fountain of all government and propriety'. Thus the right to property is dependent upon the whole system of which monarchy is the mainstay. Its basis in nature, in the *status quo* and in Scripture can be summed up in Filmer's own words:

I see not then how the children of Adam, or of any man else, can be free from subjection to their parents. And this subordination of children is the fountain of all regal authority, by the ordination of God himself.
[III, p. 57]

Filmer's work gives some indication of how inextricably religion, politics and morality were intertwined in the seventeenth century. Filmer was not a cruel man, nor was he particularly prejudiced; his premises seemed reasonable enough in his age and his ideas drew strength from tenacious social traditions. He does not present systematic argument from propositions to conclusions, but then he does not need to, since he is dealing, from his point of view, with facts, with experience, not with experimental conclusions. Nevertheless, his view was, even when he penned it, extreme, for his experience was limited by the conservative tenor of a country squire's life. Moreover, his 'country' or county was Kent, where the traditional way of life still throve vigorously among the families of minor gentry, who had been rooted there for centuries.[2] He was unacquainted with the political compromises entailed by survival in high office, and therefore surrendered nothing to the theory of a mixed monarchy favoured by Denham and the more moderate royalists, many of whom had experience of the political exigencies of court life. Filmer was, politically, an onlooker, and subsequent social, intellectual and religious changes have made his system utterly out of date.

## Hobbes

Another royalist onlooker, but of a very different kind, is the redoutable Thomas Hobbes, who claims to be steering something of a middle course, 'beset with those that contend on one side for too great Liberty, and on the other side for too much Authority'. Like Denham and Filmer, Hobbes is clearly arguing for what he sees as the *status quo*, but he is arguing in quite a different way. Filmer bases his case on the family unit and the will of God. Hobbes starts with the individual man and tries to argue with irrefutable logic upon the basis of axiomatic and undeniable observations concerning the nature of the human mind. Filmer's *Patriarcha* had been written to sustain like-minded friends, and Filmer seems to have realized the futility of attempting to convert opponents by its means, for the political pamphlets he published during his lifetime were aimed rather at destroying the logical coherence of opposing views, and aimed with some success. Hobbes was a more arrogant man intellectually and writes to convert the world to the obvious truth of his own conclusions. He is not so much discourteous as extremely impatient of opposition, which he cannot be bothered to take seriously. He is, indeed, often at his most amusing when he tries to swat his opponents in passing as if they were so many flies. Much has been written about the political myths of the social contract, etc., as they appear in *Leviathan*, but Hobbes's rigorous method starts with his account of the individual mind, and it is there that the assumptions underlying his political thinking are most clearly apparent.

Hobbes's view of the world is mechanistic. Material objects press upon man's various senses and this pressure constitutes the first stage of sensory perception, a form of motion, which, being motion, is in principle measurable. The senses passively convey this pressure to the brain and heart, and these, in resisting or producing a counter-pressure to that exerted through the senses, give rise to the subject's fancy or notion of the external body. Apart from the sensory apparatus, the two other important aspects of man's nature are reason and the passions. Reason simply adds or subtracts the basic single notions provided by sense impression, for 'When a man *Reasoneth*, hee does nothing else but conceive a summe totall, from *Addition* of parcels; or conceive a Remainder, from *Subtraction* of one summe from another.' In healthy people the original sense impressions are identical and the accuracy or inaccuracy of the reckoning or reasoning is verifiable. It is the passions that constitute the variable aspect of human nature:

The causes of this difference of Witts, are in the Passions: and the difference of Passions, proceedeth partly from the different Constitution of the body, and partly from different Education. For if the difference proceeded from the temper of the brain, and the organs of Sense, either exterior or interior, there would be no lesse difference of men in their Sight, Hearing, or other Senses, than in their Fancies, and Discretions. It proceeds therefore from the Passions; which are different, not onely from the difference of mens complexions; but also from their difference of customes, and education.

The Passions that most of all cause the differences of Wit, are principally, the more or lesse Desire of Power, of Riches, of Knowledge, and of Honour. All which may be reduced to the first, that is Desire of Power. For Riches, Knowledge and Honour are but severall sorts of Power.
    [I, viii, pp. 138 – 9][3]

The striking thing about Hobbes's version of the human consciousness is its extraordinary narrowness. The experience upon which he bases his analysis is that of the grossest level of the human mind, and even on that level he is not always accurate. He greatly underestimates the active role of the mind in sense perception. Work in the present century on visual perception has explored this in some depth, but everyday experience may illustrate it. Anybody who has been exposed to the neo-Victorian parlour game of guessing the nature of a common object photographed from an unusual angle will have noticed that an unidentified photograph is a mere blur or smudge: once, however, the object has been identified, a pattern or shape emerges, and it then becomes impossible to see the photograph as an unco-ordinated blur. The mind actively shapes our experience of the objective world. The poet Wordsworth, seeing sense perception as the co-operation of subjective mind and objective world, saw more truly than the philosopher Hobbes. Needless to say, the presence of the subjective element in perception means that statements about the nature of sense perception can have no 'objective' or fixed validity unless they emanate from someone with full knowledge of the possible range of human awareness, and here again Hobbes falls short of Wordsworth. Hobbes leaves out of account the highest aspects, the creative and intuitive aspects, of the human mind. For Hobbes, for instance, imagination is just a shadow of sense perception:

For after the object is removed, or the eye shut, wee still retain an image of the thing seen, though more obscure than when we see it. And this is it, the Latines call *Imagination*. . . . IMAGINATION therefore is nothing but *decaying sense*.

[I, ii, p. 88]

For Wordsworth imagination was the transcendent aspect of the human mind, a universal level of intelligence which lay at the basis of the individual mind and also at the basis of the objective world, the latter being instinct with life. Wordsworth drew on direct experience in what he said, but experience of that type had been conceptualized in the dawn of our civilization by Plato in his idea of the Good, the transcendent aspect of the world of ideas, underlying the subjective intelligence and the objective archetypal idea, and making possible the link between the two, the perception of the one by the other.[4] This way of thinking was, of course, powerfully present in Hobbes's own century in the Cambridge Platonists and elsewhere, and it is these potential opponents that Hobbes is trying to bypass. He cannot disprove them, since as Hobbes himself recognizes the only court of appeal is experience:

When I shall have set down my own reading orderly, and perspicuously, the
pains left another, will be onely to consider, if he also find not the same in
himself. For this kind of Doctrine, admitteth no other Demonstration.
[p. 83]

If he cannot disprove his opponents, however, he can and does
dismiss them. With the sentences 'Whatsoever we imagine, is
*Finite*. Therefore there is no Idea, or conception of anything we call
*Infinite*' [I, iii, p. 99] he attempts to dispose of the possibility of
metaphysics. He is obviously right in saying that the infinite cannot
be grasped as an object, since it transcends the subject—object relationship, but this does not logically preclude the Wordsworthian
position in which infinitude is the basis of both subject and object
and can be known subjectively when the mind unites with its own
essence. It was precisely this claim that had been made by Plotinus
and was maintained by the Cambridge Platonists. It is on the basis
of his own limited experience that Hobbes asserts that 'there is no
such thing as perpetuall Tranquillity of mind' in this world and
tetchily brushes off notions such as the beatific vision, the '*eternal-
Now*, and the like canting of Schoolemen'.

It is on this limited notion of man that Hobbes builds his
statecraft. For a Platonist, discipline could result from the pull of
the unity at the basis of man's nature. Hobbes conceded not unity,
but only similarity between discrete individuals. He therefore
grounds his discipline on fear. Fear is for him the essential con-
stituent of religion:

*Feare* of power invisible, feigned by the mind, or imagined from tales
publiquely allowed [is] RELIGION; not allowed, SUPERSTITION. And
when the power imagined, is truly such as we imagine, TRUE RELIGION.
[I, vi, p. 124]

Fear is also the basis of civil contracts and obedience of the law:

The force of Words, being (as I have formerly noted) too weak to hold men
to the performance of their Covenants. . . . The Passion to be reckoned
upon, is Fear; whereof there be two very generall Objccts: one, The Power
of Spirits Invisible; the other, The Power of those men they shall therein
[in the breaking of a contract] Offend. Of these two, though the former be
the greater Power, yet the feare of the later is commonly the greater Feare.
[I, xiv, p. 200]

From this it follows that fear of other men is the basis of the social
contract, both causing it to come into being and causing it to be
maintained.

Man's initial resort to the social contract is, then, through fear. Each man, being an utterly discrete entity according to Hobbes, acts for himself alone: the tendency is therefore towards perpetual violence, a war 'of every man, against every man', in which there is 'continuall feare, and danger of violent death; And the life of man, solitary, poore, nasty, brutish, and short'. From this state man is rescued by the law of nature, which is nothing other than the law of human reason, seeking peace. Since in the basic state of war there is no right and wrong, only expediency, force and fraud, there is no sanction to make any agreement to peace binding. Reason, therefore, dictates to each individual that for the preservation of his life and the establishment of peace he hand over his individual power to a civil authority and submit to that, and it is the coercive power of the civil authority that then provides the sanction enforcing private agreements and public laws. Of the possible types of civil constitution, democracy, aristocracy and monarchy, monarchy is the best, for 'In Monarchy, the private interest is the same with the publique. The riches, power, and honour of a Monarch arise onely from the riches, strength and reputation of his Subjects' [II, xix, pp. 241 – 2]. Other types of government lack this advantage, and a mixture of the different forms is inevitably weak. Once accepted, the social contract binds a man and his descendants, the only right that he cannot bargain away being the right to defend his own life, for it is the achievement of this that is the very aim of the social contract.

If the social contract has led to the establishment of a monarchy, then the monarch has an absolute power:

His Power cannot, without his consent, be Transferred to another: He cannot Forfeit it: He cannot be Accused by any of his Subjects, of Injury: He cannot be Punished by them: He is Judge of what is necessary for Peace; and Judge of Doctrines: He is Sole Legislator; and Supreme Judge of Controversies; and of the Times, and Occasions of Warre, and Peace: to him it belongeth to choose Magistrates, Counsellours, Commanders, and all other Officers, and Ministers; and to determine of Rewards, and Punishments, Honour, and Order.

[II, xx. pp. 252 – 3]

The allegiance of the subject is only dissolved by the military defeat of the monarch at the hands of an invading enemy and the cessation of military resistance; otherwise the social contract must be observed, and any failure to observe it will return man to his original state of war, which is what happens in a civil war. The inconveniences of being subject to a government are nothing to the evils of civil war:

But a man may here object, that the Condition of Subjects is very miserable. . . . [however] the estate of Man can never be without some incommodity or other; and . . . the greatest, that in any forme of Government can possibly happen to the people in generall, is scarce sensible, in respect of the miseries, and horrible calamities, that accompany a Civill Warre; or that [accompany the] dissolute condition of masterlesse men, without subjection to Lawes, and a coërcive Power to tye their hands from rapine, and revenge.

[II, xviii, p. 238]

It is this fear of civil war that provides the driving force behind Hobbes's desire for an absolute and powerful state. In what he was arguing for Hobbes was naive, but with the naivety of his age; he seems to have envisaged the end-product of his ideas as a more smoothly running version of the monarchical system he was used to, and he seems to have thought of a constitutional system, once established, as permanently fixed. He shows no awareness that a constitution must vary according to the geographical and climatic conditions, the technology and way of life of the people, and that it must inevitably change with time.

Hobbes's version of the motivation underlying civil society is based upon his low opinion of human nature; but, like Filmer, Hobbes drew strength from the experience of his own age. Society worked largely by coercion, with punishments ranging from the regular savage beating of children, through judicial and military floggings, to branding, maiming, hanging and ritual mutilation. Authority also tended to be intrusive and personal, the head of a 'family', or household, presiding over the private life of its members – an arrangement that lasted into the present century (a maidservant in the earlier decades of this century, for instance, would be questioned by her mistress about her associates and how she proposed to spend her time during a day off). This authority was all-pervading, extending even to the court, the 'family' of the monarch, whose permission was sought before a courtier could marry or even depart on a journey. Such control in everyday life lent credibility to, and removed some of the harshness from, Hobbes's authoritarian leanings. Moreover, his emphasis on fear drew sustenance from the unpleasant but powerful strand in the Christian tradition which seeks authority through fear (it is, perhaps, no accident that Hobbes was himself the son of a clergyman). Like Filmer, Hobbes was also paternalistic, taking so little account of women that they are seldom mentioned except as part of a man's 'propriety', coming after his own body and immediately before his goods and chattels in a list of defence interests. Children are viewed in the same light:

Nor would there be any reason, why any man should desire to have children, or take the care to nourish, and instruct them, if they were afterwards to have no other benefit from them, than from other men. And this accordeth with the fifth Commandement.
[II, xxx, p. 382]

This paternalism, deeply rooted in the social institutions of Hobbes's day, has been a dominant feature of the whole Judaeo-Christo-Islamic cultural tradition. Thus, motivation through fear, subjection to an all-embracing personal authority and a general assumption of paternalism were all readily acceptable since they were part of everyday life.

While Hobbes's ideas gained force by drawing on the conditions of the day, they nevertheless had sufficient daring and logical rigour to strike terror into the hearts of many contemporaries. If Hobbes seems, even now, relatively modern, this is due not to the content of his ideas, but to his way of thinking. He has departmentalized life in the modern manner and looks to observation and experience for the proof of his assertions. He does not deny the older view of the world, but he accepts it in a new way: thus he does not deny the validity of religion, but neither does he seek to derive his state from it, preferring in practice the experience of this world as more relevant. Similarly, he often slips into traditional patterns of thought, elaborating, for instance, the traditional image of society as a macrocosmic version of microcosmic man in the very opening of *Leviathan*:

Nature (the Art whereby God hath made and governes the World) is by the *Art* of man, as in many other things, so in this also imitated, that it can make an Artificial Animal. For seeing life is but a motion of Limbs, the begining whereof is in some principall part within; why may we not say, that all *Automata* (Engines that move themselves by springs and wheeles as doth a watch) have an artificial life? For what is the *Heart*, but a *Spring*; and the *Nerves* [that is, muscles] but so many *Strings*; and the *Joynts*, but so many *Wheeles*, giving motion to the whole Body, such as was intended by the Artificer? *Art* goes yet further, imitating that Rationall and most excellent worke of Nature, *Man*. For by Art is created that great LEVIATHAN called a COMMON-WEALTH, or STATE, (in latine CIVITAS) which is but an Artificiall Man; though of greater stature and strength than the Naturall, for whose protection and defence it was intended;

and in which, the *Soveraignty* is an Artificiall *Soul*, as giving life and motion to the whole body; The *Magistrates*, and other *Officers* of Judicature and Execution, artificiall *Joynts*; *Reward* and *Punishment* (by which fastned to the seate of the Soveraignty, every joynt and member is moved to performe his duty) are the *Nerves*, that do the same in the Body Naturall; The *Wealth* and *Riches* of all the particular members, are the *Strength*; *Salus Populi* (the *peoples safety*) its *Businesse*; *Counsellors*, by whom all things needfull for it to know, are suggested unto it, are the *Memory*; *Equity* and *Lawes*, an artificiall *Reason* and *Will*; *Concord, Health*; *Sedition, Sicknesse*; and *Civill war, Death*. Lastly, the *Pacts* and *Covenants*, by which the parts of this Body Politique were at first made, set together, and united, resemble that *Fiat*, or the *Let us make man*, pronounced by God in the Creation.

[pp. 81 – 2]

In a traditional writer this similarity would have been a correspondence, a similarity of parts and organization springing from an identity in source or essence: here it is an analogy, resulting from the imitation by society of a living body. The concept has been mechanized, and nature is being exploited for usable ideas, ideas that will work in practice. Hobbes's intellectual appeal is to observation and experience, and not ostensibly to sentiment or to accepted pieties. This attitude is one that Hobbes shared with Bacon, whose amanuensis he had been, and it was also found in Harvey and others in the vanguard of contemporary thought. The questioning of basic beliefs and assumptions causes discomfort and sometimes outrage. Hobbes managed to call into question the assumptions even of those who largely agreed with his conclusions, and many a royalist found his habit of accepting the right things for quite the wrong reasons profoundly disquieting, while the religious tended to feel that Hobbes put them out of business. He was an insidious ally and a dangerous adversary.

Nevertheless, disquieting though he might be, no one could deny that Hobbes was a 'great wit'. His interests ranged widely in mathematics and the arts, and his analytical power and knack for definition set the stamp of his rather dry mind on much of the literary criticism of the Restoration. In *Leviathan* he spoke presumably to persuade the generality of men to see reason and behave according to his wishes but, like so many philosophers that have followed him, he spoke only to the few. He does not touch the heart of the common man, for he has little instinctive sympathy with the human heart. It is to the common man, his hopes, fears and aspirations, that we must now turn.

## The Putney Debates

The events that led up to the Putney Debates at the end of 1647 are complicated. They began in March when Parliament, dominated by the Presbyterians, ordered the Army to disband. The Army refused to do so until a series of very reasonable demands were met, including the provision of a guarantee that soldiers would not be subsequently prosecuted for normally unlawful actions of military hostility, that arrears of pay would be made up, that restrictions would be placed on the future impressment of ex-soldiers and that:

Such in this Army as have lost their limbs, and the wives and children of such as have been slain in the service, and such officers or souldiers as have sustained losses, or have been prejudiced in their estates, by adhering to the Parliament; or in their persons by sickness or imprisonment under the Enemy, may have such allowances and satisfaction, as may be agreeable to Justice and equity.

They further demanded

That till the Army be disbanded as aforesaid, some course may be taken for the supply thereof with moneys, whereby we may be enabled to discharge our quarters, that so we may not for necessary food be beholden to the Parliament's Enemies, burthensome to their friends, or oppressive to the Country, whose preservation we have always endeavoured, and in whose happiness we should still rejoice.[5]

The demands highlight, on the one hand, the soldiers' distrust of those in authority, their fear of retribution from the king, who was still alive and negotiating, their misgivings about the intentions of Parliament and their lack of confidence that Parliament would meet its debts, and, on the other hand, their humane concern for the financial well-being of the wounded and the dependants of the dead and wounded, and their concern that the Parliamentarian Army should not be a burden to the families on whom soldiers were forcibly billeted. Having done their duty, they wished to discharge their debts and responsibilities with dignity. Most of their demands were turned down flat, the biggest concession from Parliament being the promise of eight weeks' back pay only. Much to-ing and fro-ing between the Army and Parliament ensued, during which the officers of the Army tried to sit on the fence. Left without a lead or even much co-operation from the officers, the common soldiery organized themselves, choosing two 'Agitators' to represent each regiment in their deliberations. Officers who stood by the orders of Parliament found themselves arrested by their own soldiers. A raid was organized (possibly with the connivance of Cromwell) to remove the king from the custody of the guards appointed by Parliament and to retain him in the hands of the Army, which feared a secret accommodation between Parliament, the king and the Presbyterian forces in Scotland.

Pushed by events, Cromwell, his son-in-law Commissary-General Ireton, and Fairfax, the Commander-in-Chief, together with many other officers, came out in support of the soldiers' cause. At a general rendezvous in June a Council of the Army was set up, consisting of officers and Agitators, and in the same month a *Declaration of the Army* was issued, outlining proposals for settling the kingdom in peace, safety and freedom. It demanded that the Army have a say in the establishment of the government, and while it granted loyalty to duly elected parliaments that sat successively, it also affirmed the right to resist Parliament in defence of just rights and liberties. It did not object to the establishment of Presbyterianism as the official religion, provided there was no enforced conformity, but it did insist that those responsible for setting Parliament and Army at odds should be removed from power, a demand that was backed by the impeachment of eleven Presbyterian leaders in Parliament. Further negotiations followed between the Army and Parliament, and while they were going on the Council, urged on by Ireton, drew up drafts of what became the *Heads of the Proposals of the Army*. As negotiations proved inconclusive, the Army marched on London, occupying the capital in July. Meanwhile, the draft *Heads of the Proposals* were submitted to the captive king and were published in a modified form early in August. Further negotiations ensued between Parliament, the king and the Army, while the common soldiery grew increasingly restive at the prolonged attempts of Ireton and Cromwell to reach a negotiated settlement. Rumours began to circulate that Cromwell and Ireton had entered on a secret agreement with Charles. Suspicion also fell on some of the elected Agitators and several of them were replaced, and the representatives of sixteen regiments signed *The Case of the Army* in October. They were joined by a number of Levellers from London, including John Wildman, who was to take part in the Putney Debates, and the *Case*, together with a summary of political demands under the title *The Agreement of the People* were submitted to the Council of the Army for its consideration in late October.

It was above all the *Agreement* which formed the subject of the Putney Debates, a series of deliberations of the Council held in Putney in October and early November 1647 (the Council met on 28 October; a prayer meeting was held on 29 October; a Committee of Officers and Agitators met on 30 October; and further meetings of the Council continued until 9 November); the proceedings were recorded in shorthand by William Clarke, who acted as secretary. After the Putney Debates the Council continued to meet sporadically until 8 January 1648, by which time Leveller demands for the cessation of negotiations with the king had been met, as the negotiators had lost all confidence in the king's good faith. On the other hand, the more extreme and democratic demands were not met, and discipline had only gradually been restored in the Army by the suppression of several incipient mutinies. After January 1648 the Agitators no longer formed part of the Army Council, but briefly, during the Putney Debates, they had had a say in the affairs of the nation, and we thus have some insight into the mind of the Parliamentarian soldiery. We can also see from the Putney Debates the divergences between Cromwell and his soldiers, and why it was that he came to gain acceptance even from many royalists as almost a defender of the middle ground.

In the discussions of the Council, Cromwell and Ireton stand out as revolutionary conservatives. Cromwell speaks little and what he does say is characterized not by the clear ordering of abstract principles, but by a kind of pragmatic groping towards a conclusion; principles, when they are introduced, appear singly, with an implied rather than explicit system behind them. The power of the intelligence is impressive in its single-minded concern with the practical issue at hand, but it is operating in the way in which an intellectually untrained mind also works, and this must have given Cromwell an ability to communicate instinctively with the common people and to grasp the way they were thinking. It was part of the reason for his power as a leader. Faced with a slippery king, an intransigent Parliament, a potentially hostile army in Scotland and division in his own ranks, his first concern was the preservation of unity within the Army. He waited and listened, seeking a way forward. He took for granted the providential view of history, and nursed the millenarian hopes of the mid century:

I am one of those whose heart God hath drawn out to wait for some extraordinary dispensations, according to those promises that he hath held forth of things to be accomplished in the later times, and I cannot but think that God is beginning of them.
[pp. 103 – 4]

Within the context of divine providence, successful action must be right action, action fulfilling the divine will. Cromwell's criteria for discerning right action included scriptural precedent, to which he would turn for support (as he did when Colonel Harrison urged the immediate prosecution of the king for causing the bloodshed of the war), and the light of God within the human mind – but 'we should take heed what we speak in the name of the Lord', for the promptings of the mind may be 'will' (that is, wilfulness) rather than the will of God. Furthermore, actions should be appropriate to time, place and agent

that if we do difficult things, we may see that the things we do, have the will of God in them, that they are not only plausible and good things, but seasonable and honest things, fit for us to do.
[p. 45]

This approach gave Cromwell a pragmatic and formidable combination of caution – even extreme caution – and decisiveness, and tempered his actions with a shrewd grasp of the practical possibilities of the moment: he worked with the times, not against them. While the others argued about government systems, he was not interested in systems as such, though he fully recognized the practical need for government to serve the happiness of the governed, thus retaining the 'affections of the people':

If I could see a visible presence of the people, either by subscriptions or number, [I should be satisfied with it]; for in the government of nations that which is to be looked after is the affections of the people. And that, [if] I find [it], would satisfy my conscience in the present thing.
    [Consider the case of the Jews.] They were first [divided into] families where they lived, and had heads of families [to govern them], and they were next under judges, and [then] they were under kings. When they came to desire a king they had a king, first elective, and secondly by succession. In all these kinds of government they were happy and contented. If you make the best of it, if you should change the government to the best of it, it is but a moral thing. It is but, as Paul says, 'dross and dung in comparison of Christ'; and [I ask] why we shall so far contest for temporal things, that if we cannot have this freedom [peacefully] we will venture life and livelihood for it. When every man shall come to this condition [of mind], I think the state will come to desolation.
    [p. 97]

Nevertheless, despite this lack of interest in political systems as such, he did recognize that 'the foundation and supremacy is in the people, radically in them, and to be set down by them in their representations' [p. 36]. This approach led to a hesitancy in the face of proposed radical reform of the constitution, a need to feel that alterations really were necessary. Thus Cromwell's immediate and instinctive reaction to the suggestion of manhood suffrage was: 'The consequence of this rule tends to anarchy, must end in anarchy', and he saw no reason utterly to abolish the traditional property qualification for voters. This laid him open to the obvious charge of looking after his own interests:

The Lieut. Generall
Spoke much to expresse the danger of their principles who had sought to devide the Army. That the first particular of that which they call'd The Agreement of the People did tend very much to Anarchy, that all those who are in the Kingedome should have a voice in electing Representatives.

Capt. Bray
Made a longe speech to take off what the Lieut. General said, and that what hee call'd Anarchy was for propriety [i.e. property].
 [*CP*, p. 411]

From Cromwell's point of view, questions of the distribution of material wealth and the widening of the franchise were purely secondary. If Bray regarded Cromwell as a hindrance to the redistribution of wealth and political power, he was not alone, for many landowners came to agree with him, hence their grudging but growing acceptance of Cromwell as guaranteeing the survival of at least some vestige of the old order. However, Cromwell's primary concerns were undoubtedly religious, and it was his reading of the will of God, plus the logic of events, that pushed him towards his more revolutionary actions and conclusions. Unlike Ireton, he was not a theoretician of systems. To a mind already weak this might have proved a weakness; to Cromwell it gave the strength to see and seize a practical opportunity, and to stun his opponents by sudden, surprising and decisive action.

In contrast to Cromwell, Ireton seems to have spoken more than anybody else in the debates of the Council. He was trained as a lawyer, had a keen interest in constitutional questions and knew clearly how far he wished to go in altering the power of the king, the Lords and Parliament and in widening the franchise. Cromwell had a concern for the practically possible, Ireton for security of life, what he called 'safety':

I wish but this, that we may have a regard to safety – safety to our persons, safety to our estates, safety to our liberty. Let's have that as the law paramount, and then let us regard [the] positive constitution as far as it can stand with safety to these.

[p. 121]

Constitutional upheaval was only acceptable if it conduced to the 'law of liberty', an all-important proviso for Ireton. Like Cromwell, he sensed the hand of God in the victories of the Army, whose integrity and reputation he was intent on protecting. Beyond that he proclaimed his readiness to do all that was God's will, but with an underlying confidence that the things of which he heartily disapproved were not the will of God:

I look upon this Army as having carried with it hitherto the name of God, and having carried with it hitherto the interest of the people of God, and the interest which is God's interest, the honour of his name, the good and freedom and safety and happiness of his people. And for my part I think that it is that that is the only thing for which God hath appeared with us, and led us, and gone before us, and honoured us, and taken delight to work by us . . . [It is] not to me so much as the vainest or lightest thing you can imagine, whether there be a king in England or no, whether there be lords in England or no. For whatever I find the work of God tending to, I should desire quietly to submit to. If God saw it good to destroy, not only King and Lords, but all distinctions of degrees – nay if it go further, to destroy all property, that there's no such thing left, that there be nothing at all of civil constitution left in the kingdom – if I see the hand of God in it I hope I shall with quietness acquiesce, and submit to it, and not resist it. But still I think that God certainly will so lead those that are his, and I hope too he will so lead this Army, that they may not incur sin, or bring scandal upon the name of God, and the name of the people of God, that are both so nearly concerned in what this Army does.

[pp. 49 – 50]

While he 'hopes to submit' to the abolition of rank and property, should this be the will of God, he tends to equate such abolition with sin. His way of thinking is also deeply imbued with an English lawyer's awareness of precedents. He had an acute sense of the historical working of the constitution as co-operation between Lords and Commons, and in his opinion the king ought, by the terms of the Coronation Oath, to confirm the laws passed by Commons and Lords. Should the king refuse to do so, then at least 'in a case of safety' the acts of Commons and Lords should be law without his consent. Except for curbing the king's effective power within these limits, Ireton saw no reason to change what he believed to be the traditional arrangement. As for franchise:

I think that no person hath a right to an interest or share in the disposing of the affairs of the kingdom, and in determining or choosing those that shall determine what laws we shall be ruled by here – no person hath a right to this, that hath not a permanent fixed interest in this kingdom.

[pp. 53 – 4]

A property qualification for the vote should therefore remain; as Ireton said, 'All the main thing that I speak for, is because I would have an eye to property.' The ostensible reason for having 'an eye to property' is that independent private property is the basis of liberty: 'If there be anything at all that is a foundation of liberty it is this, that those who shall choose the law-makers shall be men freed from dependence upon others' [p. 82]. Ireton is thus forced to the rather odd conclusion that property-less soldiers fought to ensure the democratic rights of those who did have property. This they did, he claimed, to avoid the tyranny of one man's will, to enjoy the good judgement of propertied representatives who had a stake in the kingdom and therefore its interests at heart, and because the unpropertied might in their turn acquire property and come to enjoy voting rights.

Every man that was born [in the country, that] is a denizen in it, that hath a freedom, he was capable of trading to get money, to get estates by; and therefore this man, I think, had a great deal of reason to build up such a foundation of interest to himself: that is, that the will of one man should not be a law, but that the law of this kingdom should be by a choice of persons to represent, and that choice to be made by, the generality of the kingdom. Here was a right that induced men to fight, and those men that had this interest, though this be not the utmost interest that other men have [i. e. though it did not equal the interest of propertied voters], yet they had *some* interest.

[p. 72]

Just as the royalists tended to argue that the interest of a monarch and the interests of his subjects were ultimately identical, so Ireton here assumes, without proof, that the interests of independent men of property are ultimately identical with those of the unpropertied masses. As is so often the case with ingenious and intellectual men, Ireton was in fact engaged in double-thinking, reading into the minds of the ordinary soldiery motives convenient to himself that were not there. Before his arguments about property are dismissed utterly, however, it might be remembered that his equation of property and liberty does have some substance – an independent financial base is necessary if centralized or collective power is to be resisted. Moreover, with a partially illiterate electorate secret voting would also have been difficult in the seventeenth century, and open voting did expose voters to pressure from landlords and other people with power. The abandonment of private property as such would also have meant the disruption of agriculture and the traditional economy and way of life, with the danger of starvation as a consequence. There were thus some grounds for what Ireton was saying, and he was willing to move in the direction of widening the franchise and equalizing the number of voters who elected a representative. For similar reasons Colonel Rich, another of the debaters, while suggesting that, 'there may be some other way thought of, that there may be a representative of the poor as well as the rich', nevertheless also opposed the enfranchising of property-less men, pointing out that in ancient Rome, 'the people's voices were bought and sold . . . and thence it came that he that was the richest man, and [a man] of some considerable power among the soldiers, and one they resolved on, made himself a perpetual dictator' (p. 64).

To the property-less soldiers themselves, of course, the case looked quite different, and the Agitators did not share the misgivings of Rich and Ireton and Cromwell. The latter were for adjusting the institutions of society but continuing them in some recognizable form, not rejecting them outright. The Agitators and the officers sympathetic to them started instead from a sense of the outrageous injustice of the old order. The participant called 'Buff-Coat' said succinctly:

According to my expectations and your engagements, you are resolved every one to purchase our inheritances which have been lost, and free this nation from the tyranny that lies upon us.
[p. 6]

Colonel Rainborough expostulated:

That which is dear unto me is my freedom. It is that I would enjoy, and I will enjoy if I can.
[p. 33]

And he stated as a more general principle:

Really I think that the poorest he that is in England hath a life to live, as the greatest he; and therefore truly, sir, I think it's clear, that every man that is

to live under a government ought first by his own consent to put himself
under that government; and I do think that the poorest man in England is
not at all bound in a strict sense to that government that he hath not had a
voice to put himself under. . . . I should doubt whether he was an
Englishman or no, that should doubt of these things.
    [p. 53]

In defence of this view he was forced to plead justice against
Ireton's urging of precedent:

I hear [it] said [that] it's a huge alteration, it's a bringing in of new laws,
and that this kingdom hath been under this government ever since it was a
kingdom. If writings be true there have been many scufflings between the
honest men of England and those that have tyrannized over them; and if it
be [true what I have] read, there is none of those just and equitable laws
that the people of England are born to, but are entrenchment[s on the once
enjoyed privileges of their rulers] altogether.
    [p. 14]

And he also pointed out that by being in arms they were already
breaking with the constitution:

That the Commissary Generall is willing to lay that of Constitution aside,
and that of Custome aside, and to consider the equality and reasonableness
of the thinge, and nott to stand uppon Constitution, which wee have
broken againe and againe.
    [*CP*, p. 402][6]

Mr Petty took up the same cry:

I understood your engagement was that you would use all your endeavours
for the liberties of the people, that they should be secured. If there is [such]
a constitution that the people are not free, that [constitution] should be
annulled.
    [p. 78]

'We judge,' he said, 'that all inhabitants that have not lost their
birthright should have an equal voice in elections.' Captain Clarke
also urged the mutability of constitutions:

I presume that all people, and all nations whatsoever, have a liberty and
power to alter and change their constitutions if they find them to be weak
and infirm.
    [p. 80]

Mr Wildman traced the constitution itself back to slavery introduced by Norman conquerors:

Our case is to be considered thus, that we have been under slavery. That's
acknowledged by all. Our very laws were made by our conquerors; and
whereas it's spoken much of chronicles, I conceive there is no credit to be

given to any of them; and the reason is because those that were our lords, and made us their vassals, would suffer nothing else to be chronicled. We are now engaged for our freedom. That's the end of Parliaments: not to constitute what is already [established, but to act] according to the just rules of government. Every person in England hath as clear a right to elect his representative as the greatest person in England. I conceive that's the undeniable maxim of government: that all government is in the free consent of the people.

[pp. 65 – 6]

Thus the soldiers fought for their 'birthright', which they tended to equate with rights possessed by their Saxon ancestors before the Conquest, and this birthright was freedom, specifically the freedom to have a say in the government and some control over their own lives. The Agitators and their party were absolutely clear that anything less than this would be a cheat and a betrayal. Mr Sexby's indignation is apparent:

We have engaged in this kingdom and ventured our lives, and it was all for this: to recover our birthrights and privileges as Englishmen; and by the arguments urged there is none. There are many thousands of us soldiers that have ventured our lives; we have had little propriety in the kingdom as to our estates, yet we have had a birthright. But it seems now, except a man hath a fixed estate in this kingdom, he hath no right in this kingdom. I wonder we were so much deceived. If we had not a right to the kingdom, we were mere mercenary soldiers. There are many in my condition, that have as good a condition [as I have]; it may be little estate they have at present, and yet they have as much a [birth]right as those two [Cromwell and Ireton] who are their lawgivers, as any in this place. I shall tell you in a word my resolution. I am resolved to give my birthright to none. Whatsoever may come in the way, and [whatsoever may] be thought, I will give it to none.

[p. 69]

And he later reiterated his disillusion:

Do you [not] think it were a sad and miserable condition, that we have fought all this time for nothing? . . . It had been good in you to have advertised us of it, and I believe you would have [had] fewer under your command to have commanded.

[p. 74]

A speaker simply labelled 'Agitator' pressed the same point, while denying that the meetings of the soldiery were a put-up job:

Whereas you say the Agents did it, [it was] the soldiers did put the Agents upon these meetings. It was the dissatisfactions that were in the Army

which provoked, which occasioned, those meetings, which you suppose tends so much to dividing; and the reason[s] of such dissatisfactions are because those whom they had to trust to act for them were not true to them.
[p. 88]

Ireton viewed with alarm all appeals to the law of nature and natural rights as a potential threat to property, and the Agitators tried to soothe him by insisting that an onslaught on property was not their aim. He similarly viewed with alarm the Agitators' insistence on their right to disobey unjust laws, but as he was himself rebelling against an unjust government, he was in an untenable position. The floodgates had been opened and were not easily to be closed again. When the Agitators met Ireton on the ground of constitutional precedent they were defeated; but they did represent the Army, and the Army was necessary, and it was recognized by the officers that as soldiers of the kingdom the rank and file in the Army had their dignity and their rights. Wildman claimed:

it will never satisfy the godly people in the kingdom unless that all government be in the Commons, and freely.
[p. 118]

The Council, meeting to consider the various undertakings of the Army, did resolve in favour of equalizing the number of voters in what we would now call a constituency and of ensuring that no part of the kingdom lacked representation in Parliament. They also advocated a concession in favour of their own soldiers:

That the qualifications of the people that shall have voices in the Elections . . . bee determined by the Commons in this present Parliament before the end therof, soe as to give as much inlargement to Common freedome as may bee, with a due regard had to the equality and end of the present Constitution in that point; wherein wee desire itt may bee provided, that all freeborne Englishmen, or persons made free denizons of England, who have served the Parliament in the late warre for the liberties of the Kingdome . . . bee admitted to have voices in the said elections for the respective Counties or Divisions wherein they shall inhabite, although they should nott in other respects bee within the qualifications to bee sett downe.
[*CP*, pp. 365 – 6]

In common prudence and in common justice the Council could hardly have escaped with conceding less.

The aspirations expressed by Rainborough and the common soldiery are age-old. The Leveller background of the Agitators enabled them to articulate basic human needs – the need of the individual to feel that his wishes and interests are, within reason, being consulted, that he has the basic necessities of material life and that he can live without being an undue burden to others. The most striking thing about the soldiers' representatives is not their demands, but their extreme and admirable independence of spirit.

From the clash in the Council two major factors emerge. The first is the soldiers' grasp of the relativity of political institutions; they have realized that other constitutional arrangements than the one they have are possible, that constitutions are not divine commands or the inevitable results of historical processes, but the choice of men and alterable. This is a view that even today might be considered revolutionary in East and West alike. The second factor is the unpreparedness of Ireton and Cromwell and the majority of the Parliamentarian officers for this onslaught on their own power and authority, while they were busy attacking the king's. Their cry of 'anarchy' is the habitual cry of those who find their authority challenged. It is also clear that Ireton and Cromwell are concerned for their property and the way of life that goes with it, that the soldiers are primarily concerned with freedom and a share in making decisions, not with material property, and that both sides have a tendency to recognize that the two issues are nevertheless closely interconnected. The wishes of the soldiers existed before their day and still exist – and still remain unfulfilled.

That they could make their wishes felt came about because they were soldiers in a revolution and were needed. The rift experienced by the revolutionary Army between the interests of accumulated property and of individual freedom continued during the uneasy return to earlier outward forms of government after the Restoration. It was the search for compromise rather than conflict which led to the events of 1688 and later, and it was this search that found its intellectual expression in the pragmatic political philosophy of Locke.

## Locke

Locke's *Two Treatises of Government* were published together in 1689, though composition appears to have begun in 1679 during the Exclusion Crisis and to have continued until the date of publication.[7] Both treatises were aimed primarily at Filmer, whose ideas were being widely advocated from the pulpit as the norm of orthodoxy in the early 1680s, though the second treatise glances occasionally at Hobbes. The treatises were originally independently composed and overlap to some extent, the second being of more general interest, while the first is largely given up to the tedious pursuit of Filmer through the minutiae of scriptural references. Apparently Locke had not read the Leveller tracts and he would have known nothing of the Putney Debates, though as both secretary and doctor to the Earl of Shaftesbury he would have had acquaintance with the general thinking of the Parliamentarian groups in the Civil War. However this may be, he certainly picks up in the most striking manner the major concerns of the discussions at Putney. Government by consent, the right of the people to build their constitution anew, an appeal to reason not precedent, a rejection of right by conquest, a conceding of the desirability of equality of representation, an emphasis upon the necessity of trust and a concern with the preservation of private property all feature in Locke's work. To understand accurately Locke's positive ideas on these points we must enter into his whole way of thinking, shown both in his refutation of Filmer and in the more general characteristics of his system of thought.

Locke is clearly irritated by Filmer. He refers to his work as *'so much glib Nonsense put together in well sounding* English', and finds Filmer's position preposterous, unreasonable. Nevertheless, he is forced to take it very seriously indeed. He objects that Filmer's paternalism confounds the fatherhood of God, the intentional Maker, with that of man, the mere occasional and fortuitous begetter ('What Father of a Thousand, when he begets a Child, thinks farther then the satisfying his present Appetite?'). Filmer also ignores the authority of the mother and her dominant role in generation, 'For no body can deny but that the Woman hath an equal share, if not the greater, as nourishing the Child a long time in her own Body', so that power within the family is parental rather than paternal. Moreover, Filmer ignores the admissible limits to parental power, which lasts only until the children attain the age of reason, and may only be legitimately exercised for the children's good, parents being *under an obligation to preserve, nourish, and educate the Children*, they had begotten'. Locke's appeal in these objections is really to reasonableness and common experience; nevertheless, he feels that it must be bolstered by detailed scriptural support, and hence his pursuit of Filmer through the *Genesis* and his demonstrations that Sir Robert misquotes and misinterprets

Holy Writ. Locke's instinct is, however, to move from Sir Robert Filmer's mental world of religious authority towards a modern, secular world of rational rights, and his historical importance is that he does this without flouting the old order and the social forces behind it.

Locke is the reconciler of different ways of thinking. He brings traditional religious sentiment to the support of rational argument about empirical data. His system is open-ended. Whereas Hobbes had tried to enclose his entire subject matter within a complete and perfect rational argument, so that one brick falsely placed brings the whole edifice about his ears, Locke instead launches certain general principles and criteria and leaves their exact definition and relationships vague. As the balance is shifted between them, so very different practical approaches to politics, and indeed to life, can emerge from them, yet some common communication and understanding can be retained, as will become clear from a brief survey of these major conceptions. Locke's system, possibly because of its philosophical incompleteness, is thus of immense practical use.

Locke's basic conceptions start with a distinction between the state of nature, or of man untrammelled by civil society, and the state of war.

And here we have the plain *difference between the State of Nature, and the State of War*, which however some Men have confounded, are as far distant, as a State of Peace, Good Will, Mutual Assistance, and Preservation, and a State of Enmity, Malice, Violence, and Mutual Destruction are one from another. Men living together according to reason, without a common Superior on Earth, with Authority to judge between them, is *properly the State of Nature*. But force, or a declared design of force upon the Person of another, where there is no common Superior on Earth to appeal to for relief, *is the State of War*.
[II, xix, p. 298]

This is as much as to say that man is by nature sociable. The reason for this is that a human being is both subject to, and has within him, the Law of Nature. Before that Law all men are equal, being born equal and free, and that Law obliges men to care each for others, all being equally the handiwork and property of God. The central description of the Law of Nature in Locke is simply 'reason':

But though this [the state of nature] be a *State of Liberty*, yet it is *not a State of Licence*, though Man in that State have an uncontroleable Liberty, to dispose of his Person or Possessions, yet he has not Liberty to destroy himself, or so much as any Creature in his Possession, but where some nobler use, than its bare Preservation calls for it. The *State of Nature* has a Law of Nature to govern it, which obliges every one: And Reason, which is that Law, teaches all Mankind, who will but consult it, that being all equal and independent, no one ought to harm another in his Life, Health, Liberty, or Possessions. . . . Every one as he is *bound to preserve himself*, and not to quit his Station wilfully; so by the like reason when his own Preservation comes not in competition, ought he, as much as he can, *to preserve the rest of Mankind*, and may not unless it be to do Justice on an Offender, take away, or impair the life, or what tends to the Preservation of the Life, the Liberty, Health, Limb or Goods of another.

[II, vi, pp. 288 – 9]

The Law of Nature is one of Locke's most important and profound concepts and is a restatement in contemporary terms of an idea central to the whole tradition of Western European civilization. It could indeed be said to lie behind such modern phenomena as the Declaration of Human Rights. Like all such really important and widely applicable principles, the Law of Nature has a broad range of possible interpretations, and Locke himself has a sliding scale of usage. While the central meaning of the term in Locke is reason, *'The Voice of God'* in man, it moves objectively towards ethical principles like the desirability of preserving life and the recognition of the inherent dignity of others, while it also has an interesting subjective extension:

For *Law,* in its true Notion, is not so much the Limitation as *the direction of a free and intelligent Agent* to his proper Interest, and prescribes no farther than is for the general Good of those under that Law. Could they be happier without it, the *Law,* as an useless thing would of it self vanish; and that ill deserves the Name of Confinement which hedges us in only from Bogs and Precipices. So that, however it may be mistaken, *the end of Law* is not to abolish or restrain, but *to preserve and enlarge Freedom*: For in all the states of created beings capable of Laws, *where there is no Law, there is no Freedom.*

[II, lvii, pp. 323 – 4]

Here the Law of Nature, expressed in human reason, has become the means by which man is self-directed towards his 'proper' (that is his own), his peculiarly human interest, and its aim is freedom and happiness. The Law has thus become the expression of the basic nature of man, whose realization in action brings fulfilment to him. Locke's conception thus spans the gap between the objectively oriented and ultimately Aristotelian strand in European civilization and the subjectively oriented Neo-Platonist strand. It gives a common ground and a means of communication, which are invaluable services to civilized life.

The idea of the Law of Nature also has other most important applications to politics, to family life, to society at large. Fundamentally, it sets bounds to power, or at least to legitimate power. Being by nature equal and free, all men are equally subject to the Law of Nature, and no man may repudiate that Law by placing himself utterly beneath the absolute power of another.

For a Man, not having the Power of his own Life, *cannot,* by Compact, or his own Consent, *enslave himself* to any one, nor put himself under the Absolute, Arbitrary Power of another, to take away his Life, when he pleases. No body can give more Power than he has himself; and he that cannot take away his own Life, cannot give another power over it.
     [II, xxiii, p. 302]

Each man has, moreover, the executive power of the Law of Nature within himself, though he may consign this to a civil society while that society lasts. However, within or outside civil society any bid for absolute power constitutes an act of war, and the dissolution of a civil society inevitably follows this, in which case it is the Law of Nature that force may be properly opposed by force.

And hence it is, that he who attempts to get another Man into his Absolute Power, does thereby *put himself into a State of War* with him; It being to be understood as a Declaration of a Design upon his Life . . . [and] he that in the State of Society, would take away the *Freedom* belonging to those of that Society or Common-wealth, must be supposed to design to take away from them every thing else, and so be looked on as *in a State of War.*
     [II, xvii, p. 297]

Upon this principle rests the lawfulness of rebellion against absolute rule. Similarly, parental power is not absolute, but subject to the Law of Nature. Children are potentially the equals of their parents, they 'are not born in this full state of *Equality,* though they are born to it', for, 'we are *born Free,* as we are born Rational; not that we have actually the Exercise of either: Age that brings one, brings with it the other too'. Parents are not the arbitrary lords of their children, but responsible for the wardship of their children under the Law of Nature:

*Adam* and *Eve,* and after them all *Parents* were, by the Law of Nature, *under an obligation to preserve, nourish, and educate the Children,* they had begotten, not as their own Workmanship, but the Workmanship of their own Maker, the Almighty, to whom they were to be accountable for them.

[II, lvi, p. 323]

Instances adduced by Filmer of parents sacrificing, enslaving and castrating their children are disgusting violations of natural law and not proof of absolute paternal power. However, the practical limitation of the Law of Nature in the state of nature lies in the limitations of individual power and the fallibility of the individual mind.

For though the Law of Nature be plain and intelligible to all rational Creatures; yet Men being biassed by their Interest, as well as ignorant for want of study of it, are not apt to allow of it as a Law binding to them in the application of it to their particular Cases.

[II, cxxiv, p. 369]

Were it not for 'the corruption, and vitiousness of degenerate Men', there would be no need to come out of the single community of all mankind in the state of nature and under the Law of Nature. However, given this corruption and fallibility, man's answer is the formation of civil societies.

The basis of civil society is consent: 'all peaceful beginnings of *Government* have been *laid in the Consent of the People*', and to govern by conquest is to use power illegitimately. When the people place power in the hands of governors they give it as a trust, a valid proceeding even in the state of nature, 'For Truth and keeping of Faith belongs to Men, as Men, and not as Members of Society' (this circumvents the objection to the theories of Hobbes that a social contract could not be entered into before society was there to validate it, and it also avoids altogether the narrow idea of a legal contract). The founding act in creating a civil society is creating the legislative power, which is then the supreme power within that society, though if it betrays the trust placed in it then the people retain the ultimate, supreme power of dissolving that society:

Though in a Constituted Commonwealth . . . there can be but *one Supream Power*, which is *the Legislative*, to which all the rest are and must be subordinate, yet the Legislative being only a Fiduciary Power to act for certain ends, there remains still *in the People a Supream Power* to remove or *alter the Legislative*, when they find the *Legislative* act contrary to the trust reposed in them.

[II, cxlix, pp. 384 – 5]

The judges who decide when trust has been forfeited are the people themselves, who deliver their verdict by rebelling and using force against force, or 'appealing to Heaven', that is to say the judgement of God in history. Government should serve, and be felt to serve, the purposes for which society was created: faced with the 'fears and continual dangers' of the state of nature, man

seeks out, and is willing to joyn in Society with others who are already united, or have a mind to unite for the mutual *Preservation* of their lives, Liberties and Estates, which I call by the general Name, *Property*.
[II, cxxiii, p. 368]

Property, whose preservation is society's aim, thus becomes another of Locke's sliding terms. In the state of nature all things belong to man in common, but his labour gives him a right to what he takes from the common stock, for

Though the things of Nature are given in common, yet Man (by being Master of himself, and *Proprietor of his own Person*, and the Actions or *Labour* of it) had still in himself *the great Foundation of Property*; and that which made up the great part of what he applyed to the Support or Comfort of his being, when Invention and Arts had improved the conveniences of Life, was perfectly his own, and did not belong in common to others.

Thus *Labour*, in the Beginning, *gave a Right of Property*, where-ever any one was pleased to imploy it, upon what was common, which remained, a long while, the far greater part, and is yet more than Mankind makes use of.
[II, xliv – v, pp. 316 – 17]

In the state of nature man has only the right to appropriate as much as he can use before it spoils, but by using money, which does not spoil, and by attributing to it a conventional value that is not intrinsic, men in general have consented to the accumulation of property:

Since Gold and Silver, being little useful to the Life of Man in proportion to Food, Rayment, and Carriage, has its *value* only from the consent of Men, whereof Labour yet makes, in great part, *the measure*, it is plain, that Men have agreed to disproportionate and unequal Possession of the Earth, they having by a tacit and voluntary consent found out a way, how a man may fairly possess more land than he himself can use the product of, by receiving in exchange for the overplus, Gold and Silver, which may be hoarded up without injury to any one, these metalls not spoileing or decaying in the hands of the possessor. This partage of things, in an inequality of private possessions, men have made practicable out of the bounds of Societie, and without compact, only by putting a value on gold and silver and tacitly agreeing in the use of Money. For in Governments the Laws regulate the right of property, and the possession of land is determined by positive constitutions.
[II, l, pp. 319 – 20]

Thus does Locke justify accumulated property, and the term itself slides between 'that Property which Men have in their Persons as well as Goods', something approaching basic human rights, and property in its more limited modern sense of material possessions. Thinking in terms of seventeenth-century English experience, and remembering the quarrels between king and Parliament on the subject of taxation, Locke denies the arbitrary right of government over property:

Hence it is a mistake to think, that the Supream or *Legislative Power* of any Commonwealth, can do what it will, and dispose of the Estates of the Subject *arbitrarily*, or take any part of them at pleasure. . . . In Governments, where the *Legislative* is in one lasting Assembly always in being, or in one Man, as in Absolute Monarchies, there is danger still, that they will think themselves to have a distinct interest, from the rest of the Community; and so will be apt to increase their own Riches and Power, by taking, what they think fit, from the People.

[II, cxxxviii, p. 379]

Nevertheless, the regulation of property by the law of the community is possible, 'For in Governments the laws regulate the right of property, and the possession of land is determined by positive constitutions'. The relationship between these two conflicting ideas is not clarified by Locke, but his basic feeling seems to be that an onslaught on private property is also an onslaught on individual freedom.

By recognizing, on the one hand, the rights of property and, on the other, the basis of government in consent, by upholding the supreme power of the people, and by regarding power as by nature both limited and given in trust, Locke stands between the positions of the officers and the Agitators in the Putney Debates. The Agitators were not out for equality of material goods and might have found Locke's general position acceptable. In discussing general principles Locke's whole approach (like Rainborough's and unlike Ireton's) is to argue on the basis of reasonableness and not constitutional precedent, for 'the *Municipal Laws* of Countries . . . are only so far right, as they are founded on the Law of Nature, by which they are to be regulated and interpreted'. Nevertheless, Locke clearly has his English experience and the English constitution in mind, and in some passages specifically, though not overtly, he refers to contemporary English issues.

Among the contemporary issues discussed by Locke are the legitimacy of rebellion and of the trial of superiors, the limitations necessarily implied in oaths of allegiance and the matter of equality of representation. The trial of Charles I must have been at the back of his mind, as well as the likely need for rebellion against Charles II or his successors. Given what amounts to the English constitution (Crown, house of nobles and elected assembly), then, claims Locke, the government is automatically dissolved and a state of war ensues if the 'Prince sets up his own Arbitrary Will in place of the Laws', if he 'hinders the Legislative from assembling in its due time, or from acting freely', if he arbitrarily alters 'the Electors, or ways of Election', or if either the legislature or the prince design the 'delivery . . . of the People into the subjection of a Foreign Power'. Locke has in mind the manoeuvres of Charles II, his summoning of the Commons to meet in Oxford and his use of the royal prerogative to influence elections, as well as the deep-rooted suspicion of the opposition that Charles had been willing to connive at an invasion by Louis XIV. Locke also carefully defines the royal prerogative:

This Power to act according to discretion, for the publick good, without the prescription of the Law, and sometimes even against it, *is* that which is called *Prerogative*.
[II, clx, p. 393]

Thus the prerogative is only legitimate 'whilst imployed for the benefit of the Community, and suitably to the trust and ends of the Government', and cannot therefore be 'encroached' upon, since it is not a private power. Moreover, the trial of a superior for the misuse of power is justified, a view which follows logically enough from the idea that no power should be absolute, that power goes with responsibility. Locke deals, on similar grounds, with the problem of when to break oaths of allegiance to the sovereign (the problem posed by oaths of allegiance to deposed sovereigns caused torments of conscience for innumerable Englishmen in the seventeenth and early eighteenth centuries):

though *Oaths of Allegiance* and Fealty are taken to him, 'tis not to him as Supream Legislator, but as *Supream Executor* of the Law, made by a joint Power of him with others; *Allegiance* being nothing but an *Obedience according to Law*, which when he violates, he has no right to Obedience.
[II, cli, p. 386]

Locke also advocated the idea that the majority should hold sway in a body politic (he does not specifically deal with the rights of the minority, though presumably the Law of Nature would come to his assistance here), and he supports equality of representation:

> For it being the interest, as well as intention of the People, to have a fair and *equal Representative*; whoever brings it nearest to that, is an undoubted Friend, to, and Establisher of the Government, and cannot miss the Consent and Approbation of the Community.
>
> [II, clviii, p. 391]

He also moves very close to enunciating the principle that the executive and legislative powers should be separate, again basing himself on English experience.

This reliance upon experience in a thoroughly pragmatic way, together with an ability to develop old ideas and adapt them to circumstances, gives Locke his peculiar power. His development, in particular, of the idea of natural law links his thinking with the older, traditionalist views of men like Hooker, whereas the innovations of Hobbes had disrupted tradition. Locke's is an untidy way of thinking, very organic and very English, logically imperfect but flexible in practice, and none the less reasonable for this, since logical perfection can only achieve truth if it takes into account the totality of possible information, which is unknowable to man. The central problem in Locke is the control of power, the prevention of arbitrary power and the protection of the individual against it. This central problem Locke had inherited through Shaftesbury from the England of the Civil War, but he has taken the discussion of it one stage further.

Locke's role in developing the discussions of an earlier generation and providing a compromise solution to its dilemmas has, in modern times, laid him open to the Marxist charge of being a spokesman of the rising bourgeoisie and helping to subvert a potential proletarian revolution. As Peter Laslett points out, this way of thinking does not really fit Locke:

> Locke was as free as a man could then be from solidarity with the ruling group, and yet he was not one of the ruled; this is the only intelligible definition of 'middle-class' as applied to him and it leaves out many of the things which that expression seems to imply. Ultimately the possibility of living like this did arise as a function of economic change, but Locke can only be made into the spokesman of that change by the use of a whole apparatus of unconscious motivation and rationalization. An order of free individuals is not a concerted group, not a cohesive assemblage actually bringing about change; no simple conception of 'ideology' will relate Locke's thought with social dynamics.

He is perhaps best described as an independent, free-moving intellectual, aware as others were not of the direction of social change.
[p. 44]

Indeed, the whole idea of economic change as the sole or necessarily the dominant force in the development of human society is simplistic. A theory of multiple causation involving an element of choice is nearer the reality of human experience. Nor does the view of Locke as an advocate of an economic group even do justice to seventeenth-century thought, most of which was firmly within a religious framework. Locke has human importance, for he made respectable the basic freedoms: his principles of consideration and care were to be extended by subsequent generations; he refused to treat human beings as property or as mere means to an end; his ideas on the rights of children began a long and slow process in the reform of education; his tendency to speak of women as rational creatures certainly helped in some alleviation of their lot; and his writings on toleration were a major cause of the eradication from England of the disgusting vice of religious persecution. He was undoubtedly a benign influence, and he is a major thinker whose force is by no means exhausted yet. He writes, however, out of his experience of the constitutional upheavals of the seventeenth century, and we must now turn back to look at Milton, who wrote in the middle of them, and at Dryden, whose greatest poetry deals with the Exclusion Crisis and Shaftesbury's opposition to Charles II, an opposition which led to Locke's own flight and exile in Holland.

# 5  Milton: the political pamphlets and *Paradise Lost*

A return to Milton and the political pamphleteers of the mid century discloses at once the originality and unoriginality of Locke. In
the mid-century disputes all of Locke's concepts already occur,
with the exception of his theory of property and labour. While
Locke's idea of property is important both in itself and for the
bridging role it enabled him to play, he is distinguished from the
Civil War pamphleteers above all by his unsectarian spirit and his
pragmatic flexibility, allowing a gradualist approach to reform. It
was the religious background of the earlier pamphleteers that made
them see the possibility of democracy, but it was equally their
religious background that hindered the broader application of their
ideas. Locke writes as someone aiming at a practical arrangement
to enable man to live at peace with his fellows as far as possible,
despite differences of opinion about the ultimate nature of the
universe. God is mentioned by Locke, but in a non-denominational
way that was acceptable to the vast Christian majority of the day
and would have remained acceptable to many eighteenth-century
minorities like the Deists. The Saints wrote as forwarders of the
schemes they attributed to the Almighty for the founding of heaven
on earth. They were concerned not with tolerance despite
divergences, but with establishing the practical conditions for the
triumph of truth (that is to say, the triumph of their particular conception of ultimate religious truth) in this world. If, accordingly,
tolerance was advocated, it was usually as a means to the end of
sectarian triumph. It was within this context that Milton's constitutional pamphlets were formulated.

The first major statement of Milton's political principles is *The
Tenure of Kings and Magistrates*, published in 1649, two weeks
after the execution of the king and in order to justify that act. The
opening states Milton's typical position:

If men within themselves would be govern'd by reason, and not generally
give up thir understanding to a double tyrannie, of Custom from without,

and blind affections within, they would discerne better, what it is to favour and uphold the Tyrant of a Nation. But being slaves within doors, no wonder that they strive so much to have the public State conformably govern'd to the inward vitious rule, by which they govern themselves. For indeed none can love freedom heartilie, but good men; the rest love not freedom, but licence; which never hath more scope or more indulgence then under Tyrants. Hence is it that Tyrants are not oft offended, nor stand much in doubt of bad men, as being all naturally servile; but in whom vertue and true worth most is eminent, them they feare in earnest, as by right thir Maisters, against them lies all thir hatred and suspicion. Consequentlie neither doe bad men hate Tyrants, but have been alwayes readiest with the falsifi'd names of *Loyalty*, and *Obedience*, to colour over thir base compliances.

[V, p.1, ll. 1 – 18][1]

The spirit behind this is hardly one of live and let live, though there is truth in Milton's case. It is nowadays most commonly assumed that economic and political systems make man, that reform therefore comes from manipulating systems. Milton's view that the basis of communal and political freedom is the virtue and internal freedom of individuals is equally possible and less naive. The narrowness comes rather with the conception of freedom and virtue. For Milton freedom exists in the state of divine grace – not an unreasonable idea in itself, but Milton's view of the state of grace is influenced by the Puritan experience of opposition against government and by a pervasive sense of being one of the 'Elect'. If election springs from faith, and faith is defined in terms of acceptance of tenets and propositions, then each man tends to conceive of the Elect as those who happen to agree with him, those who disagree being consigned to the devil's party. This is of course an inadequate mode of judgement and leads to such injustices as Milton's attributing a vicious servility to all the upholders of the traditional religious and social order. This sectarian attitude affects Milton's application of principles, which are in other ways strikingly similar to Locke's.

Milton, like Locke, starts from the natural freedom of man, and similarly points to a covenant as the basis of civil society:

No man who knows ought, can be so stupid to deny that all men naturally were borne free, being the image and resemblance of God himself, and were by privilege above all the creatures, born to command and not to obey: and that they liv'd so. Till from the root of *Adams* transgression, falling among themselves to doe wrong and violence, and foreseeing that such courses must needs tend to the destruction of them all, they agreed by common league to bind each other from mutual injury, and joyntly to defend themselves against any that gave disturbance or opposition to such agreement. Hence came Citties, Townes and Common-wealths. And because no faith in all was found sufficiently binding, they saw it needful to ordaine som authoritie, that might restrain by force and punishment what was violated against peace and common right. This autoritie and power of self-defence and preservation being originally and naturally in every one of them, and unitedly in them all, for ease, for order, and least each man should be his own partial Judge, they communicated and deriv'd either to one, whom for the eminence of his wisdom and integritie they chose above the rest, or to more then one whom they thought of equal deserving: the first was call'd a King; the other Magistrates. Not to be thir Lords and Maisters (though afterward those names in som places were giv'n voluntarily to such as had been Authors of inestimable good to the people) but, to be thir Deputies and Commissioners, to execute, by vertue of thir intrusted power, that justice which else every man by the bond of nature and of Cov'nant must have executed for himself, and for one another.

[V, p. 8, 1. 1 – p. 9, 1. 4]

The passage seems to imply the same existence within the individual of the executive power of the Law of Nature as is found in Locke, but Locke's explicitness makes his concept useful, whereas Milton introduces it implicitly in passing. The idea of trust, however, is spelt out more explicitly by Milton:

It being thus manifest that the power of Kings and Magistrates is nothing else, but what is only derivative, transferr'd and committed to them in trust from the People, to the Common good of them all, in whom the power yet remaines fundamentally, and cannot be tak'n from them, without a violation of thir natural birthright.

[V, p. 10, ll. 24 – 8]

The difference here is one of tone, Milton having more violence about him (inevitably, since he was engaged in justifying a revolution), and his references to the people's 'birthright' recall the language of the Agitators in the Putney Debates.

Similarly, when discussing the ultimate rule of law and the limited nature of oaths of allegiance he recalls Locke, while his specific concern with the coronation oath is part of the Agitators' case against the king:

While as the Magistrate was set above the people, so the Law was set above the Magistrate. When this would not serve, but that the Law was either not executed, or misapply'd, they were constrain'd from that time, the onely remedy left them, to put conditions and take Oaths from all Kings and

Magistrates at thir first instalment to doe impartial justice by Law: who upon those termes and no other, receav'd Allegeance from the people, that is to say, bond or Covnant to obey them in execution of those Lawes which they the people had themselves made, or assented to.
[V, p. 9, ll. 17–27]

The people have therefore in practice the power to rescind their oaths of allegiance upon sufficient provocation when they see fit. This, then, constitutes the equivalent of Locke's withdrawal of trust in the ruler. At this point in his political development Milton is thus still speaking in clearly recognizable terms within the main tradition of a developing democracy in England. His religious background, however, gives him an underlying tendency to equate the people who have rights with the people of God – that is, at this date, with the supporters of Parliament – and the ultimate sanction is military victory given by the favour of God. When he came to write his last major political pamphlet, just before the Restoration, circumstances had changed, and so had Milton's opinions.

*The Readie & Easie Way to Establish a Free Commonwealth* appeared in 1660 on the eve of the Restoration. The endless embroilment in controversy and the urgency of the situation leave their mark: Milton's style is breathless with the sincere eloquence of fanaticism. Apart from his more rational fears, Milton has an emotional loathing of kings and courts:

A king must be ador'd like a Demigod, with a dissolute and haughtie court about him, of vast expence and luxurie, masks and revels, to the debaushing of our prime gentry both male and female; not in thir passetimes only, but in earnest, by the loos imploiments of court service, which will be then thought honorable. There will be a queen also of no less charge; in most likelihood outlandish and a Papist; besides a queen mother such alreadie; together with both thir courts and numerous train: then a royal issue, and ere long severally thir sumptuous courts; to the multiplying of a servile crew, not of servants only, but of nobility and gentry, bred up then to the hopes not of public, but of court offices; to be stewards, chamberlains, ushers, grooms, even of the close-stool; and the lower thir mindes debas'd with court opinions, contrarie to all vertue and reformation, the haughtier will be thir pride and profuseness: we may well remember this not long since at home; or need but look at present into the *French* court, where enticements and preferments daily draw away and pervert the Protestant Nobilitie.
[VI, p. 120, ll. 9–28][2]

The picture is, of course, partial. It was not for nothing that the loathed court of Louis XIV was the cultural centre of Europe, and in England the cultural and artistic life of the court of Charles I had surpassed anything the Commonwealth could offer. The energetic but sternly repressive virtue of Puritanism may be admirable, but it is also narrow, hugely afraid of the more sensuous aspects of human nature, not tolerant of fundamental disagreement and open to no humour but that of scorn and derision. The Dionysian aspects of man can only emerge disguised as the headiness of the Holy Spirit: the confusion that this occasions is regrettable. Milton almost parodies himself in his contempt for the Presbyterians, who were favouring a restoration of the monarchy:

Let them but hear the insolencies, the menaces, the insultings of our newly animated common enemies crept lately out of thir holes, thir hell, I might say, by the language of thir infernal pamphlets, the spue of every drunkard, every ribald; nameless, yet not for want of licence, but for very shame of thir own vile persons, not daring to name themselves, while they traduce others by name; and give us to foresee that they intend to second thir wicked words, if ever they have power, with more wicked deeds. Let our zealous backsliders forethink now with themselves, how thir necks yok'd with these tigers of Bacchus, these new fanatics of not the preaching but the sweating-tub, inspir'd with nothing holier than the Venereal pox, can draw one way under monarchie to the establishing of church discipline with these new-disgorg'd atheismes: yet shall they not have the honor to yoke with these, but shall be yok'd under them; these shall plow on their backs.

[VI, p. 139, ll. 11 – 26]

Milton is as intemperate as the vices he castigates. But there is reason also on his side. He foresees rightly the difficulties caused by any attempt to undo the changes in the ownership of property that had taken place under the Commonwealth and also the danger of vindictive reprisals from newly returned royalists:

A new royal-revenue must be found, a new episcopal; for those are individual: both which being wholly dissipated or bought by privat persons or assign'd for service don, and especially to the Armie, cannot be recovered without a general detriment and confusion to mens estates, or a heavie imposition on all mens purses; benifit to none, but to the worst and ignoblest sort of men, whose hope is to be either the ministers of court riot and excess, or the gainers by it: But not to speak more of losses and extraordinarie levies on our estates, what will then be the revenges and offences remembered and returnd, not only by the chief person, but by all his adherents; accounts and reparations that will be requir'd, suites, inditements, inquiries, discoveries, complaints, informations, who knows against whom or how many.

[VI, p. 138, ll. 12 – 26]

That the reprisals upon the Restoration were no greater is, in fact, surprising, the result in part of Monck's shrewdness, in part of political necessity and in part of Charles's easy-going temperament, for, whatever his faults, general vindictiveness was not among them. Milton also rightly foresees the attempted suppression of the freedom of the press and the reopening of the struggle against royal autocracy. To avoid these dangers, he outlines his own plan for establishing a permanent republic.

Milton's planned republic is to be something new, not a monarchy or a traditional parliament. A rebel against monarchy, Milton had now become a rebel against parliaments, having learned to distrust them almost as much as he distrusted the king:

The main reason urg'd why popular assemblies are to be trusted with the peoples libertie, rather then a Senat of principal men, because great men will be still endeavoring to inlarge thir power, but the common sort will be contented to maintain thir own libertie, is by experience found false; none being more immoderat and ambitious to amplifie thir power, then such popularities.

[VI, p. 130, ll. 6 – 12]

Using his earlier language of democracy he advocates the setting up of a Grand Council:

For the ground and basis of every just and free government (since men have smarted so oft for commiting all to one person) is a general councel of ablest men, chosen by the people to consult of public affairs from time to time for the common good. In this Grand Councel must the sovrantie, not transferrd, but delegated only, and as it were deposited, reside.

[VI, p. 125, l. 28 – p. 126, l. 6]

However, the choice is to be a once-and-for-all affair:

And although it may seem strange at first hearing, by reason that mens mindes are prepossessd with the notion of successive Parlaments, I affirme that the Grand or General Councel being well chosen, should be perpetual.

[VI, p. 126, ll. 16 – 19]

With the experience of the Commonwealth behind him, Milton has learned to distrust the endless wrangling of parliaments:

I see not therefor, how we can be advantag'd by successive and transitorie Parlaments; but that they are much likelier continually to unsettle rather then to settle a free government; to breed commotions, changes, novelties and uncertainties; to bring neglect upon present affairs and opportunities, while all mindes are suspense with expectation of a new assemblie, and the assemblie for a good space taken up with the new setling of it self. After

which, if they finde no great work to do, they will make it, by altering or
repealing former acts, or making and multiplying new; that they may seem
to see what thir predecessors saw not, and not to have assembld for
nothing: till all law be lost in the multitude of clashing statutes.
    [VI, p. 127, ll. 4 – 16]

His Grand Council should therefore be permanent, or if this cannot
be, then a proportion of its members should periodically face new
elections. But Milton has learned to distrust elections also, so
perhaps election procedure could be modified:

Another way will be, to wel-qualifie and refine elections: not committing
all to the noise and shouting of a rude multitude, but permitting only those
of them who are rightly qualifi'd, to nominat as many as they will; and out
of that number others of a better breeding, to chuse a less number more
judiciously, till after a third or fourth sifting and refining of exactest
choice, they only be left chosen who are the due number, and seem by most
voices the worthiest.
    [VI, p. 131, ll. 21 – 8]

If elections are designed to choose the best, then they cannot, of
course, be said to work very well, but they do provide some
possibility of ousting the incompetent. A permanent Grand
Council, if incompetent or dishonest, could only be ousted by Civil
War, and since Milton was proposing that it should originally be
established by elections, there would be no guarantee that these
first elections would prove more reliable than subsequent ones.
Milton does, however, provide some counterpoise against a centralized assembly in his idea of regional assemblies governing local
affairs under the auspices of the Grand Council (again a reflection
of Interregnum experience of the difficulty of establishing central
control over the counties). This is one of the innumerable prophetic
suggestions for amending the constitution put forward during the
Commonwealth and since realized or approaching realization now.
Indeed, the whole central problem that drove Milton to new
schemes, the discovery that a parliament could be just as tyrannous
or as disastrously inefficient as an individual autocracy, is also
something that is still with us and is likely to remain so.
    In 1660 Milton's reforming suggestions were ignored – perhaps
rightly so. They were not likely to have worked in practice. His
scheme for a democratic oligarchy was not fully formulated and he
was beset with the difficulties of a democrat who distrusts the
people. The mere discussion of these issues was, however, a service,

part of a general growth of tolerance. From the first there had been within Puritanism a tendency to seek the gradual revelation of the full truth of the Lord by groping towards it, aided by prayer and full discussion with the brethren: some disagreement among the like-minded was part of the work of Christ. There was, therefore, some spirit of tolerance and liberty here. This spirit had already been carried further towards secular liberty by the Levellers, who tended to regard religious conviction as a matter of private conscience, while other aspects of life were to be regulated democratically by the state; thus equality before God could lead to ideas of toleration and political equality. The Diggers had carried similar doctrines to the conclusion of material equality and the abolition of ancient rights of property, while the Ranters had inferred from the freedom of the regenerate a sexual freedom which effectively abolished traditional marriage, removing the restraints placed by the community on the sexual life of the individual. Within the life of the sects the sheer divergence of opinion therefore exerted pressure towards toleration.

There were also other intellectual influences at work for toleration. One stemmed from the German and Dutch tradition of Christian mysticism, which tended to emphasize Christ as a principle of divine life within the souls of all men, rather than as an object of doctrinal belief. (The Familists, with their emphasis on God as Love, stood loosely within this tradition, as did the Quakers with their belief in the Inner Light.) Another major influence was the strand of intellectual scepticism bred by the Renaissance and encouraged both by the gradual emerging of an experimental method in 'natural philosophy', or science, as we would now call it, and by the increasing knowledge of strange cultures and continents, where customs and beliefs opposed to ours were equally taken for granted. (Montaigne had become a powerful propagator in England of this type of scepticism, at least in more cultivated circles.)

There were thus many currents of ideas flowing towards toleration or some measure of it. In this context Milton stands out as almost right-wing in his faith in the chosen few rather than the promiscuous many as instruments of government, and, as we have seen, it is this belief that comes to dominate in his later political thinking. That he had the courage still to publish his ideas on the very eve of the Restoration is, however, one of the acts that kept the growing spirit of tolerance alive at a time when it might have been utterly extinguished. His specific suggestions are less import-

ant than this service. Apart from his link with Cromwell's government, the reason why Milton's writings on constitutional issues still
receive the attention they do is because of his importance to us as a
poet, and his constitutional thinking can clarify some aspects of
*Paradise Lost*.

*Paradise Lost* is one of the two great feats of the Puritan
imagination, but its achievement is unequal, some aspects being far
more powerful and persuasive than others. One striking and odd
characteristic of Milton's universe is the lack of freedom within it,
and it is a characteristic that Milton certainly did not intend;
indeed, he specifically points to the freedom of his characters:

Freely they stood who stood, and fell who fell
    [III, l. 102][3]

says God himself;

To stand or fall
Free in thine own Arbitrement it lies
    [VIII, ll. 640 – 1]

Raphael warns Adam, and he comments on the lot of the angels in
heaven,

Freely we serve,
Because wee freely love, as in our will
To love or not.
    [V, ll. 538 – 40]

As a word freedom rings through the poem, but the substance of
it is lacking; that this is so is the result of a partial failure of
Milton's imagination, which is connected with the nature of his
theology. Milton understands Hell much better than he
understands heaven, the heavenly existence in *Paradise Lost* being
an endless round of pious futility. The basic reason for this lies in
Milton's whole imaginative conception of God; his God is time-
bound and present throughout space rather than free from it.
Milton does not conceive of eternity, even the eternity of God, as
timelessness, beyond time, beyond space, beyond duality. Instead,
he imagines eternity as time going on for ever except that it is
slower-moving and more long-drawn-out; his eternity is thus
indistinguishable from the temporal sequence of this world. In
Milton time is an unalterable absolute, for

Past who can recall, or don undoe?
Not God Omnipotent, nor Fate
    [IX, ll. 926 – 7]

(as the yet unfallen Adam comments). In keeping with this way of thought, God is conceived of far less as a principle of life within creatures, despite passing references to this idea, than as an external ruler and law-giver within a spatial heaven and a temporal sequence. The imaginative consequences are immense. If the divine life is the essence of man's own being, then it becomes possible to move towards the conception of law mooted at one point by Locke as 'in its true Notion . . . not so much the Limitation as *the direction of a free and intelligent Agent* to his proper Interest' (see page 69 above). In other words, law becomes humanity's own essence or fundamental nature, and individual spontaneity, law and fulfilment can become one; the individual can be free because he is fundamentally Freedom. Milton, however, can only conceive of relative freedom – that is, freedom defined in terms of an external situation, an ability merely to choose or reject certain lines of action.

Thus, freedom in *Paradise Lost* becomes the possibility of obeying or disobeying edicts that are imaginatively felt as external. This would not in itself be so cramping, were it not coupled with Milton's emphasis on his peculiarly anthropormorphic conception of God's supremacy in the affairs of men and angels. In order to make clear God's supremacy and the futility of Satan's rebellion, Milton turns the heavenly world into an autocracy, in which all decisions of any importance are made in the centre, and all power resides in the centre. The good angels do not take original initiatives of their own, in accordance with their own nature; they wait for and react to orders, and their obedience is required as proof of love, God being He 'whom to love is to obey', (for whom the proof is required is not entirely clear; the all-knowing God could hardly require it, though Book III, lines 103 – 4, seem to suggest this interpretation). Since God is imagined as an externalized and discrete entity, His power must be seen to be maintained by His being seen to act independently of His creatures' action. The result is situations like that described by Raphael:

For I that Day was absent, as befell,
Bound on a voyage uncouth and obscure,
Farr on excursion toward the Gates of Hell;
Squar'd in full Legion (such command we had)
To see that none thence issu'd forth a spie,
Or enemie, while God was in his work,
Least hee incenst at such eruption bold,

Destruction with Creation might have mixt.
Not that they durst without his leave attempt,
But us he sends upon his high behests
For state, as Sovran King, and to enure
Our prompt obedience.
       [VIII, ll, 229 – 40]

To send the angels from one end of the universe to the other on an unnecessary errand to inure them to obedience hardly befits the dignity of Almighty God – and for whose benefit is the 'state' being supplied? Milton's theological limitations prevent him from allowing his drama to speak for itself. God is made explicitly to permit Satan to rise from the lake in Book I, to approach the universe in Book III and to tempt man, and God withholds the effects of sin and limits the destructive power of all the warring angels in Book VI, so that he intrudes in, and explicitly controls, the drama of much of the poem; this removes the point of a considerable amount of the action, destroying climaxes like that at the end of Book IV, when Satan almost encounters Gabriel in a duel. Moreover, by emphasizing God's permitting of specific events, Milton draws attention to the possibility of their not having been permitted and makes God an accessory, responsible for the consequences of this permission – indeed, sometimes a deliberate actor with dubious motives:

So stretcht out huge in length the Arch-fiend lay
Chaind on the burning Lake, nor ever thence
Had ris'n or heav'd his head, but that the will
And high permission of all-ruling Heaven
Left him at large to his own dark designs,
That with reiterated crimes he might   .
Heap on himself damnation, while he sought
Evil to others, and enrag'd might see
How all his malice serv'd but to bring forth
Infinite goodness, grace and mercy shewn
On Man by him seduc't, but on himself
Treble confusion, wrauth and vengeance pourd.
       [I, ll. 209 – 20]

A God who is held to have preached forgiveness to man is here depicted as Himself on a lower moral level, deliberately seeking the triple damnation of His creatures. As a concept of God this is repugnant. God has been crudely anthropomorphized.
   Milton's anthropomorphization of God is intended as an

'accommodation', a rendering of God in terms graspable by man, and its purpose is the purpose of the poem as a whole, to 'justifie the wayes of God to men'. This justifying and glorifying is to occur through the dual victory of God in Messiah, first in the war in heaven, then through the greater triumph of love in the Incarnation foretold in Books III and XII. The battle between Satan and Messiah in heaven is, as we have seen, a foregone conclusion, since God increases or diminishes the strength of actors in the cosmic drama at will. The imaginative force of the Incarnation, however, depends on the credibility of another part of Milton's theology, his doctrine of justification. Within Christianity and within Protestantism there have always been two approaches to justification. The most common approach is that of Milton, that Adam, by sinning, offended the righteousness of God and incurred a penalty or debt beyond his power to pay, so that Christ had to step into Adam's place, paying the debt for him; this vicarious payment can then be credited to any man who believes in Jesus, belief enabling a man to benefit from the atonement of Christ and paving the way for a full influx of divine grace into his soul for inner regeneration. The objections to this belief have also been voiced with great clarity within the Christian tradition:

Some People have an *Idea*, or Notion of the Christian Religion, as if God was thereby declared so full of *Wrath* against *fallen* Man, that nothing but the *Blood* of his only begotten Son could satisfy his *Vengeance*.

Nay, some have gone such *Lengths* of Wickedness, as to assert, that God had by *immutable Decrees* reprobated, and rejected a *great Part* of the Race of *Adam,* to an *inevitable* Damnation, to show forth and magnify the *Glory* of his Justice.

But these are miserable Mistakers of the Divine Nature, and miserable Reproachers of his great Love, and Goodness in the Christian Dispensation.

For *God is Love,* yea, *all Love,* and so all Love, *that nothing* but Love can come from him; and the Christian Religion, is nothing else but an *open, full* Manifestation of his *universal* Love towards *all* Mankind. . . .

There is no *Wrath* that stands between God and us, but what is awakened in the *dark Fire* of our own fallen Nature; and to quench *this Wrath,* and not *his own,* God gave his only begotten Son to be made Man . . . The precious Blood of his Son was not poured out to *pacify* himself, (who in himself had *no Nature* towards Man but *Love*) but it was poured out, to quench the *Wrath,* and *Fire* of the fallen Soul, and kindle in it a *Birth* of Light, and Love.[4]

According to this view, the redemption of Christ is universally valid, for Christ is the ultimate principle of life in all human souls:

HEATHENS, Jews, and Christians differ not thus, that the one have a *Saviour* and are in a *redeemed* State, and the other are not . . . but they only differ in this, that one and the same Saviour is *differently* made known to them.[5]

Milton's view, on the contrary, is that most men have only the offer of vicarious atonement by Christ through belief, and he places corresponding stress upon the importance of community of belief. He is, as always, whole-hearted in his commitment, intending his poem for his fellow believers:

still govern thou my Song,
*Urania,* and fit audience find, though few.
   [VII, ll. 30 – 1]

However, as a work of art rather than religious propaganda, *Paradise Lost* claims the attention of mankind and must be judged by standards other than those that Milton would accept. For those readers not pre-convinced by religious adherence, Milton's grim doctrine of justification and his consigning of the majority of the human race to everlasting torture are repellent, and his version of God lacks the vitality and imaginative power that would make the reader feel that he was indeed in the presence of the Almighty.

A further reason for the limpness of Milton's rendering of God and heaven is Milton's Puritan rather than Christian exclusion of the feminine. Had he been working in the Catholic or Eastern Orthodox traditions, with their emphasis upon the Virgin Mary as Mother of God and a pre-eminent source of mercy and grace, it might have been easier for him. As it is, his heaven and God lack feminine softness. There seems to be no room for spontaneous joy or humour. The 'spontaneous' carollings of the angels recall the organized, 'spontaneous' political rallies of twentieth-century experience. When God does attempt humour in Book III (or, for that matter, Satan in Book VI) the results are elephantine. Neither is there sensuous or super-sensuous enjoyment in heaven, for the songs and dances are described generally and coldly (the nearest to warmth is Raphael's blushing account of love among the angels, and this is accompanied by embarrassment). Milton, suspicious of the life of the senses, was equally suspicious of woman and her sensuous attractiveness, and of the feminine side of his own nature (a point to which we will return in Part Two). The superior angels are 'without feminine' and God is harshly masculine.

Milton's vision of a stern and masculine God conforms to his views of male superiority. The unique virtue of his Heaven is its perfect but regimental orderliness. Politically, this orderliness is apparent in a precise equivalence between rank and worth. With reference to Messiah, the point is hammered home several times, but it is also true of the angelic cohorts. Thus, the great archangels each have some particular virtue or ability in its highest degree, Uriel being the most keen-sighted, Raphael the most sociable and Michael supremely gifted with martial prowess. On the just basis of His infinite virtue, God rules here supreme, and Milton, the oligarchical republican, creates a heaven that is an absolute monarchy. In Milton's view state and pomp of right belong to this monarchy because it is supreme in virtue, and he is ready to welcome Messiah at the Second Coming as the one true king. Whereas, however, a royalist would say 'As in heaven, so on earth' and derive earthly monarchies from this divine pattern, Milton dissents precisely because earthly monarchies do not correspond with an inner hierarchy of virtue. If he did not believe that Christ was present in the souls of all men, at least he believed that Christ was present to the mind of all believers. Thus, Milton is at pains to distinguish between the genuine monarchy of heaven and the false monarchy of hell, and in the last book of *Paradise Lost* he goes out of his way to derive earthly kingship from an ungodly tyrant in the Old Testament.

Hell has, in practice, a mixed constitution. The monarchical pretensions of Satan are emphasized – and their falseness:

High on a Throne of Royal State, which far
Outshon the wealth of *Ormus* and of *Ind*,
Or where the gorgeous East with richest hand
Showrs on her Kings *Barbaric* Pearl and Gold,
Satan exalted sat, by merit rais'd
To that bad eminence; and from despair
Thus high uplifted beyond hope, aspires
Beyond thus high, insatiat to persue
Vain Warr with Heav'n, and by success untaught
His proud imaginations thus displaid.
          [II, ll. 1 – 10]

There is some kind of justice in Satan's exaltation, for he is pre-eminent, but pre-eminent in vice. The glitter of the throne is a

warning to men, and the pearl and gold are barbaric because
Milton sees them not as reflecting but as falsely imitating the glory
of God. Similarly, in the war in heaven Satan is described as 'Idol
of Majestie Divine', affecting a godlike, imitated state. He is also
the 'dread Commander', the military autocrat whose voice none
dares disobey. There is a deliberate attempt, through the earlier
part of the poem, to link Satan with, among other things, the great
military sultanates of Islam, associated in the Western mind with
religious infidelity and slavery, though this is also an attempt to
build up Satan's importance by using the military prestige of a
religious civilization that had almost brought Christian Europe to
its knees. Nevertheless, hell is not entirely an autocracy, for it contains also an element of democracy that is absent from heaven. It
has been noticed more than once that Milton's experience as a
revolutionary is brought to bear in the description of the revolutionary army that is seeking to overthrow the absolute monarchy
of God. Not only does Satan have some of the qualities of
Cromwell (if not his success), but the summons calling

From every Band and squared Regiment
By place or choice the worthiest
    [I, ll. 758 – 9]

to the Council in Pandaemonium, and the ensuing discussions,
bear some trace of the procedure of the Putney Debates. The fallen
angels even vote on the policy to be pursued, and their striving for
an acceptable consensus echoes the strivings of the saints in this
world. Indeed, they are even held up as an example to man:

O shame to men! Devil with Devil damnd
Firm concord holds: men onely disagree
Of Creatures rational, though under hope
Of heav'nly Grace.
    [II, ll. 496 – 9]

This blend of military dictatorship with consultation and agreement comes precisely because Satan is superior and the natural
leader; as Milton points out, the plan finally agreed upon originates
from Satan himself. Satan's monarchy is thus partly the result of
eminence in evil and partly a jealous imitation of God, and it is
only a tyranny because Satan's superiority is not one of goodness,
the only genuine worth.

  Among fallen men no one has sufficient superiority in virtue to
claim absolute kingship by right. In the final book of his poem

Milton is careful to remove the two underpinnings of conventional royalist thinking, biblical precedent and the example of God. Whereas Filmer traces monarchy to Adam, and Dryden in *Absalom and Achitophel* uses the conventional parallel between Charles II and David, Milton picks upon Nimrod as a suitable spawner of kingship:

This second sours of Men, while yet but few . . .
Shall spend thir dayes in joy unblam'd, and dwell
Long time in peace by Families and Tribes
Under paternal rule; till one shall rise
Of proud ambitious heart, who not content
With fair equalitie, fraternal state,
Will arrogate Dominion undeserv'd
Over his brethren, and quite dispossess
Concord and law of Nature from the Earth;
Hunting (and Men not Beasts shall be his game)
With Warr and hostil snare such as refuse
Subjection to his Empire tyrannous:
A mightie Hunter thence he shall be stil'd
Before the Lord, as in despite of Heav'n,
Or from Heav'n claming second Sovrantie;
And from Rebellion shall derive his name,
Though of Rebellion others he accuse.
　　[XII, ll. 13 – 37]

The law of nature here dictates political equality among the regenerate. In anticipation of Filmer's arguments, as yet unpublished, Milton continues by having Adam deliver a diatribe against his future son:

　Whereto thus *Adam* fatherly displeas'd.
O execrable Son so to aspire
Above his Brethren, to himself assuming
Autoritie usurpt, from God not giv'n:
He gave us onely over Beast, Fish, Fowl
Dominion absolute; that right we hold
By his donation; but Man over men
He made not Lord; such title to himself
Reserving, human left from human free.
　　[XII, ll. 63 – 71]

Michael then backs this by making explicit Milton's own insistence on the link between political liberty and the inner regeneration of man:

To whom thus *Michael*. Justly thou abhorrst
That Son, who on the quiet state of men
Such trouble brought, affecting to subdue
Rational Libertie; yet know withall,
Since thy original lapse, true Libertie
Is lost, which alwayes with right Reason dwells
Twinnd, and from her hath no dividual being:
Reason in man obscur'd, or not obeyd,
Immediatly inordinate desires
And upstart Passions catch the Goverment
From Reason, and to servitude reduce
Man till then free. Therefore since hee permits
Within himself unworthie Powers to reign
Over free Reason, God in Judgement just
Subjects him from without to violent Lords;
Who oft as undeservedly enthrall
His outward freedom: Tyrannie must be,
Though to the Tyrant thereby no excuse.
          [XII, ll. 79 – 96]

Thus Milton sighs righteously under the iniquity of mortal monarchies and looks forward to the Second Coming when he, like Abdiel, will be able to round on his enemies triumphantly and, pointing to the hosts of heaven, say, 'My Sect thou seest'.

If the Second Coming were to provide the vindication of Milton's political views, it would also provide the final vindication of *Paradise Lost* itself:

Servant of God, well done, well hast thou fought
The better fight, who single hast maintaind
Against revolted multitudes the Cause
Of Truth.
          [VI, ll. 29 – 32]

For Milton the greatest merit of the poem was its literal and detailed truth, as it still was for Dr Johnson in the eighteenth century, though it also met the demands made in the criticism of Bacon and Hobbes for superhuman heroic virtue, wonderful events, surprising turns of action and precise poetic justice. Even in this century there have been critics who have regarded ultimate truth as the great merit of the poem, though the world has moved on since Milton's day, and most religious critics would feel constrained to regard much of Milton's literal fact as allegorically or mythically true. The garden, the apple, the snake, the seven days of Creation are not the literal wonders they once seemed. Milton's poem still survives, at least within the English-speaking tradition, though it has never enjoyed the broad audience of Virgil or Homer. Increasingly, its survival has come to depend not on its factual accuracy, but on its human truth, its imaginative power. It has usually and justly been praised for its grandeur. It has already been said that Milton has no sense of eternity as timelessness. He has a horror of the indefinite and undifferentiated; this is for him chaos,

> A dark
> Illimitable Ocean without bound,
> Without dimension, where length, bredth, and highth,
> And time and place are lost,
>     [II, ll. 891 – 4]

which threatens annihilation and un-being. While this is a limitation of and, to Milton's imagination, a weakness of his intelligence, it is accompanied by an architectonic strength, an ability to build a universe within space and time and, when unconstrained by theological considerations, to people it with fantastic creatures of a grotesque vitality, Sin and Death and the serpentine occupants of hell after Satan's return there, apparently victorious.

In all of this, of course, Milton built upon the achievements of Virgil and Homer and the world of the wicked dead as conceived by the ancients. Their version of heaven, the abode of the virtuous dead, was less impressive and anyway unusable if Milton were to avoid the charge of blasphemy. There is also a streak of the purely 'gothick' in Milton's imaginings, recalling the paintings of Bosch and the curious faces and figures that lurk in the carved shadows of old churches. But to this Milton has added a quality of his own; if he cannot evoke a reality beyond space and time, he is supreme in evoking a spatial vastness that is almost illimitable.

> He calld so loud, that all the hollow deep
> Of Hell resounded.
>     [I, ll. 314 – 15]

> The Thunder,
> Wingd with red Lightning and impetuous rage,
> Perhaps hath spent his shafts, and ceases now
> To bellow through the vast and boundless Deep.
>     [I, ll. 174 – 7]

The sound of the words, the choice of vowels and bounding consonants, is a physical evocation of the imaginative idea. This physical quality of Milton's language becomes almost crude at times and is used especially to evoke unpleasant sensations (Milton dare not unleash a potentially dangerous enjoyment of sensuous pleasure):

> They . . . instead of Fruit
> Chewd bitter Ashes, which th'offended taste
> With spattering noise rejected: oft they assayd,
> Hunger and thirst constraining, drugd as oft,
> With hatefullest disrelish writh'd thir jaws
> With soot and cinders fill'd.
>         [X, ll. 564 – 70]

Here even the mouth movements of reading coincide with the described action.

Milton rarely uses his physical power of language in describing the good angels or God, but when he does God too begins to come alive:

> Boundless the Deep, because I am who fill
> Infinitude.
>         [VII, ll. 168 – 9]

It was this aspect of Milton's language that Wordsworth most profited from, making possible the physical suggesting of the unphysical. However, in Milton space, though vast, is structured. There is always a sense of locality in *Paradise Lost*: even chaos, the negation of time and space, is indeterminately wedged between heaven and hell, and ultimately bridged. It has a bottom and a top, pinned between nether fire and upper light. This architectonic quality is there also in the language, in the Latinate structure of the sentences, where predicate may be separated from verb by lines of intervening clauses, and the surge of energy is necessary to complete the units of the sense. The syntactical structure indeed changes from place to place according to the exact nature of the order expressed. The violent energy of hell leads to the surging rhythmical drive of Book I; the more repressive hierarchy of the Garden of Eden is expressed in the sedate and more static balances of the syntax in Book IX, where phrase is often counterpoised against phrase and word against word. In either case the syntactical whole is a complex structure of interlinking parts, which relates to Milton's model of the physical universe and to his sense of the intricate interlinking of the events of human history, just as the vision of history at the end of the poem and the many references to the disasters of biblical and human history are tied back to the central events of the poem, which are the origin of all sin and suffering. Thus all these various elements – vocabulary, syntax, imagery and cosmography – come together, and if the poem does not have literal truth, it nevertheless has an impressive imaginative coherence.

The imaginative coherence of *Paradise Lost* conveys a profound understanding of at least the grimmer sides of human experience. Whatever the shortcomings of Milton's depiction of the angels, of God and Messiah, his description of the Devil is immensely impressive, combining courage and endurance in the face of adversity with a gradual waning of self-confidence as the limitations of hellish power become clearer, and with a constant evil rationalization and self-justification as Satan stoops to vicarious revenge, the hellish equivalent of vicarious atonement. The grander aspects of human evil are focused in this steadily diminishing but nevertheless heroic Satan. Our decaying confidence in the literal truth of our religious myths has placed Milton's epic achievement beyond our own reach. Subsequently, the epic moved inwards, into the human mind, in the longer poems of Blake and Wordsworth and the epic endeavour of Keats. Blake, indeed, interpreted all the actors in *Paradise Lost*, God, Messiah and Satan, as aspects of Milton's mind, and some of the most stimulating modern criticism of Milton has followed in Blake's footsteps.

Milton himself would undoubtedly have been appalled by this trend. His mythical drama was for him an objective reality and he was playing in one of its vital scenes. He was still sublimely confident that the history of England mattered, that the fate of the universe might have been forwarded on the battlefields of the Civil War. Nothing was the triviality it might appear. Even as Milton was writing, disillusionment was setting in. The saints of God were becoming enthusiasts and fanatics, and the noble shade of Charles I faded before the more amiable but earthy presence of his royal son. After years of life in the shadow of the *Book of Revelations*, Charles II seemed rather an anticlimax. He made no secret of his vices; he was not even ashamed of them, and they were not heroic. He was witty, charming, even affable; he had a lazy kind of good nature; he was easy-going; and he lacked the vindictive cruelty that might have raised an heroic opposition. Unreliable and deceptive he might be, but he belonged in a world of insidious intrigue rather than heroic attack. In this atmosphere reasonableness, if necessary specious, was the order of the day; the epic became the ironic, and the heroic gave way to the mock-heroic. We have left the world of Milton and have entered the world of John Dryden.

# 6  Dryden: *Absalom and Achitophel* and the Popish Plot

Dryden's greatest poem, the first part of *Absalom and Achitophel*, was occasioned by the Exclusion Crisis in the reign of Charles II. At the instigation of General Monck, Charles had been recalled from exile with general rejoicing, for the scars of the Civil War had still been green and new broils were avoided by the restoration of the monarchy. Moreover, the terms of the Restoration caused the minimum upheaval. There was a political amnesty for everyone except the regicides and questions of the ownership of confiscated estates, apart from Crown and Church lands, were decided by private litigation. Charles, however, was shifty, as he had good reason to be, trusting nobody over-much. His conduct of affairs was marked by a shrewd opportunism accompanied by a weary negligence, and his real designs were never openly declared. He generated unease; it was difficult to pin him down and unwise to rely on him. He was suspected of Papist leanings and absolutist ambitions, and his policies favoured France and the Roman Catholic Louis XIV rather than the Protestant Dutch. His wife was a Papist, and barren. Moreover, after the first euphoria the country was neither contented nor thriving. 1665 saw the great plague, unhappily terminated by the Fire of London in 1666 (an ominous year for the members of the Sects, for 666 was the number of the Beast in *Revelations*), and this was followed by the greatest naval defeat in English history when the Dutch sailed up the Medway in 1667 and sank the English fleet at leisure (it had been laid up for the winter to save money, and defence cuts had left the shore batteries devoid of powder). The flagship, the *Royal Charles*, was towed off to Holland, where its stern still remains in an Amsterdam museum. The Dissenters murmured that all this was a judgement of God on a land ungodly enough to restore a king.

Meanwhile, the incumbencies of the Church of England had been placed by Parliament in the gift of the local gentry; the Puritan ministers who had evicted the original clergy were themselves evicted; and Church and squire pursued a policy of quietly persecuting the Dissenters. Charles smiled blandly at the thwarting of his attempts to protect the Roman Catholics, many of whom had risked their lives to protect him when he was a fugitive from Cromwellian justice, and continued to await his opportunity. Then in 1668 James, Duke of York, heir apparent to the throne, who was noted for pigheadedness, fanatical loyalty and the lack of a sense of humour, defied his royal brother and publicly declared himself a convert to the Roman Catholic faith. It was a noble stand, no doubt, but politically inept, dangerous and embarrassing. As Charles grew older and still produced no legitimate child, it led to repeated attempts to debar his brother from the succession and, eventually, to the Exclusion Crisis of the early eighties. Even before then, however, both duke and king had become the targets of a great deal of satire.

From 1665 onwards a spate of lampoons and satirical verse developed. The most distinguished of this work was the series of poems offering 'Advice to a Painter' that started when Waller celebrated an inconclusive sea victory over the Dutch off Lowestoft in 1665. He issued 'Instructions to a Painter', describing graphically the picture that was to be painted of the battle between the Dutch and English fleets, the English under the conduct of the unpopular Duke of York. It was not one of Waller's best pieces: as Charles II remarked, Waller wrote best on Cromwell. Given the unpopularity of the duke and the known bungling and incompetence of naval administration, Waller's compliment was felt to overstep all bounds, and Marvell in particular replied with several other poems of 'Advice to a Painter', in which the painter was directed to produce a rather different picture of affairs. His biting comments are instanced in his description of the visit by the Duchess of York to the fleet at Harwich, an event that had also been portrayed by Waller:

But, Painter, now prepare, t'enrich thy piece,
Pencil of ermines, oil of ambergris:
See where the Duchess, with triumphant tail
Of num'rous coaches, Harwich does assail!
So the land crabs, at Nature's kindly call,
Down to engender at the sea do crawl.
    ['Second Advice to a Painter', *POAS,* I, p. 39, ll. 53 – 8]

As the Duke, though more morose than his brother, was equally lecherous, and as the Duchess had been made his wife as a result of pregnancy, the lines have great sting (there had been a previous legally binding promise of marriage, what was technically known as 'spousals', prior to her pregnancy, but the marriage itself met with great opposition and the Duchess was for a while in the shadow of disgrace). 'With triumphant tail', coming at the end of the line, at first seems a completed phrase with a purely sexual innuendo; the following phrase, 'Of num'rous coaches' then makes the sexual innuendo seem accidental or at most secondary, but the innuendo is only apparently distanced in order that it may return with re-doubled force in the verb 'assail' and the following explicit couplet. It is very good journalistic satire, of scurrilous interest and vigour, and it was not bettered until the major satirical pieces appeared in the Exclusion Crisis.

It was Dryden who turned political satire into great poetry, at the time of the Exclusion Crisis and the Popish Plot. The full background to the Plot is complicated and in part obscure, but it all stemmed from the fertile brain of Titus Oates, who had a genius worthy of Fleet Street. He had no concern for truth; he was indif-ferent to the human consequences of his lies; and he had a knack for telling people what they were prepared to believe. Oates had served as chaplain to the Protestants in the household of the Catholic Duke of Norfolk. He had been expelled from a naval chaplaincy and a living in Kent and in 1676 he had become a member of a Roman Catholic and Protestant club in London. He claimed that he had pretended conversion to Catholicism, and had assisted the Jesuits, in order to scent out the secret plottings of that order, being dispatched to Spain and becoming a Doctor of Divinity at the University of Salamanca. He had subsequently been at the College of St Omer and had been sent back in 1678 to murder Ezerel (or Israel) Tonge, rector of St Michael's, Wood Street, the author of a book against the Jesuits (and, as it happened, Oates's personal friend, the co-discoverer of the great Popish Plot).

The Jesuits, it seemed, had been deputed by the Pope to murder Charles II and, assisted by French and Spanish gold, to arrange for a massacre of Protestants and a French invasion of Ireland. The Catholic James would meanwhile ascend the throne and restore Britain to Catholicism. Tonge and Oates, having attempted to gain the ear of the king, called on Sir Edmund Berry Godfrey to take their depositions on oath. The Privy Council began an investi-gation. Oates claimed that the queen's physician, Sir George Wakeman, had been bribed to murder the king, and that there was an extensive plot afoot involving numerous English and foreign

Jesuits and even two archbishops. Despite the fact that some of the documents produced were clearly forgeries, and that the king himself exposed Oates in telling palpable lies by questioning him on the appearance of Don John of Austria, whom Oates claimed to have met, the Privy Council nevertheless believed the substance of his stories. News of the plot became public property. Then Sir Edmund Berry Godfrey was found murdered, his money intact but his pocket-book missing. A committee of the Lords was appointed to investigate the murder, and William Bedloe came forward. He also claimed that he had pretended to be a Catholic in order to discover the secrets of the Papists, and that he had been to Spain, and he added that he had been commissioned to set fire to London. (The Catholics had, of course, been credited with beginning the Great Fire in 1666, as recorded by the inscription on the Monument in London.) He was himself to have been one of Godfrey's murderers, and he identified those who had committed the crime. One of the suspects, a servant of Pepys, was able to prove an alibi. Another, less fortunate, was lodged in Newgate, where he was said to have been visited by an unknown stranger, later rumoured to have been the Earl of Shaftesbury, who told him what he must say in order to save his life. He then confessed to having shared in Godfrey's murder on the orders of an Irish priest, who had told him that Godfrey was an enemy to the queen; by turning king's evidence, he saved his life but implicated three other men, who were subsequently hanged. The plot was now in full swing. Committees were appointed to examine witnesses; the Houses of Parliament were searched for explosives; and suspected individuals were hauled up for questioning.

One of the committees lighted on Edward Coleman, a Roman Catholic convert and secretary to the Duchess of York, who had genuinely espoused the cause of converting the land to Catholicism and had written abroad asking many highly placed individuals to supply money to the duke, who was well situated to achieve this end and less likely to waste the money than the king himself. Coleman's ill-judged letters seemed to constitute proof that the plot was a reality. Bills were passed excluding Catholics from either House. Coleman was executed. Oates and Bedloe meanwhile accused the Catholic queen of complicity in the plot. Various Jesuits were executed. Oates was of necessity lodged in Whitehall and given a handsome allowance.

With Oates in Whitehall the plot was a solid political reality materialized from the vapours of fantasy. It focused the fears of the nation and was the centre of a long political duel between Charles and Anthony Ashley Cooper, Earl of Shaftesbury. Charles sought to maintain the full prerogative of the Crown and to ensure the descent of the throne to the heir apparent, the Duke of York. The extreme opposition, headed by Shaftesbury, sought to ensure that the throne could descend only to a Protestant, that the monarch should never have a standing army at his disposal and that parliaments should be regularly called. The more moderate opposition, headed by the Earl of Halifax, sought rather to limit the monarchy, possibly with some form of regency to operate during the lifetime of a Catholic king. The opposition was also divided on the question of alternative candidates for the throne, some favouring the illegitimate but Protestant Duke of Monmouth, Charles's son, others preferring William of Orange, the Calvinist husband of Mary, the Duke of York's daughter. On the sidelines stood Barrillon, the ambassador of Louis XIV, ready to bribe anybody who would be of service to his master.

The ensuing manoeuvres were complicated in the extreme. Charles played a waiting game, persuading Monmouth to accept exile in the Low Countries and packing the Duke of York off first to the Low Countries and subsequently to Scotland, summoning, proroguing and dissolving parliaments in rapid succession, offering compromises to split the opposition, talking sympathetically to Shaftesbury, to Halifax, to the other opposition leaders and to the visiting Prince of Orange, and negotiating meanwhile with Barrillon for a supply of French gold. The plot grew ever more grand, complex, subtle and incredible, as informer after informer sought payment from court or opposition in return for timely revelations. Repeated attempts to force exclusion Bills into law were repeatedly foiled, and meanwhile the list of executed victims of the plot grew steadily longer, as Shaftesbury attempted to bring political and religious hysteria to the support of a very rational opposition programme. Political hysteria is, however, an unreliable weapon; it is impermanent; it can backfire; it easily gives way to exhaustion and boredom. By waiting Charles won, at least in immediate terms. In 1681 his negotiations with Barrillon began to move towards a successful conclusion. Charles summoned Parliament to meet in March at Oxford, well away from the London mob swayed by Shaftesbury. The day after its session commenced Charles concluded a secret verbal treaty with Louix XIV and pocketed two million French crowns, a token of Louis's renewed financial support of the Stuart monarchy. The Commons meanwhile were coming out against a regency and in favour of excluding Catholic heirs to the throne. Charles promptly dissolved Parliament and moved into a counter-attack against the out-manoeuvred opposition.

Charles's counter-attack was eventually to prove all too effective, leading to the exile of Shaftesbury, the suicide of the imprisoned Essex and the execution of Algernon Sidney among the prominent Whigs, as the opposition party had come to be called. It also led to the recalling of the charters that had buttressed civil liberties in cities and boroughs, and to a vicious campaign of repression against Quakers, Dissenters and Nonconformists, many of whom froze in prison during the cold winter of 1683–4. At the beginning, however, before the charter of the City of London had been withdrawn and remodelled, Charles and the triumphant Court Party, or Tories, met with one rebuff. Shaftesbury, arraigned for high treason on suspicion of having intended to levy war against the king, was acquitted by a Middlesex grand jury selected by the Whig sheriffs of London. It was to influence this trial that Dryden's *Absalom and Achitophel* appeared, and the poem may have been commissioned by the king. The poem is thus a political document, aiming to consolidate support for the throne, to discredit the opposition by associating them with violence and disorder and to persuade the uncommitted among the moneyed and propertied public to favour a condemnation of Shaftesbury. The tone of the poem is in consequence speciously reasonable and notably different from the more hysterical abuse in 'The Medal', written after Shaftesbury's acquittal. However, while abusive satires and lampoons were commonplace, *Absalom and Achitophel* is unique, having a literary value beyond the occasion that provoked it. It manages to express the Augustan frame of mind, itself a refinement and crystallization of one aspect of our intellectual and emotional heritage, and it is no accident that the poem stems from the mock-heroic tradition.

The mock-heroic tradition is now often misunderstood, being interpreted crudely in twentieth-century terms as a vehicle for moral and political platitudes. The tradition was, in fact, much subtler than this, the mock-heroic being a highly aristocratic form, though the aristocracy sought was one of intellect not rank, and the word 'aristocratic' must retain its original sense of belonging to a dominant group distinguished by outstanding excellence. While politically *Absalom and Achitophel* supports the king, the judgements and feelings that lie behind that support are by no means as clear-cut. The mock-heroic genre lends itself to ambiguity, and this Dryden had already learned to exploit in *Mac Flecknoe*, where he developed the techniques that were later to be employed in *Absalom and Achitophel*. Shadwell, Dryden's victim in the earlier poem, was a successful dramatist of considerable calibre, and it may have been the enormous popularity of his masque *Psyche* that sparked off Dryden's revenge, though Shadwell added to the crime of success the two other crimes of Whig principles and a close association with the City. Instead of producing a straightforward lampoon, full of amusing abuse, Dryden produced in *Mac Flecknoe* a mock-heroic account of Shadwell's coronation as Emperor of Dullness, and the heroic references that are brought to bear centre on Augustus and Rome, the idea of anti-Christ contained in various biblical citations and the figure of Satan viewed through the heroic verse of *Paradise Lost*. The jokes culminate in the final lines of the poem, when Shadwell, unlike Elisha, receives a mantle wafted up from hell from the shoulders of the descending Irish Jesuit, Flecknoe himself (this is an anti-type to the Renaissance poet's stock claim to divine inspiration and thus to a lineal descent from the inspired prophets of the Old Testament).

The point about this framework is that it is not simply dismissive. Dryden has it both ways: on the one hand, Shadwell is trivial and beneath contempt; on the other, he is the Antichrist and anti-Augustus, the servant of hell standing for irreligion, political insurrection and the death of civilization. In himself trivial, he represents something far from trivial, and these two conflicting scales of measurement are reconciled not logically but emotionally, in the feeling-mind of the reader, through the wholeness of artistic reaction that subsumes and transmutes its constituents. In achieving this Dryden had taken the mock-heroic poem beyond the successes of *Le Lutrin* and its Italian predecessors, and had begun the technique that Pope was to perfect in *The Rape of the Lock* – that of taking opposite, contradictory emotional reactions and counterpoising them in such a way that the opposition is transcended while each separate part remains valid and true. Herein lies the poetic calibre of these works, for they take the reader to a level of awareness where unity predominates over diversity without destroying it, and this mere analytical reasoning based upon the separation of opposites cannot do. Hence the enduring popularity of *Mac Flecknoe* and, above all, *The Rape of the Lock*.

The mock-heroic technique developed in *Mac Flecknoe* is again used in *Absalom and Achitophel* and brought to bear on most of the characters, including Charles, so that to describe the poem simply as a heroic satire testifies to a misunderstanding. The habit of comparing monarchy with biblical precedents was, as we have seen, common; the derivation from biblical institutions was taken seriously, and the comparison of Charles and David had been made more than once before. Nevertheless, there is a difference between the man and the office. Even if kingship were of biblical origin, and even if the providential history of Charles's life did parallel that of David's, it was nevertheless difficult to think of Charles as an Old Testament patriarch and keep a straight face. Charles had a scur-rilous, low sense of humour (and any sense of humour at all is a disadvantage in such a role), while it was not the number of Charles's sexual affairs that told against him, but their lack of dig-nity. The constant bundling of prostitutes and actresses up the back stairs of Whitehall Palace and the public scenes caused by the more pretentious mistresses, together with the passing of women from hand to hand, lacked, in the context of Charles's witty court, the serious grimness or the serious frivolity of high-minded sin. The whole humour of the opening of *Absalom and Achitophel* turns upon the valid parallel with David and the contradictory awareness that the parallel is ridiculous:

In pious times, e'r Priest-craft did begin,
Before *Polygamy* was made a sin;
When man, on many, multiply'd his kind,
E'r one to one was, cursedly, confin'd;
When Nature prompted, and no law deny'd
Promiscuous use of Concubine and Bride;
Then, *Israel*'s Monarch, after Heaven's own heart,
His vigorous warmth did, variously, impart
To Wives and Slaves: And, wide as his Command,
Scatter'd his Maker's Image through the Land.
    [ll. 1 – 10][1]

It was one of Charles II's more endearing traits that he was able to appreciate this kind of humour. But the tone of the poem that is keyed in at the beginning has more to it than mere humour. We have already seen Marvell and Denham struggling to accommodate irreconcilable opposites: the frame of mind is very English and involves a large measure of pragmatism, a refusal to sacrifice the exigencies of experience to logical consistency, which tends to be a much overrated virtue. At its best, the result is openness of mind, flexibility and a certain humility in the face of experience; at its worst, the result is that hypocrisy for which we are not unjustly famous among our neighbours. In either case the quality, the way of thinking, has been central to our tradition for centuries and is only now, to all appearances, dying. In other words, Dryden's conservatism in *Absalom and Achitophel* had an appeal far wider than the ideas the poem expressed; the feeling, from which thought and ideation spring, has a validity well beyond the context of the moment, and that feeling still appeals to some of us today.

The application of the feeling is another matter. Here Dryden is much more limited by a specific political stand on issues that are, in the form in which they appeared to him, now dead. His portraits of Buckingham and Shaftesbury, or of Charles in the other direction, are as unjust as his portrait of Shadwell or Pope's portrait of Sporus. We also have the virtue of hindsight and are tempted to equate what happened with what must inevitably have happened: historically, Dryden was backing the wrong horse; the Whigs were the ones who romped past the post in 1688, when Dryden lost his stipend as court poet to his old enemy, the Whig Shadwell. Moreover, we are aware of the irony that the pragmatic conservatism which was shared by Denham and Marvell, which inspired *Absalom and Achitophel* itself and which lay behind both the moderate Whig and moderate Tory traditions was utterly opposed to the Catholic absolutism that appears to have been Charles II's occulted ideal: the Whigs were right, and the king was working against the cultural tradition, the whole way of thinking of the English people – indeed, it was probably this that ultimately defeated his policies. Nevertheless, truth in the relative world is by definition partial, and the acknowledgement of this is a virtue more fundamental than any specific political misjudgement. The recognition that the views of opponents have their validity emerged from the broad tradition in which Dryden was working; it gave him strength, since he could understand and sympathize with his opponents' position, and it also gave his imagination the ability to burst the bounds of his partisan affiliations. The portraits of Shaftesbury and Buckingham may be unjust, but they are not untrue artistically; Shaftesbury and Buckingham may not have been like this, or not only like this, but the portraits remain brilliant because they are appreciative accounts of characteristic and perennial modes of human behaviour. Even Buckingham is genially cherished as his shortcomings are enumerated. In the Taoist tradition it is said that when two warriors meet the one who has pity conquers; in the warfare of words it was Dryden's pity, his generosity of spirit, that gave his hostile portraits a vigorous life that has yet to die, whereas the vituperations of his opponents and allies have been justly consigned to virtual oblivion. For this reason *Absalom and Achitophel* was instantly recognized as the most dangerous and damaging piece of propaganda that the Tories had ever put out.

As propaganda, the poem is supremely skilful. Dryden's aim was to sway the uncommitted, to convince the seventeenth-century equivalent of the floating voter. While doing this, he had also to take account of the susceptibilities of those in power. The opening of the poem, already cited, takes Charles's sexual indulgences lightly, laughing them out of account, while leaving him as king still. Monmouth presented difficulties, being immensely popular, handsome, charming, a soldier of some distinction, something of a favourite with his father and a possible successor to the throne; it would have been unwise to offend him in case he had come to the throne, unwise to offend Charles's affection for him and unskilful to abuse him in view of his large popular following. Shaftesbury, however, was far less popular. He had tacked and veered his way through many political storms and had laid himself open to the charge of tergiversation, of ratting; he was an intriguer and was distrusted as an over-clever man. On the other hand, he stood for many very reasonable changes. Dryden was thus surrounded by shoals and barely submerged rocks that he dextrously avoided. As in *Mac Flecknoe*, there are repeated references to *Paradise Lost* and the myth of the Fall. Monmouth can thus be described as committing sin against his better judgement and is amusingly cast in the role of a male Eve, fondly overcome by Shaftesbury's political blandishments. Shaftesbury stands in for the Devil and is portrayed as brilliant but unsound – if not insane – intriguing always for himself, risking chaos in his determination 'to ruin or to rule the state'. The moderate upholders of the *status quo* are presented in such a way that an uncommitted reader could identify himself with them:

The sober part of *Israel*, free from stain,
Well knew the value of a peacefull raign:

And, looking backward with a wise afright,
Saw Seames of wounds, dishonest to the sight;
In contemplation of whose ugly Scars,
They Curst the memory of Civil Wars.
The moderate sort of Men, thus qualifi'd,
Inclin'd the Ballance to the better side:
And *David*'s mildness manag'd it so well,
The Bad found no occasion to Rebell.
    [ll. 69 – 78]

The fear of reopening the Civil War is explicitly touched on; then in
the lines that follow the moral categories are deliberately confused
to destroy any appeal to righteousness by the opposition, as pimp-
ing, literally associated with the king, is metaphorically applied to
the plotting of the Whigs:

But, when to Sin our byast Nature leans,
The carefull Devil is still at hand with means;
And providently Pimps for ill desires:
The Good old Cause reviv'd, a Plot requires.
Plots, true or false, are necessary things,
To raise up Common-wealths, and ruin Kings.
    [ll. 79 – 84]

These lines also slip in the idea that Shaftesbury aimed to establish a
commonwealth or republic (with Cromwellian overtones) rather than
to protect the traditional Protestant constitution as he claimed.

Thus, early in the poem, Dryden sides with, and tries to persuade
the reader to side with, those who uphold the present order. He
associates Shaftesbury with the horrors of civil war and thus
prepares to undermine one of the major appeals of the opposition,
who saw in the arbitrary power of the king a threat to property.
This fear of royal power is acknowledged and treated leniently in
the description of the members of the opposition:

The Best, and of the Princes some were such,
Who thought the power of Monarchy too much:
Mistaken Men, and Patriots in their Hearts;
Not Wicked, but Seduc'd by Impious Arts.
By these the Springs of Property were bent,
And wound so high, they Crack'd the Government.
    [ll. 495 – 500]

In these and similar passages Dryden soothes his audience's misgivings about Charles and exacerbates its unease about Shaftesbury. All this prepares the way for the major statement of Dryden's

political credo towards the end of the poem. Meanwhile, having established Shaftesbury and Monmouth in the roles of tempter and tempted, Dryden then, in the manner of Classical historians, places speeches in their mouths and makes them testify against themselves. Monmouth gives away his own case and casually provides a eulogy of Charles that Dryden could not have carried off if he had given it himself:

My Father Governs with unquestion'd Right;
The Faiths Defender, and Mankinds Delight:
Good, Gracious, Just, observant of the Laws;
And Heav'n by Wonders has Espous'd his Cause.
Whom has he Wrong'd in all his Peaceful Reign?
Who sues for Justice to his Throne in Vain?
What Millions has he Pardon'd of his Foes,
Whom Just Revenge did to his Wrath expose?
Mild, Easy, Humble, Studious of our Good;
Enclin'd to Mercy, and averse from Blood.
If Mildness Ill with Stubborn *Israel* Suite,
His Crime is God's beloved Attribute.
    [ll. 317 – 28]

An attack on Filmer is discredited by being placed in the mouth of Shaftesbury and made part of an argument in which Shaftesbury, for his own ends, tries to persuade Monmouth to accept a limited monarchy:

And Nobler is a limited Command,
Giv'n by the Love of all your Native Land,
Than a Successive Title, Long, and Dark,
Drawn from the Mouldy Rolls of *Noah*'s Ark.
    [ll. 299 – 302]

Similarly, the Duke of York, who was quite capable of acquiring unpopularity for himself, is made the innocent victim of Shaftesbury's machinations, and ideas that were later to be published by Locke (who was, of course, Shaftesbury's secretary at this time) are again discredited by being placed in a context of sordid intrigue conducted by Shaftesbury for Shaftesbury:

The next Successor, whom I fear and hate,
My Arts have made Obnoxious to the State;
Turn'd all his Vertues to his Overthrow . . .
Till time shall Ever-wanting *David* draw,
To pass your doubtfull Title into Law:
If not; the People have a Right Supreme

To make their Kings; for Kings are made for them.
All Empire is no more than Pow'r in Trust,
Which when resum'd, can be no longer Just.
Succession, for the general Good design'd,
In its own wrong a Nation cannot bind:
If altering that, the People can relieve,
Better one Suffer, than a Nation grieve.
[ll. 401 – 16]

Thus Dryden uses literary skill to circumnavigate the tough intellectual centre to the opposition's case. Other political ideas, such
as those of the Presbyterians, had had their day and could be
dismissed more summarily:

Hot *Levites* Headed these . . .
Resum'd their Cant, and with a Zealous Cry,
Pursu'd their old belov'd Theocracy.
Where Sanhedrin and Priest inslav'd the Nation,
And justifi'd their Spoils by Inspiration;
For who so fit for Reign as *Aaron*'s Race,
If once Dominion they could found in Grace?
[ll. 519 – 26]

While the link between politics and religion remained strong, to
attempt to link political democracy with an arbitrarily defined state
of grace, as Milton was still doing in 1660, no longer seemed a
feasible proposition. As the less reputable ideas could be dismissed
with open contempt, so too could the less reputable members of the
opposition. Oates – once all-powerful, now a known liar who had
lost all credit – is treated with a bluntly ironic reference to his habit
of remembering, when convenient, people and circumstances of
which he had earlier denied all knowledge:

Were I my self in witness *Corahs* place,
The wretch who did me such a dire disgrace,
Should whet my memory, though once forgot,
To make him an Appendix of my Plot.
[ll. 668 – 71]

Thus is the opposition made dangerously insidiously ridiculous and
the reader is invited to share Dryden's alarmed admiration for
Shaftesbury's intelligence, his sorrow at Shaftesbury's moral
perfidy, his superior understanding of the weaknesses of young
Monmouth. The reader is shamelessly flattered into an assumption
of moral strength and mature judgement. With that assumption
made, and with the poem drawing towards its close, Dryden can at

last afford to give a moderate and carefully modulated statement of his own political beliefs.

Having described Monmouth's triumphant western progress, with Monmouth himself figuring blasphemously as the crowd's 'young Messiah' and Shaftesbury calculating evilly in the background, Dryden makes the statement of his own political ideals the pivot upon which the poem turns before it moves to list the king's supporters. The first six lines of this passage reject the Hobbesian position that was such an embarrassment to the royalists:

> What shall we think! Can People give away,
> Both for themselves and Sons, their Native sway?
> Then they are left Defensless, to the Sword
> Of each unbounded Arbitrary Lord:
> And Laws are vain, by which we Right enjoy,
> If Kings unquestioned can those laws destroy.
>      [ll. 759 – 64]

Having thus disarmed a dangerous ally, Dryden turns to the equally dangerous view of kingship as given in trust and open to forfeit if abused, a view that had been expressed in the Putney Debates and became triumphant in the work of Locke:

> Yet, if the Crowd be Judge of fit and Just,
> And Kings are onely Officers in trust,
> Then this resuming Cov'nant was declar'd
> When Kings were made, or is for ever bar[r]'d.
>      [ll. 765 – 8]

The counter-argument is weak and Dryden knows it, for it depends on the figment of a legal social contract rather than an understood and reasonable agreement. Dryden therefore rapidly calls upon the support of religion to bolster his case, and by implication commends Filmer:

> If those who gave the Scepter could not tye
> By their own deed their own Posterity,
> How then could *Adam* bind his future Race?
> How could his forfeit on mankind take place?
> Or how could heavenly Justice damn us all,
> Who nere consented to our Fathers fall?
>      [ll. 769 – 74]

Dryden is intent on making it appear that those who reject his politics must reject Christianity too: that the argument carried weight in an orthodox age is borne out by the lengths Locke later went to in order to refute it. Dryden then adds to the appeal of religious sentiment an equally powerful appeal to propertied self-interest. The Whig plea that support of the king was support of absolute power, and therefore an attack on private property is turned against the opposition:

Add, that the Pow'r for Property allowd,
Is mischeivously seated in the Crowd:
For who can be secure of private Right,
If Sovereign sway may be dissolv'd by might?
    [ll. 777 – 80]

The emphasis is on 'mischievously' – it is mischievous to base property rights on the whims of the crowd, which is the case if they may dismiss kings at will. Dryden then adds the undoubtedly true points that the populace at large can be as much in error as a few people in positions of authority, and that parliaments can also make  grievous mistakes, be oppressive and commit crimes. He then appeals to the prudence of careful men:

Yet, grant our Lords the People Kings can make,
What Prudent men a setled Throne woud shake?
For whatsoe'er their Sufferings were before,
That Change they Covet makes them suffer more.
All other Errors but disturb a State;
But Innovation is the Blow of Fate.
    [ll. 795 – 800]

'Innovation', fundamental or revolutionary change, is thus classed as an 'error', a word having overtones of erroneous religious belief at the time, and Dryden then proceeds to use the metaphor of building that Marvell had employed in his poem on the first anniversary of Cromwell's government. His phrase 'ancient fabric' suggests automatically a church, the most common form of ancient public building, and reverence for antiquity is combined with reverence for religion; this emotional preparation leads into the subsequent specific linking of divine and human law, or human law and the law of nature, which appeals to the idea of the constitution as an outgrowth of a divinely ordered nature, and echoes the earlier and similar appeal in Denham's 'Cooper's Hill':

If ancient Fabricks nod, and threat to fall,
To Patch the Flaws, and Buttress up the Wall,
Thus far 't is Duty; but here fix the Mark;

For all beyond it is to touch our Ark.
To change Foundations, cast the Frame anew,
Is work for Rebels, who base Ends pursue:
At once Divine and Humane Laws controul;
And mend the Parts by ruine of the Whole.
    [ll. 801 – 8]

The practical message comes in the final couplet. Let well be!

The Tampering World is subject to this Curse,
To Physick their Disease into a worse.
    [ll. 809 – 10]

   The central political message of the poem has now been delivered. What follows is a series of panegyrics on the Court Party and a version of Charles's speech to the Oxford Parliament, in which Charles is made to claim the traditional rights of the throne as part of the government of the nation, and explicitly to base his wielding of power upon law, with the overtones the word now has of constitutional law, natural law and divine law. The poem is thus a very subtle piece of polemic, appealing to sentiment, reason and experience. Perhaps most important of all, it is civilized polemic, aiming to persuade. It communicates with those who might be inclined to support the opposition in terms that they can understand. It was the gradual dominance of this spirit in ever-widening sections of the people that has led to the degree of toleration and freedom that we now enjoy. If we are unfortunate, we may see this spirit extinguished in our civilization, for it is not always valued by those who take it for granted, but it remains one of the greatest legacies that Dryden and the succeeding age have left to us. It was a final irony, which Dryden himself might have appreciated, that the next step in the growth of a modicum of freedom came with the Whig revolution of 1688, a revolution he had himself tried so hard to prevent.

# 7 The satirical aftermath: Dryden, Oldham, Shadwell and Settle

The first part of *Absalom and Achitophel* stands unique among Dryden's works and those of his contemporaries. There were other contributions of distinction to the religious and political polemics of the Popish Plot, but none that rises above the immediate occasion. The best was the religious satire of John Oldham, whose four 'Satires upon the Jesuits' established his reputation as the most promising young poet of the time. He died young, however, and Dryden paid him the laconic tribute of his noblest elegy:

One common Note on either Lyre did strike,
And Knaves and Fools we both abhorr'd alike . . .
O early ripe! to thy abundant store
What could advancing Age have added more?
It might (what Nature never gives the young)
Have taught the numbers of thy native Tongue.
But Satyr needs not those, and Wit will shine
Through the harsh cadence of a rugged line.
A noble Error, and but seldom made,
When Poets are by too much force betray'd.
      ['To the Memory of Mr. *Oldham*', ll. 5 – 18]

Dryden's measured appraisal is accurate, but generous in its omissions. Oldham did have force enough and to spare, and his lines were rugged. He affected a Juvenalian satire of abuse and bitterness, a kind of satire that can afford to be outrageously exaggerated and unjust, but must have a core of clear truth and must be funny. The genre is seen at its best in Dryden's own translation of Juvenal's 'Sixth Satire', a diatribe against the vices of women, containing a famous onslaught on exclusively feminine religious cults:

The Secrets of the Goddess nam'd the Good,
Are ev'n by Boys and Barbers understood:
Where the Rank Matrons, Dancing to the Pipe,
Gig with their Bums, and are for Action ripe;

With Musick rais'd, they spread abroad their Hair;
And toss their Heads like an enamour'd Mare:
*Laufella* lays her Garland by, and proves
The mimick Leachery of Manly Loves.
Rank'd with the Lady, the cheap Sinner lies;
For here not Blood, but Virtue gives the prize.
Nothing is feign'd, in this Venereal Strife;
'Tis downright Lust, and Acted to the Life.
So full, so fierce, so vigorous, and so strong;
That, looking on, wou'd make old *Nestor* Young.
Impatient of delay, a genral sound,
An universal Groan of Lust goes round;
For then, and only then, the Sex sincere is found.
Now is the time of Action; now begin,
They cry, and let the lusty Lovers in.
The Whoresons are asleep; Then bring the Slaves,
And Watermen, a Race of strong-back'd Knaves.
     ['The Sixth Satyr of Juvenal', ll. 430 – 50]

This is outrageous, but funny in the sheer indignity of the lust
attributed to women. In contrast, Oldham's Juvenalian satire is
savage without being funny. His targets, the Jesuits, had a dubious
reputation even in Catholic countries, and were commonly thought
to subordinate all moral scruple to political advantage. Oldham,
however, attributes to them a frivolously complete commitment to
evil. The ghost of Garnett, who had been executed for complicity in
the Gunpowder Plot of Guy Fawkes, is made to declare in the
'Satire I' that morality and the Bible are of no account:

Let no such toys mislead you from the road
Of glory, nor infect your souls with good;
Let never bold encroaching virtue dare
With her grim holy face to enter there,
No, not in very dream: have only will
Like fiends and me to covet and act ill.
     [*POAS,* II, p. 26, ll. 110 – 15]

To make the Jesuits give their own game away in such a simple-
minded fashion destroys the credibility of the satire. Similarly, to
have Loyola in 'Satire III', the best of the *Satires,* say

Renown'd Iscariot! fit alone to be
Th'example of our great society;
Whose daring guilt despis'd the common road,
And scorn'd to stoop at sin beneath a god
     [*POAS,* II, pp. 53 – 4, ll. 281 – 4]

might at the time have provoked a shock of horror in the more bigoted adherents to the Protestant cause, but it is so exaggerated that it provokes disbelief. Oldham is too bent on the total annihilation of his enemy. Here is his onslaught on the doctrine of transubstantiation:

But nothing with the crowd does more enhance
The value of these holy charlatans
Than when the wonders of the mass they view,
Where spir'tual jugglers their chief mast'ry shew –
Hey jingo, Sirs! What's this? 'tis bread you see?
Presto, be gone! 'tis now a deity.
Two grains of dough, with cross and stamp of priest
And five small words pronounc'd, make up their Christ.
To this they all fall down, this all adore,
And straight devour what they ador'd before.
Down goes the tiny Savior at a bit,
To be digested, and at length beshit:
From altar to close-stool or jakes preferr'd,
First wafer, next a god, and then a turd!
          [*POAS*, II, pp. 78 – 9, ll. 259 – 72]

This attack was traditional – it had been used by the Lollards, and Milton employed it in one of his pamphlets – but it is abusive rather then persuasive. Its ineffectiveness as satire becomes apparent if it is compared with the passages in *A Tale of a Tub* in which Swift attacks the Dissenters' claims to inspiration from the Holy Spirit, taking 'inspiration' in its literal sense of a breathing or blowing in:

Into this *Barrel* [the pulpit], upon Solemn Days, the Priest enters; where, having before duly prepared himself by the methods already described, a secret Funnel is also convey'd from his Posteriors, to the Bottom of the Barrel, which admits new Supplies of Inspiration from a *Northern* Chink or Crany. Whereupon, you behold him swell immediately to the Shape and Size of his *Vessel*. In this Posture he disembogues whole Tempests upon his Auditory, as the Spirit from beneath gives him Utterance; which issuing *ex adytis*, and *penetralibus*, is not performed without much Pain and Gripings. And the *Wind* in breaking forth, deals with his Face, as it does with that of the Sea; first *blackning*, then *wrinkling*, and at last, *bursting it into a Foam*. It is in this Guise, the Sacred *Aeolist* delivers his oracular *Belches* to his panting Disciples; Of whom, some are greedily gaping after the sanctified Breath; others are all the while hymning out the Praises of the *Winds*; and gently wafted to and fro by their own Humming, do thus represent the soft Breezes of their Deities appeased.[1]

This attack on the emotional preaching of Protestant extremists also shows no mercy for the cherished beliefs of the victims. Swift, however, is funny as Oldham is not, having a Heath Robinson inventiveness in the anal funnel used to catch the inspiration imparted by the Presbyterians of Scotland; the ludicrous humour softens the tone and gives permanent life to the passage. Oldham's onslaught on the Jesuits could effectively stir up emotional prejudice in his time, but it has sadly dated.

The same can be said of the remaining political satires of the period, including Dryden's own, despite their technical brilliance. After Shaftesbury's acquittal, celebrated by the striking of the medal in his honour, Dryden was again asked by the king to right the balance of public opinion. The result was 'The Medal', in which Dryden adds to scurrilous attack the old polemical trick of righteous indignation, which can, like charity, be used to cover a multitude of sins. A tone of righteous indignation tends to sweep a reader along, so that its justification is taken for granted. Moreover, the device enables Dryden to retain his own dignity while engaged in the undignified activity of blackening his enemy's character:

> But thou, the Pander of the Peoples hearts,
> (O Crooked Soul, and Serpentine in Arts,)
> Whose blandishments a Loyal Land have whor'd,
> And broke the Bonds she plighted to her Lord;
> What Curses on thy blasted Name will fall!
> Which Age to Age their Legacy shall call;
> For all must curse the Woes that must descend on all.
> Religion thou hast none: thy *Mercury*
> Has pass'd through every Sect, or theirs through Thee.
> But what thou giv'st, that Venom still remains;
> And the pox'd Nation feels Thee in their Brains.
> [ll. 256 – 66]

This makes unscrupulous use of Shaftesbury's physical infirmity, linking his crooked spine with his devilish ('serpentine') counsels. The pervasive image makes out that Shaftesbury, illogically both pander and adulterer, is afflicted with the pox; he not only seduces the nation, lawfully wedded to the king, but infects her so that she subsequently goes mad with syphilis. The unscrupulousness of Dryden's tactic is apparent. The miracle is that he gets away with it – the tone of moral indignation is maintained, and is greatly assisted by the skill of Dryden's versification. The Alexandrine capping the triplet in line 262 gives a terrible sense of recurrence and inevitability through the repetitions of the mid-line and the echoing of 'For all' by 'on all' (this, of course, leads on to the disease image and the implication of inherited pox echoing from generation to generation). Above all, Dryden knows how to pause, as Oldham does not; a point made, he allows silence for it to sink in. There are very carefully graded pauses at the ends of lines 259 – 62, followed by the strong caesura after 'none' in the middle of line 263. And within the verse the rhythm is varied and telling, line 259 having a slight caesura after 'bonds', but being otherwise smooth, whereas the following verse has a rougher, more emphatic rhythm. The light pause after 'curses', coming in the middle of the second iamb of line 260, cuts across the metrical pattern of the verse; the spoken stressing on 'curses' and 'fall' thus submerges the metrical pattern without destroying it, giving the verse a forceful elegance typical of Dryden at his best. Like all good poetry his verse has a superb audible quality that is half its pleasure. Nevertheless, it remains inferior, if not in technique, then in kind, to the achievement of *Absalom and Achitophel*. 'The Medal' makes the best of the limitations of the occasion; Part 1 of *Absalom and Achitophel* rises above it. There may be truth in the suggestion, made by Howard H. Schless in *POAS*, III, that the first part of *Absalom and Achitophel* was a long time in preparation, which might account for its unusual maturity.

Both *Absalom and Achitophel* and 'The Medal' provoked replies. 'The Medal Revers'd', of uncertain authorship, launches an attack on Persecution, personified as a hag, and ends with a prognostication of the ills consequent on James's succession, in contrast to the ills foretold by Dryden should Shaftesbury have his way. Compared with Dryden's, the poem is limp, as can be seen from the opening lines, a very distant parody of the opening of *Mac Flecknoe*:

How easy 'tis to sail with wind and tide!
Small force will serve upon the stronger side;
Power serves for law, the wrong too oft's made right,
And they are damn'd who against power dare fight.
Wit rides triumphant, in Power's chariot borne,
And depress'd opposites beholds with scorn.
This well the author of *The Medal* knew,
When Oliver he for an hero drew.

[*POAS*, III, p. 61, ll. 1 – 8]

Dryden's technical skill stands out in contrast to the relative crudity of these lines. The first four verses all have a caesura after the second iamb, a monotonous effect. Moreover, while the opening verse has an easy lilt to it, the first two couplets are wasted, for the second and fourth verses stand as independent statements, like the first and third, instead of clinching a point made in the two-line unit and driving it home with the force of the rhyme. The inversion in the third foot of verses 4 and 8 is awkward in both cases. It serves no purpose of emphasis, and the lurching movement of the lines decreases cohesion without adding force. In short, this poet is simply not in Dryden's class as a verse technician.

Shadwell's 'The Medal of John Bayes' is more skilfully written and contains such amusing couplets as:

Though with thy sword, thou art the last of men,
Thou art a damn'd Boroski with thy pen
  [*POAS*, III, p. 81, ll. 23 – 4]

(as Boroski had assassinated a man by letting fly at him with a blunderbuss in a coach, the comparison is telling). The opening, which has clearly been worked over very carefully, has spirit and life:

How long shall I endure, without reply,
To hear this Bayes, this hackney-railer, lie?
The fool, uncudgell'd, for one libel swells,
Where not his wit, but sauciness excels;
Whilst with foul words and names which he lets fly,
He quite defiles the satire's dignity.
  [*POAS*, III, p. 81, ll. 1 – 6]

The references to the satirical portrayal of Dryden as Bayes in Buckingham's *Rehearsal* and to Dryden's cudgelling in Rose Alley, and the charge that he is a 'hackney-railer' writing for hire not principle, are deftly introduced in passing; the caesuras are varied; the verse moves; and the couplets have point. Shadwell was a competent professional with a good ear and a clear recognition of Dryden's superiority at writing verse:

In verse, thou hast a knack with words to chime,
And had'st a kind of excellence in rhyme:
With rhymes like leading-strings, thou walk'dst; but those
Laid by, at every step thou brok'st thy nose.
  [*POAS*, III, p. 83, ll. 54 – 7]

A good deal of 'The Medal of John Bayes' is, however, a personal attack on Dryden's private life, an attempt to destroy Dryden's personal standing and thereby undermine his case. Also Shadwell's grip on his verse medium is uncertain; the following rather lame passage should have been the positive climax of the piece:

Those miscreants who hate a parliament
Would soon destroy our ancient government.
Those slaves would make us fit to be o'ercome,
And gladly sell the land to France or Rome.
But Heaven preserve our legal monarchy
And all those laws that keep the people free.
Of all mankind, for ever curs'd be they
Who would or king's or people's rights betray,
Or aught would change but by a legislative way.
       [*POAS*, III, p. 94, ll. 364 – 72]

While not without skill, the verse nevertheless hobbles; the unit of the couplet is too isolated while the spoken rhythm of the sentences is too closely attached to the stress patterns of the metre, and in these circumstances verse invariably moves towards doggerel, for the harmony of English verse comes from a living interplay between the metrical and spoken stress patterns. Shadwell's performance is spirited, but the match is unequal.

   'The Medal', then, elicited no really effective reply. The best of the replies to Dryden was an answer to *Absalom and Achitophel*, Settle's *Absalom Senior*. It starts with a parody of the opening lines of the original:

In gloomy times, when priestcraft bore the sway
And made Heav'n's gate a lock to their own key;
When ignorant devotes did blindly bow,
All groping to be sav'd they knew not how:
Whilst this Egyptian darkness did o'erwhelm,
The priest sat pilot even at empire's helm.
Then royal necks were yok'd, and monarchs still
Held but their crowns at his almighty will.
       [*POAS*, III, pp. 107 – 8, ll. 1 – 8]

The parallels with biblical personages are recast, the Duke of York becoming Absalom, Shaftesbury Barrillai and Monmouth Ithream, and Halifax being given the role of Achitophel. The many echoes of Dryden's poem reallocate his praise and blame, much of his description of Shaftesbury, for instance, being deliberately brought to mind by Settle's description of the Duke of York. While the character sketches fall short of the definitive perfection of Dryden's and therefore lack Dryden's universal range of application, they are nevertheless vivid and well formulated. Settle also has an ability to handle long passages of couplets, giving a sustained ascent to a rhetorical climax, and this is a very necessary art in a polemical poem of nearly fifteen hundred verses. At his best he combines vividness and vigour, as in his description of the supposed Catholic murderers of Sir Edmund Berry Godfrey taking the sacrament at the duke's altar:

Here draw, bold painter (if thy pencil dare
Unshaking write what Israel quak'd to hear),
A royal altar pregnant with a load
Of human bones beneath a breaden god.
Altars so rich not Moloch's temples show;
'Twas Heaven above, and Golgotha Below.
  [*POAS,* III, p. 128, ll. 466 – 71]

His colloquial freedom in handling the formal couplet allows him to give a statement a twist that will make it stick, as in his imputing to the duke's party the tactic of inventing false plots to cover the traces of the old:

To this were twenty underplots contriv'd
By malice and by ignorance believ'd,
Till shams met shams, and plots with plots so cross'd,
That the true Plot amongst the false was lost.
  [*POAS,* III, p. 157, ll. 1170 – 3]

Settle also takes up the constitutional arguments in Dryden, introducing a prolonged attack on Filmer (lines 786 – 825), and using a panegyric on parliaments to make an ingenious but shaky claim to divine precedent for the institution, as well as appealing to the traditional and Denhamesque notion of the constitution as an outgrowth of nature harmoniously combining opposed qualities:

But ere their hands this glorious work can crown,
Their long-known foe, the Sanedrin, must down:
Sanedrins, the free-born Israel's sacred right,
That God-like balance of imperial might,
Where subjects are from tyrant-lords set free
From that wild thing unbounded man would be,
Where pow'r and clemency are pois'd so even,
A constitution that resembles Heav'n.
So in th'united great Three-One we find
A saving with a dooming Godhead join'd.

(But why, oh why! if such restraining pow'r
Can bind Omnipotence, should kings wish more?)
A constitution so divinely mix'd,
Not Nature's bounded elements more fix'd.
Thus earth's vast frame, with firm and solid ground,
Stands in a foaming ocean circl'd round;
Yet this not overflowing, that not drown'd.
        [*POAS*, III, pp. 123 – 4, ll. 370 – 86]

However, despite its solid competence, *Absalom Senior* is now largely unread. It lacks the subtlety and rich ambiguity of Dryden's masterpiece, and it does not have Dryden's human insight or his political persuasiveness.

That Settle could not equal Dryden at Dryden's best is not surprising. When Dryden joined Nahum Tate in adding a second part to *Absalom and Achitophel*, he was himself unable to equal his earlier achievement, despite all his technical brilliance and the scurrilous skill of portraits like that of Og, Dryden's old enemy, Shadwell. Little from the political polemics of the succeeding years has endured. When the Prince of Orange invaded England in 1688 he brought a complete printing press to ensure that his Calvinist sense of destiny should have every chance of proving its necessity; however, it is not the printed word that has survived, but the jubilant Whig tune of 'Lilli burlero'. It was not so much persuasion as the intransigence of James and the shrewd but flexible firmness of the Prince of Orange, or perhaps a Calvinist predestination, that finally decided the issues in dispute.

# Part Two
# The Woman's Workhouse

Home is the girl's prison and the woman's workhouse.

BERNARD SHAW

England is a paradise for women.

ROBERT BURTON, JOHN FLORIO and various other men

# 8 Prologue: 'Love, the Life of Life'

The stage is more beholding to love than the life of man. For as to the stage, love is ever matter of comedies, and now and then of tragedies: but in life it doth much mischief; sometimes like a siren, sometimes like a fury. You may observe, that amongst all the great and worthy persons (whereof the memory remaineth, either ancient or recent), there is not one that hath been transported to the mad degree of love; which shows that great spirits and great business do keep out this weak passion. . . . As if man, made for the contemplation of heaven and all noble objects, should do nothing but kneel before a little idol, and make himself subject, though not of the mouth (as beasts are), yet of the eye, which was given him for higher purposes.

Thus wrote Sir Francis Bacon on the subject 'Of Love', an emotion which, he felt, should give way to more serious considerations. In other essays he deals with marriage and with parents and children, though very much from the man's point of view: 'Wives are young men's mistresses; companions for middle age; and old men's nurses. So as a man may have a quarrel to marry when he will' ['Of Marriage and Single Life']. From a modern point of view, this may be felt to grant woman less than her intrinsic dignity, but at least it does not deny her utility. Given the high mortality rates of earlier society, her most obvious social usefulness was, however, as a mother and, given male dominance of public life, her second and associated role was that of wife. Her sphere of activity was thus domestic, though there was a slight increase in other types of opportunity open to her later in the century. Attitudes to women and to love were part of a complex of attitudes to marriage and the family, and these, as E. A. Wrigley has pointed out, are as much a public and social as a private matter:

The act of marriage is necessarily one which stands centrally in the whole complex of social behaviour. The family is a basic unit in all cultures and the creation of a new family by marriage is bound to interest society as a whole as well as the individuals and families most directly involved.

[*WPH*, pp. 116 – 17]

Marriage, propagation and love are separable factors, any one of which may exist independently of the others. The accepted norm or norms for the interrelationship of the three are, however, part of a society's strategy for survival and relate in turn to its modes of thought, its economic and technological condition and its place in the broader ecology of nature. A change in any one aspect of this whole is likely to produce repercussions in others: the human need for emotional fulfilment affects and is affected by the availability of food, water, air, living space, raw materials and leisure, and the use that can be made of any of these is affected by technology and economics. Love and attitudes to women, to marriage, to children, to relatives cannot therefore be taken in isolation, and there is no absolute standard of rightness by which these things can be judged. The assessment of the interplay of all these factors in history also poses the difficulty that institutions and attitudes are not the same thing: it is a delicate task to extract from the facts known about sexual relations and marriage in seventeenth-century England a tolerable understanding of what they mean, of the range of emotional experience they imply. In order to establish and assess the facts, and then bring them to bear on the literature of the time, it is necessary first to glance back at the inheritance handed down from the Middle Ages, and then to examine household and family organization in the context of seventeenth-century society.

# 9 The inheritance from the Middle Ages

Among the Teutonic tribes that settled in the far west of the Roman Empire, women appear originally to have taken some part in warfare and to have undertaken the major part of the drudgery of agriculture. This latter habit they continued into the early Middle Ages, in which period they died off before men, possibly as a result of hard labour, and consequently had a scarcity value. David Herlihy records that in traditional legal codes the *wergild* exacted for killing a woman, unless she was old, was twice that demanded for killing a man. Moreover, upon marriage a man was expected to make a *Morgengabe* to his wife, and some of the women appear to have demanded extortionate sums. After about 1150, however, the balance of the sexes within the population shifted, possibly because of the decrease in raiding and violence, the dwindling of the European slave trade – a source of income to the Vikings and others, which had taken its toll of able-bodied and attractive women – and because of the development of urban settlement and the associated trades that women could pursue without unduly heavy physical labour. The ethos of chivalry may also have reduced open physical violence to women. Their lot was lightened and they lived longer, but their scarcity value disappeared. Instead of a wife requiring a *Morgengabe* from her husband, a father had now to find a dowry to marry his daughters off or, alternatively, to buy them entrance to a convent (many convents were, in fact, under-endowed and needed the money to survive, so this was not entirely a matter of greed).[1]

With changes in the numerical balance of the sexes and the general mode of life, attitudes to women also changed, tending to polarize. The adoration of the Virgin had become a dominant feature of religious life by the eleventh century, and it lent to women some participation in the divine. The cult of chivalry, with its feudal service of the lady, became an aristocratic fashion in the twelfth and thirteenth centuries. Both led to an idealization of women and had a profound effect on the European imagination. On the other hand, there was also within Christianity a tradition of contempt for women, sanctioned by the work of St Augustine, a lecher reluctantly reformed, and by St Jerome: according to this, women were the sinful daughters of mother Eve, who had been the first to fall and had then tempted Adam. In the case of women who were living in the world rather than in a convent, it gained strength from the high evaluation of virginity in the Catholic tradition, and it may have been given additional impetus by the attempts made from the eleventh century onwards to enforce celibacy in practice among the clergy, the guilt associated with sexual longing being transferred to its cause, woman. Together with the male tendency to claim superiority on the basis of muscular strength and the presence of a surplus of women in the population, this may be enough to explain the development of the literary denigration of women, especially in the *fabliaux*. There thus developed the syndrome of what Eileen Power has called the pit and throne, a bifurcated attitude towards women alternating between idealization and contempt.[2]

While bifurcation marked the literary attitude to women, their position in real life was a much more complex matter. Where property was concerned, men and women alike were treated as appendages to it and married off according to considerations of finance and family influence. Once she was married a woman lost control of her property to her husband. Nevertheless, a gentle- or noblewoman would be expected, in the absence of her husband at court, at war or on business, to defend the family estates by recourse to law or, if necessary, by directing a military defence, as a number of women of rank were to do later in the English Civil War. Further down the social hierarchy women in the artisan and trading classes enjoyed a considerable measure of freedom, despite their legal subjection to their husbands. Daughters were usually apprenticed to the family trade; wives often worked with husbands at the same trade; and widows would continue the family business after their husbands' deaths. Women might also ply trades in their own right if they were single or follow trades different from those of their husbands, and they were then able to take out and defend legal actions on their own accounts. Some trades, like silk-weaving, spinning and brewing, were almost entirely feminine preserves, but there are also records of women following a large diversity of other trades as butchers, chandlers, ironmongers, goldsmiths, and so on.

Women were thus often essential contributors to the family income. Among the peasantry women again shared in all the agricultural work except the very heavy labour of ploughing, and here also their by-industries might help the family income. It was, however, among the artisan and trading classes in the urban centres that the small freedom allowed to women seems to have been at its maximum, and here also the Middle Ages anticipated the situation in seventeenth-century England.

While in economic life women could enjoy some measure of autonomy, they were usually only able to gain access to the professional guilds as widows of men who had been members, and their education was directed towards domestic duties, apart from the training they might receive in the family trade. Noblewomen were taught the social graces they would need in the management of large households containing many male courtiers, servants and administrators. The treatises aimed primarily at women of slightly lower rank emphasized the pious wifely duties, which also had practical value in a male-dominated world where links of kinship were vitally important (Christine de Pisan's warnings against love affairs and admonitions to maintain good relations with the husband's relatives, for instance, were sound practical sense as well as pious exhortation in the society of the time).[3] The common assumption of education was that women were more stupid than men, and there was a general prejudice against training their more abstract intellectual powers. Again, this prejudice continued in the sixteenth and seventeenth centuries (Lord Burghley more than once complained about the naturally inferior intellectual powers of the most intelligent monarch to have sat upon the English throne) and is not unknown today. Many (indeed, most) later institutions and attitudes had recognizable roots in the Middle Ages.

# 10  Propagation and contraception in the seventeenth century

The age structure, or 'age pyramid', of the population of seventeenth-century England was very different from the one that exists now and was shaped by the mores and medicine of the period. Contemporary standards of hygiene were appalling; it was not uncommon to defecate in fireplaces and sometimes about rooms and staircases if no chamber or close-stool were available, and when privies were used their contents were removed by the night cart and often dumped outside the town or thrown into the rivers which were one of the sources for drinking water. Fleas, lice and intestinal worms abounded; the poor suffered from inadequate and the rich from unbalanced diet; and the diseases that struck met with no effective medical resistance – indeed, they may well have been assisted by medical counter-measures. Almost a quarter of the children born died in their first year (more than a quarter in London, or anywhere else during epidemics). After the first year prospects improved, but a steady toll was taken of growing children and young adults by a variety of infectious diseases, so that death struck relentlessly at all age groups; it is this demographic fact that lies behind the steady production of elegies upon the young, from Ben Jonson's poems on his son and daughter to Cowley's tribute to William Hervey and Dryden's elegies on Lord Hastings, John Oldham and Mrs Anne Killigrew at the other end of the century. Since dearth limited the number of conceptions and marriages and bouts of plague vastly increased mortality, there could be sharp, localized fluctuations in the birth and death rates and in the overall age structure of the population, but in very general terms the picture is clear. Gregory King estimated in 1695 that almost 11 per cent of the population of England and Wales was over sixty years old, but nearly 28 per cent was under ten and 75 per cent was under forty. The difference from our own situation today is striking: the younger age groups were proportionately much larger, and while the population would have aged more quickly than it now does, this would have softened but not removed the effect. There was also, presumably, a visible difference between the physical underdevelopment of the poorest sections of society and the growth of those who were better placed: 'The privileged were no doubt taller, heavier and better developed than the rest just as they were in Victorian times.'[1] The increase in expectation of life, even for the wealthy was, however, marginal, and during the first year or so of life their children were put out to wet-nurses to share the general high rate of infantile mortality.[2]

The high mortality rates of earlier society affected the family by removing not only children but also parents. The remarriage of a surviving parent was common and usually prompt, often only a few weeks after bereavement. Something like a quarter of marriages were, in fact, remarriages, and many of those who remarried had been married several times before. It has been estimated by Peter Laslett that most marriages lasted for about twenty years, though other authorities would put the figure lower.[3] In England, as in northern France, western Germany and Scandinavia, the family was usually nuclear (a couple and their children in a separate household) rather than multi-generational, though the pattern is complicated by resident servants and apprentices. A poorer household would probably have something like four or five people in it, as older children would be sent into service; but the higher the rank, the larger the 'family' or household, the greater the number of resident servants and the higher the likelihood that relations would live with the nuclear family. The acceptance of the nuclear family as the norm had important repercussions: 'In pre-industrial western European societies . . . Marriage normally meant the creation of a new household immediately and could therefore not take place unless the economic basis for a new household existed' [*WPH*, p. 117]. Age at marriage, in consequence, tended to hover around the mid-twenties, a little earlier for women, a little later for men, and naturally fluctuated according to circumstances. This was quite late, given the expectation of life at the time, and much later than in some eastern societies. The young appear to have had to wait, either to amass savings or to inherit a smallholding or family business.[4]

Until marriage the majority of the population appear, on the evidence available, to have been chaste, or at least much more chaste than the experience of our own age would have led us to expect. It is difficult to know what practices were adopted for contraception or family limitation. Statistical evidence suggests that contraception was practised within marriage at certain periods, and Keith Thomas notes 'the numerous potions and medicines to procure abortion' and also records that in the 1690s 'Henry Coley . . . in his astrological practice, was said to be selling astrological sigils at four shillings each, for use as contraceptives by servant-girls'.[5] Since the ecclesiastical authorities imposed upon midwives an oath forswearing practices designed to induce abortion, they clearly felt that abortion was widespread, or at the very least a common temptation. It is often assumed that contraception could only have taken the form of interrupted coition, but there may, in fact, have been other methods. Occasional scattered and very vague hints have survived. E. A. Wrigley cites the indictment of Edward Shawcross, vicar of Weaverham, during the visitation of the diocese of Chester in 1580:

He is vehementlie suspected for committinge adulterye with dyvers and sundrie women. He is also an instructor of yoong folkes how to comyt the syn of adultrie or fornication and not to beget or bring forth children.
[*WPH*, p. 127]

There is another intriguing passage in the account of Major Weir and his sister that was published in 1685. He was burned and she was hanged in Edinburgh for witchcraft, but she also claimed that they had had an incestuous relationship:

*She avouched*, that from her being sixteen years of age, to her fiftieth, her Brother had the incestuous use of her body, and then loathed her for her age. . . . *He* [ a minister] *asked her*, if ever she was with Child to him? *She declared with great confidence*, he hindred that by means abominable, *which she beginning to relate, the Preacher stopped her. Some bystanders were desirous to hear the rest, but saies he (Gentlemen)* the speculation of this iniquity is in it self to be punished.[6]

Evidence drawn from witchcraft trials is notoriously unreliable, since it was commonly suggested to victims who were psychologically unbalanced or undergoing torture. This is, in addition, hearsay. Nevertheless, the author of the tale was a seventeenth-century man or woman who seems to have thought some method of contraception possible, and it is not very likely in this case to have been interrupted coition, a practice hardly unmentionable since it occurred in the Old Testament. *The School of Venus*, published in 1655 and translated into English in 1680, mentions linen contraceptives, presumably ineffective, and in the following century sheaths of sheep gut and oiled silk were in use.[7] Other factors such as diet, herbal drugs and psychological attitude may have had some effect, and it was certainly not beyond the ingenuity of seventeenth-century man to devise mechanical contraceptive methods. The available scraps of evidence may indicate a sexual subculture which at least thought it commanded methods of discouraging contraception.

The possibility of really widespread contraception does not, however, loom large, and there were enormous social and religious pressures enforcing abstinence. The discipline in the patriarchal household was strict, and there was little conception of personal privacy. The attitude of religion to sexuality outside matrimony was strongly repressive and the influence of religion very pervasive, since in theory at least everyone was legally obliged to attend church, and family prayers were a regular part of life in many households. Nevertheless, the illegitimacy ratios (the number of baptisms of children recorded in a sample of parish registers as illegitimate, expressed as a percentage of total baptisms) ran at about 3 per cent in the earlier decades of the century, dropping to 0.5 per cent from 1651–60 and remaining below 2 per cent for the rest of the century: since infanticide, abortion, subterfuge and flight would hide a good many illegitimate births, the real totals were probably higher. The rates, except during 1651–60, are much higher than those in France at the same period, but lower than those of the late eighteenth century and much lower than those for Victorian England. Despite the punishment of public whipping for the bearing or spawning of bastards, despite constant surveillance and sheer exhaustion from long hours of hard work and despite moral exhortation and threats of divine retribution, human nature was, it would seem, impossible utterly to suppress.[8]

These were the conditions in the settled village communities most open to official coercion. Beyond them, as Christopher Hill has pointed out, lay much more shadowy areas of the country and segments of the population. The outskirts of the kingdom, the north-west, the south-east and Wales still adhered to the traditions of medieval Catholicism, and the less accessible areas were reputedly hardly Christian at all. Keith Thomas cites a number of records of ignorance of Christianity among the poorest and most independent members of the population and also documents the persistence of scepticism of religion among the common people. There are indications of a subculture indifferent to the ways of official religion and pursuing its own way of life, and from it there may have stemmed the traditions of urban folk marriage recorded of the eighteenth century and handed on to the irreligious poor of the nineteenth.[9]

If the poorest had their own ways of ordering sexual relationships, so, at the opposite extreme, did the aristocratic. Courts and the houses of the great provided the maximum opportunity for philandering. Many court offices entailed a great deal of waiting around. The time had to be spent somehow, and men and women naturally turned to one another in order to spend it agreeably. Even Queen Elizabeth, who was strict in these matters, had had a good deal of trouble from time to time because of the indiscretions of her ladies-in-waiting, and the courts of the Stuarts were far less austere. Among the male courtiers hard drinking, gambling and whoring were established habits well before the reign of Charles II, and the diseases which resulted from this way of life were taken with a buoyant nonchalance born of an everyday familiarity with medical horrors and a determination simply to survive. Sir John Suckling, for instance, wrote a witty poem of metaphysical conceits, 'To Thomas Carew Having the Pox', and Sir William Davenant, having consorted with a Westminster whore, a 'black handsome wench',[10] lost part of his nose in consequence and was mercilessly twitted ever after. (He appears as a butt of Suckling's humour in 'A Sessions of the Poets': his fate may have been unpleasant, but that of the whore was presumably worse; he lived on to become a courtier of Charles II and the greatest theatrical impresario of the Restoration.) It was from this side of courtly tradition that the obscene political satire of the Restoration derived, as well as poems of sceptical libertinism like Rochester's 'A Maim'd Debauchee'. This whole attitude of indulgence and enjoyment, even if at a price, might be applied to sexual relations but was far removed from the serious-minded concern with finance and the will of God that governed the approach to marriage. It was said earlier that love, propagation and marriage are separable factors. Milton and the Protestant tradition of the seventeenth century tried to pull the three inextricably together, with important consequences for Milton's poetry and long-term results for Anglo-American culture and the world. Before proceeding to this attempt and Milton's part in it, however, we must briefly look at seventeenth-century poetry on love and women, a curious mixture of libertine sexuality, medieval prejudice and, occasionally, a fuller human responsiveness.

# Love, sex and attitudes to women in the poetry

Most seventeenth-century poems on women and sexual relationships were written by men; many were genre pieces composed by courtiers or poets with strong court sympathies. Carew and Sir John Suckling held minor office in the court of Charles I; Waller, Cotton and Lovelace were country gentlemen, part of the group that by hereditary right conducted much of the local government in the shires; Herrick was of wealthy London stock and moved into court circles, becoming chaplain to the Duke of Buckingham before retiring to his remote Devonshire living; Cowley, similarly of London stock, became cipher-secretary to Queen Henrietta Maria and a royalist agent before making his peace with Cromwell; while Rochester was born into the aristocracy. With the exception of Rochester, the taste of these poets was largely formed before the Restoration and, despite differences in rank, profession and generation, there is a considerable degree of uniformity in their attitudes towards women. Attitudes to mistresses, wives and prospective wives are clearly distinguished and do not seem to interact; the man who is a libertine hedonist to his mistress proves a very old-fashioned husband.

The bulk, especially of the court poems, is addressed to mistresses and plays on the obvious variants – extravagant compliment, humorous comment or incitement to pleasure. Much of the poetry has elegance and charm, and sometimes other virtues too. For instance, Carew's 'A Rapture', a poem which circulated widely in manuscript and was probably designed to achieve an interesting notoriety for its author, has his distinctive delicate sensuousness, which prevents it from becoming mere pornography. The seductive poetry usually throws out the lure of mutual pleasure. As Carew says rather smugly:

Did the thing for which I sue
Onely concerne my selfe not you,
Were men so fram'd as they alone
Reap'd all the pleasure, women none,

Then had you reason to be scant;
But 'twere a madnesse not to grant
That which affords (if you consent)
To you the giver, more content
Then me the beggar; Oh then bee
Kinde to your selfe, if not to me.
   ['To A.L.: Perswasions to Love', ll. 17 – 26]

This, of course, ignores the risk to the woman of pregnancy or disgrace, though the risks involved were lessened if the woman was married. However, it holds out the only practical temptation in the circumstances of court life, where, like the men, women were relatively independent agents with time on their hands (it also constitutes part of the evidence against the contention of some modern social historians that men of earlier centuries ignored the physical needs of women).[1] The anti-hedonistic cult of Platonic love, introduced to the court by Henrietta Maria, may have owed some of its limited success to its usefulness as a counter-strategy prolonging male attention by postponing gratification, while minimizing or eliminating risks from pregnancy and scandal. The recalcitrance of women in the face of male blandishments is one of the sources of humour, as in Suckling's lines:

If of her selfe shee will not Love,
   Nothing can make her,
   The Devill take her!
   ['Song, "Why so pale and wan" ', ll. 13 – 15]

With Herrick and Cotton, neither of them courtiers, the humour is more likely to come from a pose as a sly lecher reaping pleasure while avoiding matrimony:

Which done, forsooth, she talks of wedding,
   But what will that avail her?
For though I am old Dog at Bedding,
I'm yet a man of so much reading,
   That there I sure shall fail her.
   ['Ode, "Was ever man" ', ll. 16 – 20]

The bachelor clergyman Herrick, indeed, advocates the felicities of fornication with all the zest of a farmyard cock:

Ile praise, and Ile approve
Those maids that never vary;
And fervently Ile love;
But yet I would not marry.

Ile hug, Ile kisse, Ile play,
And Cock-like Hens Ile tread:
And sport it any way;
But in the Bridall Bed.
 ['The Poet loves a Mistresse, but not to Marry', ll. 5 – 12]

In Herrick, in particular, the lechery has very much the air of a pose, lacking the sensuous conviction of the poetry of Carew. Only Henry King, a scion of an ecclesiastical family who became a bishop, seems to have encouraged conventional chastity in his verse:

Fond Lunatick forbear, why do'st thou sue
For thy affections pay e're it is due?
Loves fruits are legal use; and therefore may
Be onely taken on the marriage day.
 Who for this interest too early call,
  By that exaction lose the Principall.

Then gather not those immature delights,
Untill their riper Autumn thee invites.
He that abortive Corn cuts off his ground,
No Husband but a Ravisher is found:
 So those that reap their love before they wed,
  Do in effect but Cuckold their own Bed.
 ['Loves Harvest', ll. 1 – 12]

If an Ovidian enjoyment of sexual pleasure was the dominant pose when mistresses were being addressed, the attitude to wives or prospective wives was very different. Carew, of all people, spared a moment from gambling and debauches to say:

When I shall marry, if I doe not find
A wife thus moulded, I'll create this mind:
Nor from her noble birth, nor ample dower,
Beauty, or wit, shall she derive a power
To prejudice my Right; but if she be
A subject borne, she shall be so to me:
As to the soule the flesh, as Appetite
To reason is, which shall our wils unite;
In habits so confirm'd, as no rough sway
Shall once appeare, if she but learne t'obay.
 ['A married Woman', ll. 1 – 10]

Instinctively, the notion of hierarchy is introduced and a parallel drawn between the hierarchies in the state, in marriage and in the mind, the latter being conceptualized according to the old faculty psychology as a range of disparate powers rather than as a unified consciousness with differing modes of operation. The woman is the subject, like body to soul or feminine appetite to masculine reason. This way of thinking will have to be examined further in connection with Milton and the Protestant ideal of marriage, but it was pervasive in the seventeenth century. As Donne put it in 'Aire and Angels',

> Just such disparitie
> As is twixt Aire and Angells puritie,
> 'Twixt womens love, and mens will ever bee.
> [ll. 25 – 7]

The polite Waller puts the conventional idea even less flatteringly, comparing the woman he is wooing to a horse waiting to recognize the overmastering mettle of its rider:

> Women, (born to be controul'd,)
> Stoop to the forward, and the bold:
> Affect the haughty, and the proud,
> The gay, the frolick, and the loud.
> Who first the gen'rous steed opprest,
> Not kneeling did salute the beast;
> But with high courage, life, and force,
> Approaching, tam'd th'unruly horse.
> ['Of Love', ll. 13 – 20]

(There is a saving humour in that 'mighty Love' later in the poem forces Waller to bow lower than the bowing lovers he had previously despised, but the humour works on the assumption that the natural order of things has been reversed.) Interestingly, in his bid for mastery Carew seems to anticipate feminine resistance after marriage:

> No rough sway
> Shall once appeare, if she but learne t'obay.
> For in habituall vertues, sense is wrought
> To that calme temper, as the bodie's thought
> To have nor blood, nor gall, if wild and rude
> Passions of Lust, and Anger, are subdu'd;
> When 'tis the faire obedience to the soule,
> Doth in the birth those swelling Acts controule.
> If I in murder steepe my furious rage,
> Or with Adult'ry my hot lust asswage,
> Will it suffice to say my sense, the Beast

ɔvokt me to't? Could I my soule devest,
ꟙy plea were good, Lyons and Buls commit
Both freely, but man must in judgement sit,
And tame this Beast, for Adam was not free,
When in excuse he said, Eve gave it me:
Had he not eaten, she perhaps had beene
Vnpunisht, his consent made hers a sinne.
        ['A married Woman', ll. 9 – 26]

While woman is again the mastered beast tamed by the rational masculine soul, it is Carew's assumption that such a relationship is natural, that through it he will be able to establish a gentle marriage marked by 'no rough sway'. He was, in fact, gifted with a discriminating sensibility, and he could envisage marriage as a relationship of lyrical splendour, as he does in his 'Hymeneall Song' to Lady Wentworth and Lord Lovelace:

They know no night, nor glaring noone,
Measure no houres of Sunne or Moone,
    Nor mark times restlesse Glasse:

Their kisses measure as they flow,
Minutes, and their embraces show
    The howers as they passe.
        [ll. 28 – 33]

Carew's emphasis on personal and emotional fulfilment in marriage is forward-looking. Herrick is more matter-of-fact and traditional. A bachelor himself, he thinks of a wife in terms of physical comforts, a well run house and propagation:

Fat be my Hinde; unlearned be my wife;
Peacefull my night; my day devoid of strife:
To these a comely off-spring I desire,
Singing about my everlasting fire.
        ['His Wish', ll. 1 – 4]

The implications of 'unlearned' are clear – learning enables a woman to rise above her station and is therefore not to be encouraged. The virtues that he would wish a daughter of his to have so that she might make a good wife are also suitably subservient:

*Obedience, Wise-Distrust, Peace*, shy
*Distance* and sweet *Vrbanitie,*
*Safe Modestie, Lou'd Patience, Feare*
*Of offending, Temperance, Deare*

*Constancie, Bashfullnes*, and all
The *Vertues Lesse*, or *Cardinall*.
   ['Mr Hericke his Daughter's Dowrye', ll. 95 – 100]

In keeping with his markedly conservative attitude to marriage
Herrick records many of the older superstitions and customs
surrounding it, including, in 'Julia's *Churching*', the ceremony for
the ritual purification of a woman after childbirth (she was not
supposed to look upward to the sunlight until it had been completed): the latter ceremony, in particular, was offensive to the
Puritans. In his epithalamiums, apart from giving graphic
encouragement to the new husband to force the virginity of the
reluctant wife, Herrick is most intent on the practical purposes of
breeding and the continuance of a gentle family. As he assures the
bride in one of them:

   Some repeat
Your praise, and bless you, sprinkling you with Wheat:
   While that others doe divine;
*Blest is the Bride, on whom the Sun doth shine;*
   And thousands gladly wish
You multiply, as doth a Fish.
   ['A Nuptiall Song on Sir Clipseby Crew and his Lady', ll. 45 – 50]

These attitudes were all of them conventional and deeply rooted in
tradition.

Just as marriage and extra-marital liaisons tended to provoke
conventional responses, so also did courtship, which was regarded
as an atypical and temporary disturbance of the normal order of
things. As Carew instinctively turned to the constitution of a state
when searching for a correspondence to the hierarchy of marriage,
so Cotton turns to Roman institutions to elucidate the relationship
between a woman and her suitor, a relationship that is, in this
instance, now giving way to marriage:

But your six months are now expir'd,
   'Tis time I now should reign,
And if from you obedience be requir'd
   You must not to submit disdain,
But practise what y'ave seen me doe,
And love and honour me as I did you;
   That will an everlasting peace maintain,
And make me crown you Sovereign once again.
   ['To Chloris: Stanzes Irreguliers', ll. 31 – 8]

The immediate reference is, of course, to the Roman habit of appointing an absolute dictator for a limited period of six months at a time of military crisis. Behind this reference lurks the then popular adage that only he who has learned to obey is fit to command, an illogical assumption, though useful for maintaining the social order, since it encouraged subservience in underlings by holding out the veiled promise that they might come to exercise power in their turn, and tended equally to perpetuate the demand for blind obedience, those who have had it exacted from themselves being likely to exact it from others when they have the opportunity (for this reason the adage was flaunted in English schools within living memory). Like relationships in the state and in marriage, courtship is being thought of in terms of authority and obedience, not consultation and consent.

It is the widespread, commonplace assumptions about marriage that make sense of Suckling's satirical onslaughts on the whole institution. He rejects the universal application of the idea that it is a social duty to marry and to propagate:

The World is of a vast extent we see,
And must be peopled; Children then must be;
So must bread too; but since there are enough
Born to the drudgery, what need we plough?
　　['Against Fruition I', ll. 15 – 18]

He shows no sign of sharing Carew's perception of marriage as a possible means to personal fulfilment. In his best and perhaps funniest poem, 'A Ballade. Upon a Wedding', he explodes the whole notion of married bliss as a figment produced by an overheated sexual imagination. Assuming a persona as a naive rustic, Suckling gives a wondering description of the marvels of a fashionable wedding. The undertone is, however, one of unflattering innuendo. There is uncomprehending surprise that the handsome groom, a man who would 'have first been taken out/By all the Maids i' th' Town' at course-a-park, should be going 'To make an end of all his wooing'. He then turns to the bride, described as a fruit on the verge of overripeness and a woman urgent with sexual desire, and comments on her marriage ring:

Her fingers were so small, the Ring
Would not stay on which they did bring,
　　It was too wide a Peck.
　　[ll. 37 – 9]

According to the superstitions of the time, this was an omen implying that she would be less than chaste; hence the shift in the second
half of the stanza:

And to say truth (for out it must)
It lookt like the great Collar (just)
  About our young Colts neck.
    [ll. 40 – 2]

The idea of the wedding ring becomes merged with that of the fine
collar on the groom's marriage suit and the collar round the neck of
the rustic's horse: the groom is destined to drag through life the
load of an unfaithful wife. The succulent bride, redolent of
flowers, fruit and the fertilizing bee, provokes the mental lust of
parson and guest alike, but whereas that cannot be sated, hunger is
permissible:

When all the meat was on the Table,
What man of knife, or teeth, was able
  To stay to be intreated?
And this the very reason was,
Before the Parson could say Grace
  The Company was seated.
    [ll. 91 – 6]

As the guests get steadily drunker there follows an alternation of
dreamy longing and physical contact, humorously described as
abrupt changes:

O'th' sodain up they rise and dance,
Then sit again and sigh, and glance;
  Then dance again and kisse:
Thus sev'ral waies the time did passe,
Whilst ev'ry Woman wisht her place,
  And ev'ry Man wisht his.
    [ll. 103 – 8]

By this time the bride is being undressed and lodged in bed to await
the groom, according to custom. No sooner, however, does the
groom arrive, intent on consummating (he had already been impatient at the beginning of the poem) than he is interrupted by the
arrival of the bridesmaids with posset, a kind of alcoholic yoghurt
much prized as a general tonic and a provocative to lust and
fertility. In order to get rid of the bridesmaids the groom is forced
to gobble posset, and it is only in the final stanza that the groom at
last consummates:

> $_\text{G}$th the candles out, and now
> $_\text{f}$at they had not done, they do:
> $_\text{t}$at that is, who can tell?
> But I beleeve it was no more
> Then thou and I have done before
> With *Bridget*, and with *Nell*.
> [ll. 127 – 32]

The anticlimax is deliberate; a man may commit fornication without committing matrimony. Suckling's humorous scepticism was developed in a wittier savage and more fundamental way by Rochester later in the century, just as his awareness of the gap between social pretence and human nature was exploited more ruthlessly and with a far deeper social probing by the writers of Restoration comedy: it was not for nothing that 'natural easy Suckling' was Millamant's favourite poet.

In contrast to the work of Suckling and the poets associated with the court, metaphysical love poetry, apart from Donne's, is difficult to place socially. This is partly because the metaphysicals were often socially more retired, being scholarly men in scholarly professions, and partly because the element of wit, which may magnify the immediate situation histrionically (as it does in Donne) may equally distance the immediate external reality. This is the case with Marvell's 'To his Coy Mistress', perhaps the most famous love poem of the mid century, for in it any occasioning situation has been left far behind. It starts with a hypothetical generalization, 'Had we but World enough, and Time,' and the generalization turns out to include the major part of geographical space and temporal history as these were understood by the seventeenth-century European mind, stretching from the Ganges to Marvell's home river, the Humber, and from Marvell's own day to the conversion of the Jews, an event expected to herald the approach of Doomsday. From the twinning of time and space as the medium through which the slow ritual of pastoral love might lead to the final revelation of the lady's heart, an almost religious conception with overtones of the Christian idea of the revelation of God through history, the poem turns to the actual ineluctable divorce between time and eternity – eternity conceived of as an empty desert or trackless wilderness, time as the brief moment before the poet is overtaken and hunted down by the winged chariot approaching from behind. The resolution posits the 'now' of hectic love as the means by which time itself can be turned into the prey, torn apart and devoured by the lovers, who combine feminine sweetness and masculine strength into the 'ball' or sphere, the symbol of perfection, and tear it with the violence of 'rough strife' through the iron and locked 'gates of life', an obscure image which may suggest the locked gates of Paradise. The overtones are possibly those of Hermetic ideas contacted when Marvell was in the employment of Fairfax, and suggest an underlying concern with the need for commitment to action beneath the overt subject matter of seduction (the same concern that was detected by Christopher Hill behind the 'Horatian Ode'). While the *carpe diem* theme is a seventeenth-century commonplace, this expansive treatment of it is not, and it raises 'To his Coy Mistress' out of the ordinary category of love poetry, giving it a tone at once personal and general, yet divorcing it from the specifics of social context.

The metaphysical wit of Marvell is but one specialized instance of a general wittiness in the sensibility of his period. A *pro* and *contra* attitude of mind was inherent in the educational system, both at the Inns of Court and in the universities, where degrees were awarded for the defence of a thesis in a disputation. This was one of the roots of the endless paired poems of the century, for and against hope, for and against sexual fruition, and so on: even 'L'Allegro' and 'Il Penseroso' follow this pattern. The habit of mind was also expressed in the dialogue poems of the period, ranging from Marvell's rather portentous 'Dialogue between the Resolved Soul, and Created Pleasure' to the Duchess of Newcastle's 'Dialogue betwixt Wit and Beauty'. Beyond this was a baroque sensibility, already apparent in the Jacobeans, which delighted in strong and poignant contrasts, often exaggerated to the point of corruption. In the poetry of the mid century and later this led to work such as Cleveland's 'A young Man to an Old Woman Courting Him' and 'A Faire Nimph scorning a Black Boy Courting Her', Henry Rainolds's 'A Black-moor Maid Wooing a Fair Boy', together with King's reply, 'The Boyes Answer to the Blackmoor', and Rochester's 'Song of a Young Lady to her Ancient Lover'. Both the liking for strong contrast and the logical appreciation of contrary lines of argument merge in the substance of the metaphysical poem, the dominant line of argument providing the logical thrust, while the clashing contrasts in the imagery imply a possible and contradictory line of argument. It is because metaphysical poetry grows out of the sensibility of the age that it tends to constitute less a separate school than one end of the available poetic spectrum, towards which most poets of the period move at some point in their work. The metaphysicals themselves diverge widely from one another, and just as Marvell's treatment of love differs from that of his predecessor Donne, so it differs from that of Cowley, whose work dominated the poetic world in the years immediately following the Restoration.

Cowley has a pellucid clarity and a great facility in his verse. Unlike Marvell's love poetry, his is distanced from the occasioning situation not by mysterious ambiguities but by a precise generalization. The nature of his gift means that he produces no poetry of great passion, but he can offer a quizzical insight into the absurdities of being in love; this is a slightly middle-aged virtue – but then middle age does have decided advantages over the hot self-absorption of youth. Any lover who wants to see what it all looks like from the outside might do worse than read Cowley; the wit with which he describes generalized situations shapes them up admirably. Above all, his precision, wit and slightly serene generalization make him a superb author of poetic compliments. He picks up, for instance, the traditional tropes of trees along garden walks ranging themselves about a mistress and bowing to her beauty, of flowers and plants borrowing their beauty from hers and the sun being eclipsed by her radiance, the kind of trope that Waller could handle with such elegance:

Had Dorothea liv'd when mortals made
Choice of their Deities, this sacred shade
Had held an altar to her pow'r, that gave
The peace, and glory, which these alleys have:
Embroider'd so with flowers where she stood,
That it became a garden of a wood.
Her presence has such more than human grace,
That it can civilize the rudest place:
And beauty too, and order can impart,
Where nature ne'er intended it, nor art.
The plants acknowledge this, and her admire,
No less than those of old did Orpheus' lyre:
If she sit down, with tops all tow'rds her bow'd,
They round about her into arbors crowd:
Or if she walk, in even ranks they stand,
Like some well-marshal'd and obsequious band.
     ['At Pens-Hurst', ll. 1 – 16]

Cowley takes the same tropes but rejects their stiff falsity:

Though you be absent here, I needs must say
The *Trees* as beauteous are, and *flowers* as gay,
  As ever they were wont to be;
  Nay the *Birds* rural musick too
  Is as melodious and free,
  As if they sung to pleasure you:
I saw a *Rose-Bud* o'pe this morn; I'll swear
The blushing *Morning* open'd not more fair.

How could it be so fair, and you away?
How could the *Trees* be beauteous, *Flowers* so gay?
   ['The Spring', ll. 1 – 10]

From this opening Cowley turns back to the previous year, when
his mistress was present:

Where ere you walk'd trees were as reverend made,
As when of old *Gods* dwelt in every shade.
  Is't possible they should not know,
  What loss of honor they sustain,
  That thus they smile and flourish now,
  And still their former pride retain?
Dull *Creatures*! 'tis not without Cause that she,
Who fled the *God of wit*, was made a *Tree*.
   [ll. 17 – 24]

The power of the pathetic fallacy is drawn from the recognition of
the fact of nature's indifference. Similarly, it is the untruth of the
story of Orpheus's charming the trees that is used to support the
truth of the poet's feeling:

When *Orpheus* had his song begun,
They call'd their wondring *roots* away,
And bad them silent to him run.
How would those learned trees have followed you?
You would have drawn *Them*, and their *Poet* too.
   [ll. 28 – 32]

All this leads up to the final complimentary, yet factually true
distinction between the present spring and the time of her arrival:

'Tis you the best of *Seasons* with you bring;
This is for *Beasts*, and that for *Men* the *Spring*.
   [ll. 47 – 8]

Cowley thus moves metaphysical poetry towards the world of the
Restoration and the later Augustans,[2] distinguishing between fact
and fiction, searching carefully beneath common exaggerations for
their substratum of truth and expressing feeling through a polished

intellectual wit. But the feeling has in the process become generalized; it is the generic feeling of a lover, not of one particular person
in love (it contrasts strongly with the more personalized wit of
Millamant and Mirabell in this respect). It tells us much about
the surface conventions of seventeenth-century life, the habitual
exaggerated flattery of women, of aristocrats, of princes and
generals – in short, of anyone who had something that the flatterer
wanted – a flattery so habitual that the elegance of the game, rather
than the undeceiving substance of what was said, often seems to
have been the point of it. The flattery also served as a signal of
social compliance – the norms and expectations of the situation
would be observed: in this respect it could be reassuring. Applied to
women by an unintelligent male mind, however, it could easily lose
its lightness of touch and become coarsely condescending, con-
firming the worst suspicions of the modern feminist.

   At least the flattery of women cannot be numbered among the
habitual vices of the Earl of Rochester; he is more likely to insult
them for pretending to conventional chastity or, alternatively, for
indulging in an undiscriminating promiscuity. He has an outraged
amusement at the democracy of lust that cuts across the social
strata:

Unto this all-sin-sheltering grove
Whores of the bulk and the alcove,
Great ladies, chambermaids, and drudges,
The ragpicker, and heiress trudges.
Carmen, divines, great lords, and tailors,
Prentices, poets, pimps and jailers,
Footmen, fine fops do here arrive,
And here promiscuously they swive.
   ['A Ramble in St. James's Park', ll. 25 – 32]

It is not for the number of their sexual partners that he attacks
women, but for their copulations with servile fools devoid of
intelligence or honest physical passion:

There's something generous in mere lust.
But to turn damned abandoned jade
When neither head nor tail persuade;
To be a whore in understanding,
A passive pot for fools to spend in!
   [ll. 98 – 102]

He places in the mouth of Artemisia a similar condemnation of
women who do not use their natural liberty to go to bed with men

who have aroused their admiration, but instead go to bed with any man at all:

Our silly sex! who, born like monarchs free,
Turn gypsies for a meaner liberty,
And hate restraint, though but from infamy.
They call whatever is not common, nice,
And deaf to nature's rule, or love's advice,
Forsake the pleasure to pursue the vice.
To an exact perfection they have wrought
The action, love; the passion is forgot.
      ['A Letter from Artemisia in the Town to Chloe in the Country',
      ll. 56 – 63]

While the idea of a sexual elect among males, though based on their merit rather than arbitrary choice, may owe something to Rochester's Calvinist upbringing (Byron, it may be remembered, was another rakish product of Calvinist education), it accords well enough with the hedonism of 'A Satyr against Reason and Mankind':

I own right reason, which I would obey:
That reason which distinguishes by sense
And gives us rules of good and ill from thence,
That bounds desires with a reforming will
To keep 'em more in vigor, not to kill.
Your reason hinders, mine helps to enjoy,
Renewing appetites yours would destroy.
      [ll. 99 – 105][3]

This philosophy was not confined to theory or to the male sex in the court and the town of the Restoration, but it was for obvious reasons easier for a man to practise than for a woman. While women who were too low in society to have much to lose or too high to have much to fear might pursue it with a measure of impunity, the majority of women, as we shall see when we come to consider Restoration comedy, had to think in hard-headed terms of a freedom that was more limited but perhaps, in the long run, more rewarding.

While hedonistic poetry satirizing or conducing to the seduction of women is abundant in the seventeenth century, and while poetry on marriage and courtship is not uncommon, poems from husband to wife or vice versa are rare. It is not in the nature of things for man and wife to sit around writing poems to each other: the need is usually lacking, and they have other things to do. However, in a

iod when the men were frequently away fighting in the wars or
ere imprisoned, in exile or in hiding, it often fell to the wife to
maintain the family business or estates and even, occasionally, to
defend the family house against a military siege. Whatever the conventional assumptions about the inferiority of women, in practice
many men depended on their intelligence and persistence. The love
and gratitude that were evoked by the faith and loyalty of the wives
of the period seldom found its way into verse until the wives
themselves were dead and the husbands were left alone to write of
their absent worth. Poems like Milton's sonnet 'Methought I saw
my late espoused Saint', or King's 'Exequy' do give a sense of the
love that is in marriage:

So close the ground, and 'bout her shade
Black curtains draw, my *Bride* is laid.

Sleep on my *Love* in thy cold bed
Never to be disquieted!
My last good night! Thou wilt not wake
Till I thy fate shall overtake:
Till age, or grief, or sickness must
Marry my body to that dust
It so much loves; and fill the room
My heart keeps empty in thy Tomb.
Stay for me there; I will not faile
To meet thee in that hollow Vale.
[ 'The Exequy', ll. 79 – 90]

It was in letters, composed in the haste of business during an
absence from home, that a man was most likely to express in
writing his love for his wife during her lifetime.

While there was often a recognition in fact of the worth of an
able wife, the theory of female inferiority continued to dominate.
Towards the end of the century it provoked a spirit of feminist
rebellion which found at least some outlet in Restoration drama.
Before coming to this, however, we must first turn to a consideration of the Protestant ideal of marriage and its interpretation in
the works of John Milton.

# 12 The theory and practice of Protestant marriage

There is no doubt that marriage underwent a major change in England during the seventeenth and eighteenth centuries, but there is considerable doubt about the exact nature of the change. The sources for the traditional concept of marriage were the Scriptures, canon law, and behind canon law Roman law, all superimposed on the native customs of the tribes that invaded Western Europe. Marriage was a contract, its aims before the Reformation being two, the propagation of the species and the avoidance of fornication: the woman contracted to grant sexual access to her husband, the man to enter her sexually. When marriage also became a sacrament at the Council of Florence in 1439, the contractual basis remained fundamental; if the contract could not in principle be fulfilled, usually because of impotence on the part of the male, then the sacrament was invalid and the marriage could be annulled. All this, of course, lies behind the high jinks in *Tristram Shandy*, where a formal contract is legally drawn up granting ingress, egress (lest the man, having entered, should not be allowed to withdraw) and regress (lest, having withdrawn, he should not be allowed to re-enter), and a contractual attitude also lay behind English divorce law until a few years ago.[1]

Protestant thinking retained the contractual basis of marriage, but reinterpreted virtually everything else about it. Medieval Catholicism had been, for the general populace, a religion of efficacious ceremonies administered by a properly qualified priesthood, but Protestantism emphasized the direct contact between the individual and his God, was suspicious of intermediary priests and ceremonies and laid great stress on the importance of the faith of the individual participant in the ceremonies it did allow. The resulting shift in the notion of religion is thus summed up by Keith Thomas:

Today we think of religion as a belief, rather than a practice, as definable in terms of creeds rather than in modes of behaviour. But . . . a medieval

nt's knowledge of Biblical history or Church doctrine was, so far as
ın tell, usually extremely slight. The Church was important to him not
because of its formalised code of belief, but because its rites were an
essential accompaniment to the important events in his own life – birth,
marriage and death. It solemnised these occasions by providing
appropriate rites of passage to emphasize their social significance. Religion
was a ritual method of living, not a set of dogmas.
[*TRDM*, p. 76]

The ritual aspect of Christianity was transformed by the
thoroughgoing Protestants; as Calvin put it, the Papists 'pretend
there is a magical force in the sacraments, independent of
efficacious faith'.[2] The Protestants had no time for such magic, a
point Milton was to employ in his advocacy of divorce. Thus the
sacramental nature of marriage shifted away from church
ceremonies and towards the quality of the religious life lived by the
married couple. The *Book of Common Prayer* of 1549 adds to the
two original aims of marriage a third, 'mutual society, help and
comfort'. There is here a potential conflict: procreation and the
avoidance of fornication could be regarded as social duties; the
provision of help and comfort is a personal matter, even if the help
and comfort are considered to be primarily of a spiritual kind.
Also, help and comfort are not easy to define contractually.

The potential conflict took a long while to become actual, but
sooner or later Protestants were bound to face the difficulty of
attempting to legislate upon attitudes rather than rights and duties.
Meanwhile, the various elements in marriage remained in uneasy
balance. Centralized national authority in Church and state,
accompanied by paternalistic overtones, was paralleled by the
development of the paternalistic religious household, in which a
regular round of prayers, psalm-singing and catechizing was
directed by the father of the family; the mother was hierarchically
inferior and expected to show deference, yet she was a free spiritual
individual, ultimately responsible for working out her own sal-
vation. Pleasure as such was suspect; as Schücking said, 'At the end
of the sixteenth century, we find Puritans who would not permit
themselves even to stroke their dogs.'[3] Mere physical pleasure even
in marriage was beneath the dignity of a Christian, but pleasure,
suitably chaperoned by some higher purpose, might be admitted.
The degree of pleasure and the circumstances that admitted it were
a matter of individual conscience. The anonymous author of *The
Whole Duty of Man* (1659) was of the opinion that:

Even there [in lawful marriage] men are not to think themselves let loose to please their brutish appetites, but are to keep themselves within such rules of moderation, as agree to the end of Marriage, which being these two, the begetting of children, and the avoiding of fornication, nothing must be done which may hinder the first of these ends; and the second aiming onely at the subduing of lust, the keeping men from any sinful effects of it, is very contrary to that end to make marriage an occasion of heightening, and enflaming it.[4]

On the other hand, the Anglican clergyman Jeremy Taylor took a much gentler view in giving as reasons for marital intercourse, '*a Desire of children, or to avoid fornication, or to lighten and ease the cares and sadness of household affairs, or to endear each other*'.[5] If restraint and a desire for pleasure needed to be reconciled, so also did husbandly power and love, and on this matter Taylor took a similarly gentle view: 'A husband's power over his wife is paternal and friendly, not magisterial and despotic . . . For the power a man hath is founded in the understanding, not in the will or force; it is not a power of coercion.'[6] Behind this lie the two injunctions of St Paul, 'Wives, obey your husbands' and 'Husbands, love your wives', but the resulting compromise was often harsher. Formal deference in marriage was recommended by Gouge and other Puritan divines, who criticized the use by wives of familiarities such as 'Ducks' and 'Pigsnie' rather than 'Master' followed by the surname; usage, however, seems eventually to have settled on a more friendly mode of address, the simple titles 'husband' and 'wife'.

Within the family formal deference was demanded even more strongly of children. They knelt morning and evening to receive their parents' blessing, and even when forty years of age or more were still expected to kneel in the presence of their fathers. While on the whole the divines came out against wife-beating, and while the beating of servants also declined during the seventeenth century, there were no misgivings about the thrashing of children. Original sin, taken at all seriously, means that a baby is possessed by the devil. As Walter Hilton said in the fourteenth century:

The remedy against original sin is the sacrament of Baptism, and that against actual sin is the sacrament of Penance. The soul of an unbaptized child bears no likeness to God because of original sin; it is nothing but an image of the devil and a brand of hell. But as soon as it is baptized, it is reformed into the likeness of God.[7]

Hence, presumably, the medieval habit of exorcizing children before they were baptized. All were agreed that self-will was corrupt; therefore the first aim of education was to break the child's will. Beatings were administered to this end for the good of the child. The only question was how much beating he or she could be expected to take. Robert Mannyng, in 1345, had only been concerned that no bone should be broken, and Batty, translated into English in 1581, rejoiced that the providence of Almighty God had provided posteriors which could be beaten without the infliction of serious injury, while Rogers in a much-quoted passage says that the mother 'holdes not his [the father's] hand from due stroakes, but bares their [the children's] skins with delight, to his fatherly stripes'.[8] After being savagely beaten the medieval child was expected to kiss the rod (an acknowledgement of the justice of the proceedings), while the seventeenth-century child was more commonly expected to kneel and offer up public thanks to God for such timely correction. Thrashings were backed up by threats of torment and death in this world and of damnation in the next, allotted

To him that breaks his father's law
Or mocks his mother's word.[9]

The result could be certain coolness in the parent – child relationship, encouraged by the parents' habit of keeping their distance from their children in order to retain dignity and authority. Aubrey, remarking on the improvement in the relationships between children and parents late in the century, said that in the earlier generation 'the child perfectly loathed the sight of his parents as the slave his torturer'.[10]

The harsh treatment of children and the suppression of wives, at least in theory, have led many commentators to feel that marriage in the sixteenth and earlier seventeenth centuries must have been a gloomy and loveless business. The case has been most cogently argued by Lawrence Stone in *The Family Sex and Marriage in England, 1500–1800*, one of his slim volumes on the early modern period of English history. It records virtually all that is known on its subject, and its argument is intricate and erudite. Its main thesis concerns the development of the traditional 'open-lineage family', which was dominated by a kinship network for support and defence and was directed by the senior males in the family, acting in the interests of the kinship group as a whole; this, Stone believes, gave way in the sixteenth and seventeenth centuries to a 'restricted patriarchal nuclear family', controlled by the *pater familias* in increasing independence of the wider kinship network; and this in turn developed during the later seventeenth and eighteenth centuries into a 'closed domesticated nuclear family', bonded closely by personal affection, in which children were given increasing external autonomy, after they had been brought up in such a way that they in fact internalized their parents' standards of behaviour. Coercion and the authority of the kin were thus relaxed in favour of a private conscience implanted by upbringing. The general thesis is very persuasive. The derivative modern system of upbringing certainly employs moral blackmail in preference to brute force. Nevertheless, the picture of the two earlier types of family as very cold, brutally unaffectionate, seems exaggeratedly gloomy, even though many exceptions are allowed for in Stone's account. Parents were probably more distant from children than they now are, even in our upper classes, but the relationship between man and wife often seems to have been very close. The main piece of evidence for this view is the popularity of Shakespearian romantic comedy, a matter to which we must return later. Also, even in a marriage arranged by the kin, there is a probability that any frequency of physical intercourse would give rise to some human affection. Possibly very affectionate marriages like that of Sir Simon D'Ewes, detailed at length by Stone himself, were not utterly exceptional. Certainly, other records of the gentry, such as Henry Oxinden's lines to his wife, 'Dear Heart, this is only to let thee know how infinitely I long to be with thee', or Sir Edward Dering's description of his period in hiding in 1642:

[I enjoyed] so happy a privacy as that nothing could add to the sweet satisfaction thereof but the sight and company of my children. . . . My wife at chosen times came into my study, and made my stolen commons a feast with her society

do not suggest emotional chilliness.[11] However, it is only fair to point out that Stone, who has done so much original work on this subject, has made a contrary judgement in full awareness of the evidence.[12]

Apart from the personal documentation of marriage, there are more general accounts which indicate some gap between wifely subjection in theory and the marriage relationship in practice. The Dutch Resident in London and the visiting Frederick of Würtemburg both commented on the extraordinary freedom enjoyed by

English women, and the Puritan Gouge alludes to wives who 'give the scoff at the very hearing of subjection', and was himself forced to climb down by a rebellion of the wives in his congregation against talk of feminine subservience. The radical currents of thought that had encouraged religious toleration also worked towards feminine equality. As they drew upon very different sources, ranging from the belief in an innate Christ seed in all human souls to rational pragmatism or intellectual scepticism, so they also found a wide variety of expressions. Leveller women mobbed Parliament in 1643 and had to be dispersed by troops, and while in some of the petitions they delivered to Parliament between 1641 and 1653 they accepted their inferiority in authority and wisdom to men, in others they spoke of their 'equal share and interest' in the Commonwealth and refused to be fobbed off with unsatisfactory replies pointedly directed by Parliament at their menfolk.[13] A string of pro- and anti-feminist books and pamphlets appeared in the 1640s and 1650s, culminating later in the century with the 1677 translation of Poulain de la Barre's *The Woman as Good as the Man*, a piece of rationalist feminism based on common sense and fact instead of on the Bible.[14] Finally, the extremely radical sects drew upon the long tradition of European subversive millenarianism in which women had played a prominent part. Among the most notorious of these sects were the Ranters, who combined in some cases profound spiritual insight (more profound than in the official churches) with a great deal of humbug; they confused the freedom of spiritual enlightenment with a sometimes crass amorality, some of their members seeking to justify theft and murder, and their more reprehensible excesses were used by their opponents to discredit all that they stood for, good and bad alike. One of the things which greatly shocked their right-minded contemporaries was their advocacy and practice of free love, for they took Blake's view that desire is not to be restrained, that the road of excess leads to the palace of wisdom. Richard Baxter expressed the common reaction:

Many of them committed Whoredoms commonly: Insomuch that a Matron of great Note for Godliness and Sobriety, being perverted by them, turned so shameless a Whore, that she was Carted [i.e. exposed on a cart, usually prior to flogging] in the streets of London.[15]

If the same standard were applied today, half the population would be without skin to their backs. The women of other left-wing sects contented themselves with less than stripping naked and dancing in congenial meetings, insisting merely on the right to preach the Word as if they were men. It was all very shocking.

After the Restoration the sects were severely repressed, and indeed the Ranters were already being persecuted in the Interregnum; extremist feminine freedom went underground with them. Within society generally, however, there was some softening of the atmosphere surrounding marriage. By 1660 it was common for children to be granted a veto of proposed marriage partners, and this arrangement then gradually gave way to one in which children chose their own prospective partners while parents retained the right of veto. Romantic love or a powerful sexual attraction were regarded as inadequate bases for marriage, esteem and some assessment of character being required; but this was only sensible, since strong physical attraction passes, and falling in love is a transient glamorized condition of the emotions by no means necessarily associated with clarity of perception. If a practical hard-headedness of choices was encouraged, this again was no bad thing; it is an advantage, in marriage, to have an income. Meanwhile, architectural fashion accommodated itself to greater privacy, suites of rooms that opened out on one another giving way to corridors with rooms opening off them, and sexual pleasure within marriage gradually became respectable. The scene was set fair for the arrival of the modern love nest.

# 13 Milton: from tracts on divorce to *Paradise Lost*

It is the mid seventeenth century in England that provides the natural habitat for Milton's divorce pamphlets and the matrimonial passages in *Paradise Lost*. Milton takes for granted the inherent wickedness of the human heart and the natural inferiority of the human female, for 'Who can be ignorant that woman was created for man, and not man for woman?' Throughout *The Doctrine and Discipline of Divorce*, which appeared in 1643 and was enlarged for the second edition of 1644 (dated 1645 on the title page), he refers to marriage as a covenant or contract, rejects the superstitious notion of marriage as a sacrament and deplores the fact that 'for many ages . . . marriage lay in disgrace with most of the ancient Doctors, as a work of the flesh, almost a defilement, wholly deny'd to Priests, and the second time disswaded to all'. While he accepts the three Protestant aims of marriage, he clearly has misgivings about its role as a remedy for incontinence, feeling that this is too negative a formulation for its high dignity, and he accordingly reinterprets St Paul's saying, 'It is better to marry than to burn', in a novel fashion: 'But what might this burning mean? Certainly not the meer motion of carnall lust, not the meer goad of a sensitive desire' [III, ii, p. 396, ll. 15 – 17]. Similarly, when God saw that it was not good for Adam to be alone, Milton takes this to mean that Adam requires spiritual companionship rather than domestic assistance (a sense that was actually given to the passage by others). This, the last aim of marriage in the *Book of Common Prayer*, Milton makes first in importance, placing it above procreation, for 'Out of question the cheerfull help that may be in mariage toward sanctity of life, is the purest, and so the noblest end of that contract.'

Upon this order of importance Milton bases his case for divorce on the grounds of incompatibility: if the main aim of marriage cannot be fulfilled because of incompatibility, then the contract is void; 'casuall adultery', the traditional cause of divorce, is a far less

serious matter. It has taken the laws of England over three centuries to catch up with this position. Nevertheless, Milton is still
thinking in a religious, not a secular, context; the danger of having
an incompatible wife is that she may 'disinable him [her husband]
in the whole service of God through the disturbance of her
unhelpfull and unfit society; and so drive him at last through mur-
muring and despair to thoughts of Atheisme'. Unfit matrimony
thus 'doth the same in effect that an Idolatrous match' does, and is
objectionable because irreligious rather than unpleasant. Milton
insists that, divorce having been effected, 'liberal conditions'
should be granted to the ex-wife, but gives no serious consideration
to children, only mentioning them in passing; however, given the
rapidity of remarriage in the seventeenth century, and the number
of children living with step-parents because of the death of their
own parents, children after a Miltonic divorce would have been in a
common enough situation. Also, Milton probably assumed that
any fixed incompatibility must manifest itself early on in marriage.
In deciding upon a divorce, power lay not with any Church court,
and not with the wife, but with the husband, in whose hands God
had placed it:

Another act of papall encroachment it was, to pluck the power and arbitrement of divorce from the master of the family, into whose hands God and
the law of all Nations had put it, and Christ so left it, preaching onely to the
conscience, and not authorizing a judiciall Court to tosse about and divulge
the unaccountable and secret reasons of disaffection between man and
wife, as a thing most improperly answerable to any such kind of triall.
    [III, ii, p. 497, l. 19 – p. 498, l. 2]¹

It was, Milton stated, the restraint of the 'lawfull liberty' of
humane divorce that encouraged men to whore rather than marry,
or thrust the genuinely spiritual into the arms of Anabaptist groups
like the Ranters. This careful defensive stratagem to number
himself among the respectable did not save Milton from a storm of
abuse, and he had to produce *The Judgement of Martin Bucer* and
then *Tetrachordon* to support his case by appeal to authority and
scriptural exegesis. Finally, in *Colasterion*, he exploded with irri-
tation at an attack from an adversary who was, he had heard, an
ex-servingman, and at the epithets '*Anabaptistical, Antinomian,
Heretical, Atheistical*', heaped upon him.

    In his plea for divorce Milton was opposing the authority of
Church and state and, with the authority of a Puritan head of family,
exercising his legitimate right to interpret the Scriptures for

himself; hence his outrage at being accused of proposing 'divorce at pleasure', divorce on the grounds of individual inclination. Mere inclination was anathema to Milton; he advocated distrust of 'our own hearts, for they are evill', a distrust that gained respectability and force from the evil doctrine of original sin and from Calvinist harpings on the utter depravity of all save the 'Elect' among Christians (that is, of all save themselves). Milton's counter-thrusting instincts for repressive authority and religious individualism were maintained in uneasy equilibrium by his refusal to question the ultimate presuppositions behind his religion and the Puritan system; final intellectual freedom was not within his reach – such questionings he viewed as sacrilege. The hierarchy of the Puritan family, with the rational male at its head, was internalized in Milton's distrust of the heart, of emotion and feeling and also pleasant sensation, and this was read back into man and angel before the Fall, for it is this internalized sensibility that shapes the cosmogenic vision of *Paradise Lost*. In unfallen Adam reason should dominate, and B. Rajan has traced man's fall in *Paradise Lost* as the crumbling of that dominion.[2] Reason for Milton is, at least theoretically, synonymous with intelligence or understanding and, as Raphael says in Book V, lines 486–90, intelligence ranges from the intuitive mind of the angels to the discursive ratiocination that is the dominant mode of thinking among humans. In practice, however, he tends to reduce reason to reasoning (Christopher Hill perceptively notes that the thought processes of Raphael and Adam before the Fall are post-lapsarian, indistinguishable from those of Adam in discussion with Michael in Book XII, though he explains this in terms of a confusion between ignorance and innocence on Milton's part;[3] in fact, the most intuitive passages often occur when Milton speaks directly, as in the opening to Book III). The heart Milton tends to equate with passionate emotion and he allows no place for the higher perceptive intelligence of intuitive feeling. In fact, he does not think of feeling as intelligent at all, seeing it simply as something to be controlled by reason; this is a great loss to his perception of life, since the intelligence of the heart is ultimately unitive, whereas ratiocination by its very nature is restricted to duality. This is the ultimate reason for the jarring discords in Milton's cosmology.

The cosmology of *Paradise Lost* encompasses the universal hierarchy of God, angel and man, and the lesser hierarchy of man and woman ruling over the animal creation. Both are theoretically hierarchies of love, but both are flawed by Milton's undervaluing of the female and of the feminine side of his own nature. If feeling is conceived as something unintelligent, which must be subjected to reason in the sense of ratiocination, then love must be something deliberate, a deliberate choice, for 'Reason also is choice'. Hence the danger of woman, whose attractiveness threatens superior deliberation. Given Eve's less-than-masculine rationality, she cannot add to Adam's understanding, but she can easily cloud it. The consequence is an imbalance in Milton's version of the relationship between the sexes in Paradise, and a related imbalance in the cosmos of *Paradise Lost* as a whole, where the only female personages apart from the beasts are Eve and the figure of Sin.[4]

In Milton's universe the supreme intelligence is, of course, male, God the Father. The second Person in the divine hierarchy is also male, the Son, the agent of the Father in both love and wrath, the Creator of the world, the scourge of the rebellious army of Satan, the blood sacrifice to the justice of the Father through love for man, and in his turn a 'Father of his Familie' when he clothes fallen Adam and Eve in the skin of beasts. The son is the father-king-priest, who will, as head, ultimately unite the whole Puritan family of the cosmos, man and angel alike, in an eternal round of psalm-singing and blessing. While the Holy Ghost appears as rarely in *Paradise Lost* as it does in the New Testament (Urania, apparently female, may or may not be the Holy Spirit), the conventional idea of the Trinity is parodied in the trinity of Hell, Satan, Sin and Death. The Son of the divine Trinity here becomes a daughter, Sin, whose beauty symbolizes her alluring power, while the serpentine folds of her nether limbs show her true nature. This true nature only becomes obvious when she has been experienced, hence she becomes serpentine in giving birth to Death, the consequence of sin, while the hell-hounds indicate the unrest that accompanies this. Sin is born from Satan's head, indicating the overweening ambition that is her nature (this is an extension of the exegetical tradition of Genesis, which interpreted Eve's formation from Adam's rib as indicative of a degree of companionship, the head denoting rule, the feet utter subjection). The disordered relationships of the hellish trinity are violent and incestuous, Sin, the daughter-mistress of Satan, being raped by her own son Death. While the three are in unison when hunting prey, the ultimate outcome is foretold by Michael, for Sin and Death will fix 'in [Satan's] head thir stings'. All this parodies the more conventional family relationships established by God among men. The details are allegorically impeccable; Sin would have been less effective as a man. The antifeminist ethos comes not from the infernal trinity in itself, but from the lack of counterbalancing female goodness elsewhere in the poem. God is male, and the angels (though they may, according to Raphael, mingle utterly in loving ecstasy) nevertheless appear to be, as Adam says, 'without feminine'. The sole representative of female goodness is therefore Eve, and any pro-feminist feeling must stem from the presentation of her and her relationship with Adam.

The relationship of Adam and Eve in Paradise, which now seems so dated, was boldly original when *Paradise Lost* first appeared. Milton describes the ideals of Protestant marriage in operation before the Fall, physical love as having a place in the Garden of Eden. Adam and Eve copulate in their bower for mutual delight and not merely to beget progeny, and their copulation before the Fall is contrasted with their copulation afterwards. The copulation after the Fall is sensual:

For never did thy Beautie since the day
I saw thee first and wedded thee, adornd
With all perfections, so enflame my sense
With ardor to enjoy thee.
       [IX, ll. 1029 – 32]

What then is the difference between this and copulation before the Fall? In Book IV, lines 737 – 73, Milton stresses that it was then 'Founded in Reason, Loyal, Just and Pure'. Its rational nature seems to consist in three things. First, conception is not prevented, a rational feature in accordance with the law of God, for

Our Maker bids increase, who bids abstain
But our Destroyer, foe to God and Man?

Catholic and Protestant theology alike condemned contraception in the seventeenth century. Second, copulation takes place within marriage; but this, like the absence of contraception, is true of Adam and Eve's lovemaking after as before the Fall. Formal marriage must therefore be extended to take in the inner condition of marriage; this recalls the insistence in the divorce tracts on the innerness of marriage:

When is it that God may bee said to joyn, when the parties and their friends consent? No surely, for that may concurre to lewdest

ends. Or is it when Church rites are finisht? Neither; for the efficacie of those depends upon the presupposed fitnesse of either party.
        [III, ii, p. 479, ll. 12 – 16]

The efficacy of the outer service depends, to Milton's Protestant mind, on inner faith, and the main aim of the institution of marriage is a condition of mutual solace which depends on an attitude of mind. That attitude gone, marriage has gone with it. Hence the contrast between married love and its opposites, whoredom and courtly love:

Here [in marriage] Love his gold'n shafts imploies, here lights
His constant Lamp, and waves his purple wings,
Reigns here and revels; not in the bought smile
Of Harlots, loveless, joyless, unindeard,
Casual fruition, nor in Court Amours,
Mixt Dance, or wanton Mask, or Midnight Ball,
Or Serenate, which the starv'd Lover sings
To his proud fair, but quitted with disdain.
        [IV, ll. 763 – 70]

He objects to whoredom that it is not 'constant' (unlike the 'constant' lamp of love in marriage – constant in the senses of enduring and unwavering), that it is therefore chance enjoyment, 'casual fruition', and 'unindeard' without affection. He therefore requires a current of settled affection in a relationship before copulation is acceptable to him. He objects to courtly love because the 'proud fair', starving her admirer, is using sexual attraction as a means to manipulate and control him; the wife should submit herself willingly to a good man. Sex should not be a matter of power politics but of personal regard; neither husband nor wife is simply a means to an end. (Milton's tendency to refer to Eve as the 'mother of mankind', which has provoked feminist hostility, is not intended to reduce her to a means of reproduction, but to praise her by reference to her highest and most important role.) The limitation in the relationship comes not from the treatment of either partner as merely a means to an end, but from Milton's deep-rooted idea that a woman is naturally less intelligent than a man. This stultifies the whole relationship. Having recognized the superior intelligence of Adam, Eve

what was Honour knew,
And with obsequious Majestie approv'd
[His] pleaded reason.
        [VIII, ll. 508 – 10]

She can therefore give herself without stint to Adam. Not so Adam, however, in return. Having superior intelligence, he is responsible for Eve, and while her feebler intelligence makes her liable to wayward, irrational inclination, yet her attractive power is dangerously great, so that

> Wisdom in discourse with her
> Looses discount'nanc't, and like folly shewes.
> [VIII, ll. 552 – 3]

The price that Adam pays for marriage is therefore eternal vigilance; he cannot simply give himself emotionally to Eve, but is required consciously to judge the fitness of all that she feels and does and suggests. He can never be at rest in her nature; he cannot be simply spontaneous. The element of trust and confidence in Eve is thus less than sufficient for fullness of love, for 'perfect love casteth out fear'. There is a constant strained self-consciousness about Adam: when Eve, half-embracing, leaned on 'our first Father', Adam typically 'Smil'd with superior Love' in return. He can only let himself go by giving way to sensual passion, to the 'fierce desire' which unsatiated, perhaps insatiable, is a torment of the damned. There is in consequence no playfulness and no ease in the relationship between Adam and Eve. On the one occasion when love does flow spontaneously between them, Adam is already falling:

> If Death
> Consort with thee, Death is to mee as Life;
> So forcible within my heart I feel
> The Bond of Nature draw me to my owne.
> [IX, 953 – 6]

Adam is being irrational here, and is in due course censured by Almighty God for it.

The strain in Adam and in his relationship with his wife is not an inevitable consequence of hierarchy as such, but rather of the rigidity, the falsity, of Milton's notion of hierarchy. Hierarchies of innumerable kinds are natural to life and no hindrance to freedom or spontaneity. A mother can play spontaneously with her child, who is not her equal, because she fulfils, instead of violating, the child's nature. Her superiority is obvious, and if she has to insist upon it, an unnatural strain has crept into the relationship. The superiority of man to woman is not obvious, and Milton's marital hierarchy is, in contrast, rigid and external; it can only be imposed

by emotional violence. The same strain occurs in his inner hierarchy of faculties. The Puritan emphasis on self-consciousness
stems from the idea that we must force order upon our recalcitrant
nature, and it inhibits the natural flow of intelligence and living
affection. This reflects on to the legalistic nature of Puritan
theology, in which God is to be seized as an object by man's reason.
As Eckhart says: 'We ought not to have or let ourselves be satisfied
with any thought of God: when the thought goes our God goes with
it.'[5] God as a gentle presence, the basis rather than the object of
awareness, is difficult of access for those who are convinced of the
utter corruption of the human heart. The basis of Adam's nature is
not, in fact, reason, intuitive or discursive, otherwise he would
inevitably be rational. Reason for Adam is instead the recognition
of a superior law to be imposed on his nature and against his
nature; obedience is a forced submission, not a harmonious
recognition of superior wisdom. Moreover, ignorance is a virtue;
the mind at conflict with itself is to curb its desire for knowledge, to
obey the behests of superiors without understanding why. The flow
of intelligence and affection is inhibited; love and blind obedience
become closely linked, hence the kind of obedience owed by Adam
to God, by Eve to Adam. It is an obedience to 'commands', not
inner impulses, to external laws which are not an expression of
one's own fundamental nature. The result is the cold feel of
Paradise before the Fall and a self-contained hardness in the egos
of its two inhabitants. This related to a fundamental trait of
Puritanism isolated by Schücking:

Although . . . continual self-examination was fundamentally nothing than
a more intensive form of mediaeval Catholic practice, it nevertheless differed most strikingly from the full loss of self in the religious life and from
true contemplation. Religion for the Puritan was not really surrender at all;
meditation and recollection were ultimately only valued in so far as they
contributed to practical achievements; his mind was wholly fixed on action.
   [*SPF*, p. 14]

Schücking's observation is very perceptive. It is noticeable that
Milton not only imports work into the Garden of Eden before the
Fall, but makes it typically the 'delightful task' of constantly
cutting back a natural growth 'Tending to wilde'. The plants also
must be subjected to a negative and rational discipline.
   The discipline and action beloved of Puritanism, even if regarded
cynically as repression and go-getting (a view taken by Blake and

sympathetic to modern Marxists), have, undeniably, some practical value. They place, however, a terrible strain on human nature, a strain that has taken its toll in our country down to the present day. Puritanism is, however, only one wing of Protestantism, and the Protestant ideal of marriage did find gentler expression than in Milton's Garden of Eden. Moreover, Milton's insistence on the dignity of marriage and his advocacy of divorce for incompatibility, though intended within the context of a life of Puritan godliness, had a wider and beneficial influence. Together with the bids for feminine freedom and the loosening of social convention during the Civil War, they contributed to developments in the comedy of the Restoration period which have often been misunderstood and often misjudged.

# 14 'Imparadist in One Anothers Arms' or 'The Ecclesiastical Mouse-trap': marriage in Restoration comedy

*Rains.*  Marriage is the worst of Prisons.

*Bevil.*  But by your leave, *Rains*, though Marriage be a Prison, yet you may make the Rules as large as those of the *King's-Bench*, that extend to the *East Indies*.

*Rains.*  O hang it. No more of that Ecclesiastical Mouse-Trap.

*Woodly.*  Prethee, speak more reverently of the happiest Condition of Life.

*Rains.*  A married man is not to be believ'd. You are like the Fox in the Fable that had lost his Tail, and would have persuaded all others to lose theirs.

[Thomas Shadwell, *Epsom-Wells*, 1 (*SWS*, II, p. 117)]

Restoration comedy starts in essentials with Shakespeare, for he initiated the intelligent and down-to-earth discussion of sexual relationships on the English stage, and his women often played an active and educative part in these relationships. There are also, of course, very obvious differences; Shakespeare wrote for the public theatres of Elizabethan and early Jacobean London, and English society in his day was very different from Restoration society. He lacked the elegance of Restoration playwrights at their best, a consequence of the age in which he lived, for the formality of the Elizabethans had the stiffness of a starched ruff. Also, unlike his successors, he is disinclined to question the institutions of society, including matrimony. His successors had behind them the experience of the Civil War and looked back at the Elizabethans rather as we look at the Victorians, for they had been forced to develop a sophisticated intellectual awareness that institutions change and evolve.

Despite these differences, however, there is an underlying link between the two. Whereas Shakespeare ended some of his triter comedies with a symbolic marriage as a solution to all problems, he could equally bring prodigious psychological insight to bear on the relationship between the sexes in marriage. *As You Like It*, for example, ends with a whole range of different marriages differently arrived at, and the main marriage has had to be worked for through an education in love. The centre of the play turns on the relationship between the inner person and the outer personality (the latter changing according to company and circumstances, time and place) and the bearing this relationship has on the experience of love. The playing of the role of lover may lead to enduring fulfilment or to self-entrapment, the role becoming a prison house. Rosalind plays – plays at Ganymede playing at Rosalind – and her detachment gives her flexibility and truth. Orlando's sensing of the real Rosalind behind the double mask is an education in life. All the characters, moreover, are actors on a stage which Jacques likens to the world, and Jacques himself gives expression to the gamut of the world's experience of love by detailing the seamier aspects that Rosalind must subsume to be successful. Jacques has not only been a libertine but, to judge from the words of the Duke in Act II, scene vii, lines 65–70, he has turned moralist in consequence of the pox and has retreated from the world in disgust – a kind of wisdom, but dearly bought. The Forest of Arden, the masque of Hymen, the pervading sense of the world as a theatre are successful make-believe and enable *As You Like It* to express lightly and playfully a concern, ultimately metaphysical, with the fundamental nature of human life, but this is achieved at the cost of a sense of immediate social reality. Dinner walks on four legs in the Forest of Arden, and the characters either have money or get along well enough without it; the hardness of their lot is more talked about than felt. The social possibility of forty years of wedlock on a restricted income is not one of Shakespeare's concerns. Restoration comedy, in contrast, lacks the metaphysical overtones of *As You Like It*, but is far more incisive in its treatment of immediate social realities and more willing to survey the practical alternatives to holy matrimony. It is in the context of the everyday world that it develops the kind of interest in love found in *As You Like It*. In some ways it is more limited, but within the limitations of its surface realism Restoration comedy is more open-minded and funnier.

The presence of the love interest in *As You Like It* suggests that the idea at least of marriage as based on love was widely popular by the end of the sixteenth century. *As You Like It* would hardly have succeeded in the public theatre if this had not been so. Peter Laslett has pointed out that Elizabethan plays are not always realistic, and that, for instance, Juliet marries very early by Elizabethan standards, at least for England.[1] An adjustment in the age of characters for dramatic purposes is one thing, however, and the adoption of an emotional climate foreign to an audience quite another. The art of the theatre is an art of communication, and while an audience's normal emotional reactions may be extended, they cannot be ignored. *As You Like It* does not seem to strive to create an interest in romantic love, but rather takes it for granted and builds upon it. If this is so, then some of the gloomier interpretations of Lawrence Stone and Edward Shorter (discussed in Chapter 12) would seem to need modification. However, the Elizabethan vogue for romantic comedy was a fashion confined to the public theatres; it did not extend to the more intellectually self-conscious private houses or private theatres that gradually began to dominate in the Jacobean period, and it only affected the Restoration stage as a contributory influence to Restoration comedy (unlike the scenes involving Falstaff, Shakespeare's romantic comedies were not revived later in the century).[2] The audiences at the private houses, for which Jonson and Chapman wrote, were too aware of social subterfuge to accept a delicate intimacy of feeling without taking full account of the social context in which it must find expression. During the first decade of the century that audience was also more interested in the corruption behind the social façades, and it found difficulty in identifying itself with the standards of any social group. According to Alfred Harbage, it was an audience composed largely of social in-betweens, who longed for entrance to the fashionable world of the court and scorned commercial London, from which many of them sprang. It was an audience of precarious elegance and avant-garde intellectual tastes, fascinated by a high society from which it was excluded.[3]

The social wariness and intellectual self-consciousness attributed to this Jacobean audience were shared by later Restoration audiences, though in other ways the two differed. The tone of Restoration plays suggests social assurance, not social misgivings, on the part of the audiences, and the slight evidence available indicates that audiences were, in fact, drawn not only from the court and the penumbra of fashionable life, but also from among professional men, administrators and the leaders in the intellectual life of the nation.[4] But, like their Jacobean predecessors, they were aware of the hollowness of the social façade. Unlike Shakespeare's plays, the comedies of the Restoration do not take the institution of matrimony for granted. Instead they tend to convey a sense that it is an impediment with possibilities. There is no real equivalent to

Rosalind on the Restoration stage, but Hippolita in Wycherley's *Gentleman-Dancing-Master* has some similarities. She escapes an arranged marriage to a fool by arousing the interest of an intelligent man with the promise of her person and £1200 per annum, and then withdraws the promise of the money to see whether the stranger loves only that. Rosalind worked in a social world capable of harbouring corruption, but not itself fundamentally corrupt: Hippolita's physical base, the headquarters of her campaign, is her father's house, in which she is a prisoner, and it represents a whole social order that is pursuing values which make her personal fulfilment an irrelevance. Hippolita must outwit not only her father, but also the society in which she lives.

The beginning of the evolution from the world of Rosalind to that of Hippolita starts early in the century. It can already be seen in *The Knight of the Burning Pestle*, produced for the private theatres, probably in 1607. Here the citizen and his wife pretend to support romantic love; in fact, they and their champion Ralph support the paternal power and financial interest of Venturewell against the love of Jasper and Luce, while the pocky incidents and references in the play, and the innuendoes that the citizen's wife may know Ralph a little too intimately, further undermine their standing. Opposed to the sordid calculation and self-reliance of the citizenry, its Puritan ethos and sexual hypocrisy, stands the genuine love and the prodigality of Jasper, which is both generous and genteel. Jasper's attitude has behind it a Renaissance tradition of lavishness that gained respectability from Aristotle's *Nichomachean Ethics*, where it is pointed out that a noble soul will err towards prodigality not frugality. It also demonstrates reliance on divine Providence as opposed to calculating self-sufficiency (the attitude came to be embodied in the Cavalier emblem of the grasshopper, in contrast to the Puritan ant, in some later poetry;[5] its less noble side can be seen in, for instance, the savage treatment of tradesman creditors in Killigrew's *The Parson's Wedding*, Act III, scene v). Love is thus beginning to be seen as opposed to financial interest, opposed to society and opposed to a conventional morality that is full of hypocrisy.

These foreshadowings in *The Knight of the Burning Pestle* are, of course, still slight. The play is a burlesque; its world is as make-believe as the Forest of Arden, and we have yet to see love defined in the real world of taverns and brothels and fashionable houses, where a man and a woman need to eat as well as feel fine things.

The shift is one of sentiment only, in a play designed for a coterie theatre. Nevertheless, it is a portent of things to come. The traditional, settled country world, which survived into the Restoration among the small gentleman farmers of Kent, may have had some similarity in feeling to the world of Shakespeare's romantic comedies; when it came to marriage probably some attention at least was usually paid to a girl's wishes, and most of the suitors would have been local men who were known to her. Also, horizons were small and choice was limited. But this world was coming increasingly under threat from accumulated financial power, from inflation, from the pressures of centralized government, from war, from new ideas. Moreover, the narrow horizons, especially of country gentlewomen, were widened by the development during the century of a national life of fashion, first in London, then further afield in modish spas and watering-places.

The development of 'the Town' started early in the century as country gentlemen began to use their coaches to take their women folk to London. James I was already declaiming against

those swarms of gentry who, through the instigation of their wives and to new model and fashion their daughters (who, if they were unmarried marred their reputations, and if married lost them), neglect their country hospitality and are a burden to the city and a general nuisance to the kingdom.[6]

It was for political reasons that the crown disliked the development of the town as a social centre in addition to the court and the country houses, for it provided a central meeting place for opposition leaders. Charles I tried to prevent its establishment, just as Charles II tried by edict to close its coffee houses, and with as little success. The women saw it differently, and their attitudes are reflected in the plays of the period. The advantage of the town for them is summarized in the exchange that opens Shirley's *The Lady of Pleasure*:

*Steward.* Be patient, madam; you may have your pleasure.
*Aretina.* 'Tis that I came to town for.

In the town they were at last, relatively speaking, free. They escaped from local communities where everybody knew everybody else and where their every move could be reported back to the patriarchal head of the household, and they escaped into the anonymous throng of a stupendous city whose population rose from about 200,000 in 1600 to well over 500,000 by 1700. At first they were chaperoned by their parents on short visits, but by Etherege's time a regular season had developed:

*Sentry.*   My Lady's so glad she's come to enjoy the freedom of this place
         again. . . . Our Lodgings are in *James-street* at the Black-Posts,
         where we lay the last Summer.
     [*She Would if She Could*, I, i, ll. 47 – 57 (*BSDWE*, II, p. 92)]

Modern critics have cultivated the idea of the countryside as a place inherently virtuous. In the seventeenth century an estate with its farms and timber was a basis of wealth, but the women in particular, and especially the young women, knew only too well the utter tedium of the endlessly repeated routine of a working country household. Outside contacts and social occasions were few, and while the men might drink immoderately, harass foxes or retire to higher pursuits in their libraries, the diversions of the women were too often confined to backgammon, gossip and country walks. Bellinda's Welsh gentlewomen might 'complain of the stinks of the Town,' with its open sewers and the decaying ordure in the side streets, with its mazed courtyards and their narrow tunnel entrances, but the new and fashionable areas spreading westwards after the Great Fire and centring on the Italian-style 'Piazza' of Covent Garden were more open. Commodiously lodged in these, visiting ladies could enjoy not only the public pleasure of the theatres, the Spring Gardens and other places of public resort, where wine and refreshments could be taken out of doors, but also the more select dances and gatherings of the fashionable drawing-rooms. They could also enjoy the blessed anonymity of a vizard mask, which enabled them to accost strange men with an unaccustomed boldness (for this very reason the vizard later became one of the signs of a professional prostitute, and ceased to be so frequently worn by fashionable ladies, though the latter did not deny themselves the pleasure of a masquerade, a fancy-dress dancing party of masked participants).

In these circumstances it became proverbially difficult to control daughters and wives once they had reached the town. This idea echoes through *The Country Wife*, from Pinchwife's remarks on Margery: 'So! the obstinacy already of a Town-wife, and I must, while she's here, humour her like one' [III, *WPW*, p. 293] to Alithea's account of the ill-treatment commonly meted out by a jealous husband to his wife, who may suffer 'the loss of this Town, that is, she is sent into the Country, which is the last ill usage of a

Husband to a Wife, I think'[V, *WPW*, p. 313].

The town offered freedom, especially to women, and freedom is a very desirable thing, more desirable than security (the ultimate in security is a padded cell); but it inevitably brings with it responsibility and risk. The most obvious risk, where a woman was concerned, was pregnancy, given the lack of generally available and reliable means of contraception, and it was particularly a risk for unmarried gentlewomen. Among the gentry the respectable reason for marriage was still financial, the forwarding of family interest, and thus it could be used as a face-saver even by so 'modern' a rake as Dorimant:

> The Wise will find a difference in our Fate,
> You wed a Woman, I a good Estate.
> [*The Man of Mode*, IV, ii, ll. 192 – 3 (*BSDWE*, II, p. 263)]

(Despite her jealousy, Loveit too seems to accept this as a valid excuse for Dorimant's marriage at the end of *The Man of Mode*.) Since the inheritance of property was bound up with a future wife's chastity, an unmarried mother would be ostracized and would find difficulty in marrying into her own class. A gentlewoman who wished to retain maximum freedom therefore took care to remain a virgin until marriage; as Aphra Behn's Hellena says to an amorous Willmore in *The Rover*, 'And . . . what shall I get? A Cradle full of Noise and Mischief, with a Pack of Repentance at my Back?' [V, i, ll. 453 – 4]. There is, therefore, a practical basis for the traditional sexual morality of the typical Restoration heroine, that of Harriet and Millamant, Gatty, Ariana and their like. Their chastity, however, was in the last resort a matter of their own choice; Willmore expresses a Restoration opinion when he says: 'Faith, Sir, I am of a Nation, that are of opinion a Woman's Honour is not worth guarding when she has a mind to part with it' [V, i, ll. 533 – 5].

This recognition of the choice of the individual, however partial, was a move towards the modern world. However, those unmarried women who chose promiscuity or unchastity found it difficult to do so openly. This is reflected in the drama. Thus in *The Man of Mode* Loveit's reputation is unsavoury (she is known about the Town as '*Dorimant's* convenient'), and the more discreet Bellinda also finds herself involved in a network of dangerous subterfuge. Hence Loveit's unintentionally ironic advice to her unknown rival Bellinda, recommending conventional morality for the unconventional reason that it pays: 'Take example from my misfortunes, *Bellinda*; if thou would'st be happy, give thy self wholly up to goodness' [V, ii, ll. 385 – 7 (*BSDWE*, II, p. 286)]. Once pregnant, the best a woman could hope for was a hasty marriage, probably with a fortune-hunter, the fate of Mrs Fainall in *The Way of the World*. The constraints upon women of the propertied classes did not apply equally to men or to women lower in the social order. Since men could produce bastards without endangering the inheritance of property, and since it was difficult to prove paternity, society was more tolerant of sexual activity among the young males of the town (the country was a slightly different matter, since in its more stable society younger women were likely to be the financial and social responsibility of some local gentleman; Sir Oliver Cockwood laments that in the country he can drink but not fornicate). Nevertheless, a young man might well be (or feel) obliged to marry a gentlewoman whom he had made pregnant if she could not be settled in some other way (Mirabell in *The Way of the World* seems to have married Mrs Fainall off to Fainall). It was therefore wiser for a man to choose the wife of one of his friends or acquaintances if he was to have a gentle mistress (thus Congreve himself is presumed to have fathered one of the children of the Duchess of Marlborough). A woman of lower status, on the other hand, was vulnerable less to loss of caste than to the financial charges of later pregnancy and the earlier period of child-rearing. A 'man of honour' with a regular kept mistress who was faithful to him was expected to take responsibility for these charges if he could; Valentine in *Love for Love* has a bastard out with a wet-nurse, the normal practice also in rearing the legitimate children of the gentry, and in *The Squire of Alsatia* Belfond Junior's bastard by Mrs Termagant (Mrs stood for Mistress and did not necessarily imply a married woman) is to be reared as a gentlewoman. Such bastards might see little of their parents, but the same was usually true of the legitimate children at the time. In *Love in a Tub* Sir Frederick, who is about to marry the Widow Rich, takes the trouble to marry off his old kept mistress, possibly pregnant, to Sir Nicholas Cully, while Grace, whose favours he has also enjoyed, and her maid Jenny are also provided with husbands. The mere town whore was left to shift for herself, with results described in the opening passage of Shadwell's *Epsom-Wells*:

*Cuff.* How the white Aprons scuttle, and leap, and dance yonder; some of 'em are dancing the Hey.

*Kick.* Many a *London* Strumpet comes to Jump and wash down her unlawful Issue, to prevent shame; but more especially charges.
[I, i, (*SWS*, II, p. 107)]

A poor woman would obviously face terrible difficulty in trying to earn a living for herself and her bastard, and a parish would often go to great lengths to be relieved of the responsibility of rearing a child on the poor rates. Abortion was one of the ways out.

There was one other way in which a man was expected to take responsibility for a woman (other than a whore) who had been his sexual partner, and that was through the code of duelling. It became a young man's duty to protect his mistress's reputation, if necessary at the cost of his own or somebody else's life. He might even, like Horner at the end of *The Country Wife*, have to face the prospect of fighting a close friend and defaming an innocent woman for the sake of his own mistress. (*The Country Wife* is a comedy, and Horner is saved from his unpleasant duty, in fact, by the blundering emergence of Margery Pinchwife from her hiding place.) The underlying principle in operation here is one equally applicable to our own or any other society – the principle that what everybody ignores may be said not to exist. The lover or husband prepared to fight would not be exposed to public scorn or insult, and similarly the woman would be free of it, except possibly from other women. The duty, however, fell heavily, and was recognized to fall heavily, on a cuckolded husband. Sir Oliver in *She Would if She Could* is alarmed at the prospect, and the generally unsympathetic Sir John Brute in Vanbrugh's *The Provok'd Wife* has some quite moving passages on the subject:

He comes to my house; eats my meat; lies with my wife; dishonors my family; gets a bastard to inherit my estate; and when I ask a civil account of all this – sir, says he, I wear a sword.
[V, ii, ll. 92 – 5]

The men who fought, if they survived, could hold their heads high in society. Duelling was technically illegal, but to refuse to fight, or to invoke the law and call in a file of musketeers to prevent the duel, was considered gross cowardice and might expose one to public insult and bullying. While there was some sympathy for a man in Sir John's plight, the general opinion seems to have been that of Constant in the same play:

A man of real worth scarce ever is a cuckold, but by his own fault. Women are not naturally lewd; there must be something to urge 'em to it. They'll cuckold a churl out of revenge; a fool, because they despise him; a beast, because they loathe him. But when they make bold with a man they once had a well-grounded value for, 'tis because they first see themselves neglected by him.

[V, iv, ll. 40 – 7]

While the playwrights are not always so generous in their appreciation of female constancy (this play is very late in the genre of Restoration comedy), similar sentiments occur frequently, and it was also open to a husband to resort to religious exhortation or a family exodus to the dreaded country.

The situation we have in Restoration comedy is therefore one in which the institutions and individuals of a society are at odds. Neither religion nor the law sanctioned duelling or adultery, but both existed because an influential mass of people wanted them. The problem was particularly acute in the higher echelons of society, because the lower strata, at least in the metropolis and the larger centres of population, were more anonymous. In the higher orders marriage was final; in the lower orders a man could abandon a wife he did not like, remove elsewhere and marry again bigamously without much fear of detection, or he might join one of the sects with freer ideas about marriage, or not bother to marry at all. Among the gentlemen of the town, therefore, there grew up an unofficial set of institutions or code of conduct which mediated between the official religion and law and the needs of the individual. The situation was paralleled in the high society of other Western European states and existed until recently (in nineteenth-century Vienna, for instance, there was an elaborate code governing the invitation of husbands and mistresses, wives and lovers to grand receptions). In England a more 'moral' tone was enforced early in the eighteenth century and rose to a deafening crescendo in Victorian society, accompanied by a rise in the illegitimacy rate and an increase in hypocrisy and prostitution (the present generation seems to be experimenting in the opposite direction by abandoning traditional morals in favour of a cheerful promiscuity, but the 'pill' probably has much to do with this). Briefly, in the post-Restoration period England was relatively free from hypocrisy, and it is this that makes the literature from Etherege to Swift so interesting; there is less moral cant and more observation of truth.

The present freedom of women, again relative, owes much to the disruption of traditional society by two world wars: the Civil War of the seventeenth century had a similar though smaller effect; it took a while before the official controls could be screwed down again, and they were never quite what they had been. The younger generation of the Restoration found themselves in a world where the pretences of their elders had been revealed as false. There was no restitution of property to the families of the more idealistic old Cavaliers who had sacrificed their all for their king. The old Cromwellians who had made good in the Commonwealth suddenly appeared as monarchists. The sects were rabidly religious and their creeds tended to be intellectually narrow and unsuited to life in society. Roman Catholicism was a banned political force and the Church of England a net of preferment largely controlled by the gentry for its own social ends. The king was an absolutist pretending to be a constitutional monarch and in league with the country's greatest enemy, while the law was not only obscure and expensive, as it still is, but was being used as a political weapon by king and Parliament. The younger generation was acutely conscious of the gap between the pretences of the social institutions and the reality, and one of the gaps was between the pretences of marriage and the facts. While they did not have the power to change institutions, they did have sufficient freedom to live, at least in part, in defiance of them. In the comedies of the Restoration the most interesting policy of calculated defiance is that pursued by the heroines, who are women of integrity and intelligence, though not always over-abundantly endowed with compassion, and who share with the intelligent younger men an awareness of the great generation gap that separates them from their elders, the upholders of the discredited pretences of the traditional social order.

The unenlightened and enlightened traditional approaches to marriage are expressed in the argument between the brothers Sir William and Sir Edward Belfond about the match arranged for Belfond Senior and Scrapeall's niece in Act IV of the *The Squire of Alsatia*:

*Scrapeall.*   Look you Sir *William*, I am glad you like my Neece: and I hope also that she may look lovely in your Sons Eyes. . . .

*Sir William.*   He like her! What's matter whether he like her, or no? Is it not enough for him, that I do? Is a Son, a Boy, a Jackanapes, to have a will of his own? . . .

[Scrapeall exits]

*Sir Edward.*   The person of this Girl is well chosen for your Son, if she were not so precise and pure.

*Sir William.*   Prethee, what matter what she is, has she not Fifteen
         Thousand Pounds clear?
*Sir Edward.*   For a husband to differ in Religion from a Wife.
*Sir William.*   What, with Fifteen Thousand Pound?
*Sir Edward.*   A precise Wife will think herself so pure, she will be apt
         to contemn her Husband.
*Sir William.*   Ay, but Fifteen Thousand Pound, brother.
         [IV, i (*SWS*, IV, pp. 253 – 4)]

Sir Edward is following the moderate Puritan divines in paying
attention to religious compatibility (the extreme of Puritan money-
grubbing and hypocrisy is satirized in Scrapeall, whose standards
are in practice close to Sir William's and are being rejected by Sir
Edward); Sir William is expressing the traditional property interest
(the clash recurs in Fielding's Allworthy and Squire Western).
Neither seeks the opinion of the woman, though Sir Edward shows
himself in the course of the play happy enough to accede to the
matrimonial wishes of the other son, Belfond Junior, who is his
ward. Shadwell favours a rather flat, Jonsonian type of caricature
and his Sir William is unusually blunt and direct, unself-
consciously aware of his own standards. Etherege's Old Bellair and
Lady Woodvill, both of whom are in a complete muddle and quite
unable to distinguish truth from moral fiction, are probably nearer
the common reality in the everyday life of the time. Old Bellair,
posting to town to marry off his son to a convenient fortune, is
himself caught with an old man's longing for Emilia, the very girl
his son has picked on as wife, and is willing to disinherit his son for
doing what he tries to do himself; his attempt to marry Emilia is
indeed foiled because she is already his daughter-in-law. Lady
Woodvill, endlessly praising the good manners of a bygone age,
sees the external ceremony of the past as truth: 'Well! this is not the
Womens Age, let 'em think what they will: Lewdness is the business
now, Love was the bus'ness in my Time' [IV, i, ll. 16 – 18
(*BSDWE*, II, p. 245)]. She is herself busy making an arranged
marriage for her daughter against the girl's wishes, and she
immediately succumbs to the judicious flatteries of the dreaded
Dorimant, disguised as 'Mr Courtage'. The world here is very
much that of *The Man of Mode* as a whole, where nothing is what
it seems, and the characters divide between the men and women of
sense, who discern the falseness of social appearances, including
the conventional version of matrimony, and the rest of the world,
including almost all the older generation, who do not. Thus there is

a generation gap in both plays, but Shadwell's presentation of it is much tamer.

The discernment and use of the difference between social appearances and truth, the distinguishing characteristic of Dorimant and Harriet and the intelligent younger generation in *The Man of Mode*, is essential to the treatment of marriage in the play. The treatment of the social role, including the social role in marriage, is partially analogous to the treatment of role-playing in *As You Like It*, more superficially accurate but more limited. It begins with the symbolic extension to the main physical action of Act I, the dressing of Dorimant:

*Dorimant.*  Leave your unnecessary fidling: a Wasp that's buzzing about a Man's Nose at Dinner, is not more troublesome than thou art. [To Handy, *who is fidling about him.*

*Handy.*  You love to have your Cloaths hang just, Sir.

*Dorimant.*  I love to be well dress'd, Sir: and think it no scandal to my understanding.

  [I, i, ll. 346 – 51 (*BSDWE*, II, p. 199)]

This is deliberately paralleled at the opening of Act III, when Harriet is similarly plagued by the attention to her dress by her woman Busy, and the use of clothing by Dorimant and Harriet to express intelligence is contrasted to the treatment of good clothes as an end in themselves by Sir Fopling, who exists to hold up a perruque or display a cravat. Their attitude to clothes, the material outward symbol of their social roles, is precisely the same as their attitude to their roles as a whole, Sir Fopling being utterly absorbed by his social appearance, Harriet being the most detached, and Dorimant using his status and role, but also depending very much upon it. The theme is extended in Act I into the underlying significance of superficial actions when Foggy Nan enters with her fruit basket. Ostensibly, she comes to sell fruit, but in fact she is going through what is clearly a regular morning ritual (a gentleman's morning starting at eleven or twelve o'clock) of passing on the latest gossip about the town and information about any newly arrived young ladies to Dorimant, and it is really for her news that she is paid. What ensues is a battle of wits, a bargaining session such as you might encounter in an Arab *suq*. The session is enjoyed for its own sake, and the aim of each participant is to hold off for as long as possible and bargain as skilfully as possible, the seller enhancing the value of the wares (the news) by withholding them, the buyer pretending contempt and rejection. The opening gambit is a blunt attack skilfully diverted:

*Dorimant.*    How now, double Tripe, what news do you bring?
*Orange Woman.*   News! Here's the best Fruit has come to Town t'year, Gad I was up before Four a Clock this Morning, and bought all the Choice i' the Market.
*Dorimant.*    The nasty refuse of your Shop.
    [I, i, ll. 28 – 32 (*BSDWE*, II, p. 190)]

The two understand one another very well. The insult is to dislodge Foggy Nan from her guard, and it is followed by a crude, direct question; Foggy Nan observes the basic rule in this kind of contest by retaining her poise, and she answers the question by setting down the basket of fruit. The fruit basket then becomes a diversion from, and symbol for, news of the young ladies who are the centre of Dorimant's interest (this parallels the double use of clothes as a diversion from, or expression of, cultivated intellect). Dorimant and Foggy Nan both have a self-esteem based upon the security of their respective niches in society: his good-humoured contempt for an orange-woman is countered by her good-humoured contempt for gentlemen, expressed in such lines as 'Lord, what a filthy trick these men have got of kissing one another!' [*she spits*] [I, i, ll. 69 – 70 (*BSDWE*, II, p. 191)] (spitting was an accepted sign of contempt, used by ladies also; Olivia spits in contempt in Act II, scene i, of *The Plain Dealer*) and her superb comment on the drunken shoemaker: 'That foul-mouth'd Rogue; what you Gentlemen say it matters not much, but such a dirty Fellow does one more disgrace' [I, i, ll. 164 – 7 (*BSDWE*, II, p. 194)]. On the only occasion when Foggy Nan flags under the combined onslaught of Dorimant and Medley, Dorimant urges her on to keep the conflict going: 'To him, give him as good as he brings' [I, i, l. 84 (*BSDWE*, II, p. 192)].

Here is a situation typical of *The Man of Mode*, apparent surface enmity expressing real human understanding and contact, just as friendship (that of Bellinda and Loveit, for instance) often cloaks enmity, and the ritual admiration offered to Sir Fopling manifests the contempt the others feel for him. In this kind of world, which is not so far from our own, skill is needed in the manipulation of surface appearance, and the unskilful are hurt. The first prerequisite of skill is the separation of oneself from the role one is playing in order that it may be controlled (there is a partial parallel here with Rosalind, who is playing herself). The most disastrous mistake to make is that of Loveit, who is simply swallowed up by her passion for Dorimant and makes herself a laughing-stock. Intolerably possessive, she is nevertheless simply used by Dorimant; the tavern haunters of the Town know her as '*Dorimant's* convenient'; Bellinda betrays her; Harriet jeers at her; and Lady Townley expresses misgivings in case Bellinda is spoilt, made socially unacceptable, by associating with her. Loveit is, of course, sincere, but sincerity is not enough. Her conduct, through the public flaunting of her passion, even places her, unlike Bellinda, beyond the protection of the 'code of honour' (Dorimant takes good care that news of Bellinda's affair with him is not leaked to Young Bellair in Act I and to Loveit at the end of the play; Loveit herself has made her own affair the talk of the town). The only time she has success is when she briefly gains sufficient control to pretend to be attracted by Sir Fopling, thus temporarily rousing Dorimant's jealousy and endangering his standing in the town. Young Bellair, 'by much the most tolerable of all the young men that do not abound in wit', is nevertheless not entirely without it; he stands on the edge of the men of sense, unaware of Dorimant's designs on Emilia or of how attractive Emilia finds Dorimant, inclined to sink inertly into the fopperies of romantic love but able, when pushed, to play the game of subterfuge needed to outwit his father. Supreme in mastery of the social role and in shrewd human insight is Harriet, who knows exactly what she wants and intends to get it. Dorimant wants her as a mistress, but is dangerously attracted by her intelligence or 'wit'; he attempts not to show his love because to do so would mean capitulating to her terms and entering the ecclesiastical mousetrap. She is the stronger of the two and immediately sees his weak point, vanity, and plays on it (his vanity, in fact, begins to be undermined from the moment he first hears of her – 'Fool'd did she say?'). Her luring of him as her suitor to the boredom of the countryside at the end of the play is not, as has been suggested, an exodus to the land of virtue; the point of it is that it will expose him to ridicule. As Harriet says to him on an earlier occasion: 'When your Love's grown strong enough to make you bear being laugh'd at, I'll give you leave to trouble me with it' [IV, i, ll. 181 – 3 (*BSDWE*, II, pp. 249 – 50)]. It follows her consistent and very successful policy of meeting his advances with a storm of mockery. She is no Loveit, nor even Bellinda; she knows her worth, and so does Dorimant.

The ending of *The Man of Mode* is known for its openness; happy marriage in this deceptive world is no foregone conclusion. Shortly before his final protestations Dorimant leaves for his bed and Bellinda in it – but then it is common enough for a man to love one woman and desire another, and while regard for Harriet's feelings might eventually lead Dorimant to refrain from acting in this way, his attachment to her wit has yet to carry him that far. There is a general feeling in the play that sexual love and vows of constancy are unreliable. Emilia and Young Bellair put the two sides of the matter clearly enough:

*Emilia.*          The knowledge I have of my Rival, gives me a little cause
                 to fear your Constancy.
*Young Bellair.* My Constancy! I vow –
*Emilia.*          Do not vow – Our love is frail as is our life, and full as
                 little in our power; and are you sure you shall out-live
                 this day?
*Young Bellair.* I am not; but when we are in perfect health, 'twere an
                 idle thing to fright our selves with the thoughts of sudden
                 death.
          [II, i, ll. 27 – 35 (*BSDWE*, II, pp. 205 – 6)]

This is an exchange resonant with ironies, considering Emilia's secrecy about Dorimant's advances to her and Dorimant's plan to encourage her marriage in order to be the better able to seduce her. Dorimant puts the matter more bluntly to Loveit: 'To say truth, in Love there is no security to be given for the future.' In this dangerous world of transient emotions and unreliable appearances Harriet is the new Restoration woman, determined to make a bid for personal happiness, and using her intelligence to make the best of her opportunities. Her first step is to reach the town, which is achieved by a false promise of obedience to her mother's wishes. In fact, she rejects the older, mercenary, arranged marriage, having sufficient money of her own for an agreeable style of life: 'Shall I be paid down by a covetous Parent for a purchase? I need no Land; no, I'le lay myself out all in love. It is decreed – ' [III, i, ll. 73 – 5 (*BSDWE*, II, p. 221)]. The next stages are to attract an intelligent and entertaining man. This Dorimant certainly is, for, as Lady Townley says, 'What he may be for a Lover I know not, but he's a very pleasant acquaintance I am sure' [III, ii, ll. 39 – 40 (*BSDWE*, II, p. 226)]. To turn the pleasant acquaintance into the agreeable lover and satisfactory husband is what Harriet is about in the play. She may succeed, but it is a hazardous undertaking. Nevertheless, her resolution is typical of the Restoration heroine and was most clearly expressed by Aphra Behn's Hellena: 'I don't intend every he that likes me shall have me, but he that I like' [*The Rover*, III, i, ll. 40 – 1].

The taking of Dorimant on trial as a lover is paralleled by a similar procedure in *She Would if She Could*, Shadwell's *Epsom-Wells* and many other plays. The last hurdle was, then, parental agreement. If a woman's fortune was left to her irrespective of her parents' wishes, she might defy them with financial impunity, as Hippolita does in Wycherley's *Gentleman-Dancing-Master*. Harriet's position – that she will not marry against her own wishes, but neither will she marry without her mother's consent – was usually the more reasonable one and gradually became accepted as a kind of norm (Sophia adopts it and thus avoids the disasters of her cousin Mrs Fitzpatrick in Fielding's *Tom Jones*, and it was even recommended as the reasonable position in *The Lady's Companion: Or, an infallible Guide to the Fair Sex. Containing, Rules, Directions, and Observations, for their Conduct and Behaviour through all Ages and Circumstances of life, as* VIRGINS, WIVES, or WIDOWS, surely the last accolade of respectability).

The realistic assessment of marriage found in *The Man of Mode* is typical of the group of plays we now think of as Restoration comedy, primarily the work of Etherege, Wycherley, Congreve and Vanbrugh. In fact, they form only a very small portion even of the comic repertoire of the time, and many of them were written long after the Restoration, but they do constitute a genre and they do have in common an awareness of social role-playing. It is the presence of this awareness that makes *The Man of Mode* superior to Shadwell's *Squire of Alsatia*. *The Squire of Alsatia* is certainly a very good play. It had one of the record Restoration runs of thirteen consecutive days (the repertory system meant that runs were usually much shorter than this), and it made Shadwell a lot of money. The dialogue is lively and often very amusing, and there are some outstandingly good character roles and very funny situations. The play, however, does not linger in the mind because in the last resort it shirks truth. With the exception of the transparent hypocrisy of Scrapeall and Ruth, the Governess, the characters are what they seem – the cheats are cheats, the boobies are boobies and fine gentlemen are finely genteel. The categories of conventional morality are never seriously probed or questioned, even though an enlightened version of them is recommended in the person of Sir Edward, and the psychology of sexual relationships is not really entered into at all. Instead, after four acts of wild oats, Belfond Junior, an amiable but flat character, reforms with resounding pomposity:

A long farewell to all the Vanity and Lewdness of Youth . . . I call Heav'n to witness, I will hereafter be entirely yours. I look on Marriage as the most solemn Vow a Man can make; and 'tis by consequence, the basest Perjury to break it.

[V, *SWS*, IV, p. 279]

If solemn vows were an antidote to human nature, the world would be a different place. Lady Cockwood's similar resolution at the end of *She Would if She Could* is very differently handled:

| | |
|---|---|
| *Sentry.* | What a miraculous come off is this, Madam! |
| *Lady Cockwood.* | It has made me so truly sensible of those dangers to which an aspiring Lady must expose her Honour, that I am resolv'd to give over the great business of this Town, and hereafter modestly confine myself to the humble Affairs of my own Family. |
| *Courtal.* | 'Tis a very pious resolution, Madam, and the better to confirm you in it, pray entertain an able Chaplain. |

[V, i, ll. 597 – 604 (*BSDWE*, II, p. 178)]

The quality of mind that rejects trite resolutions in the plot is also expressed in Etherege's language, which moves much more lightly, being instinct with the liveliness of his perception. The delicacy of his perception is at its finest in *The Man of Mode*, where the shimmering surface both hides and reveals the depths beneath. Delicacy of this kind was completely beyond the range of Shadwell. *The Man of Mode* also has an amiability which is surprising, given the ruthlessness of characters like Dorimant and Harriet. It comes from Etherege's sheer delight in the quirks and contradictions of human nature, his detached appreciation of the wild vitality of Harriet, the elegantly malicious intelligence of Dorimant, the extravagant display of Sir Fopling. A cruder moralist would have rushed in to judge and impose categories, too often the projection of his own ego. Etherege was more selfless; it was but just that 'gentle George' was reckoned a paragon of amiable indolence.

Wycherley, having none of Etherege's amiability, is more sardonic and less detached. He is, however, just as aware of the deceptiveness of social appearances, and his best comedy, *The Country Wife*, more crude but more forceful than *The Man of Mode*, ruthlessly exposes the gap between human nature and the conventions of society and religion. The philosophy of Horner, the most successful character in the play, is explicit in his expostulation, 'A Pox on 'em, and all that force Nature, and wou'd be still what she forbids 'em; Affectation is her greatest Monster' [I, *WPW*, p. 265]. Not forcing nature means not going against the grain of one's own nature, recognizing one's own abilities and limitations and being clear about what one actually wants: But this basic prerequisite for avoiding frustration is not in itself enough. Most human aims can only be achieved in society, with the co-operation of others. This poses the difficulty not only of accommodating the real desires of others, but also of circumventing the hindrances of social pretence. Most people do not know what they want, being misled into pretence by imposed social and religious ideas of what they ought to want; or, if they do know what they want, they may try to achieve their aims by forcing the wills and natures of others into their own mould, thus forcing pretence on others; or they may ignore their own natures by adopting some unsuitable role in order to impress others, thus becoming objects of contempt. Where such falsity has become the norm, truth itself constitutes a threat to society and is socially unacceptable, for it endangers all relationships based on dishonesty.

Horner, therefore, honest about what he wants himself and honest in his recognition that most of those about him do not want what they have got, is forced to adopt disguise. His disguise is, however, different in kind and actually superior in morality to the less deliberate pretences adopted by almost all the other characters, who are usually also less accurate in their assessment of their own desires and abilities. Thus Lady Fidget, that gem of honour, is goatishly lascivious, and her sexual enthusiasm is shared by Mrs Squeamish and Mrs Dainty Fidget. Sparkish is a blockhead masquerading as a wit. Alithea is misled by a false idea of honour and obligation, backed by an equally mistaken estimate of Sparkish's character, into trying to reject what she knows she wants; she stupidly believes that love will flow from the vows of marriage, instead of trying to square matrimony with the love and esteem she has for Harcourt. Sir Jaspar, priding himself on his knowledge of business and the wise management of men and women, and Pinchwife priding himself on his knowledge of the town and its ways, both lead their own wives, step by step, to Horner's bed. In contrast to these stand Horner and the Country Wife herself. Margery Pinchwife knows, or rather discovers, what she wants in Horner (though she is unaware of much that she does not want, her intelligence and experience being too limited for her to grasp his relative complexity). Her naive ignorance of social pretence, however, leads to the débâcle of the final scene, where her truthful outbursts have to be smothered; she cannot simply take Horner as her husband, since according to society and religion she is already married to someone else, and anyway Horner does not want her (or anybody else, for that matter) as a wife. In disregarding the general desire for pretence and Horner's disinclination to marry, she attempts to violate the wills of others, just as Pinchwife violates hers by marrying her young and attempting to hold her to him whether she will or no.

Horner also knows what he wants: an agreeable rotation of females in his bed. He does not, however, attempt to force the wills of others by persuading them to act in ways they find disagreeable (though he has no objection to acting himself in ways they may find disagreeable). His whole disguise as a eunuch is a device to penetrate through the layers of pretence and to distinguish those women who are on the look-out for sexual satisfaction from those who are not. He molests nobody. Moreover, he recognizes that permanence in a relationship depends on the good will of the participants, hence his views on keeping and marriage and the folly of Pinchwife's policy:

*Horner.*     But prethee, was not the way you were in better, is not keeping better than Marriage?

*Pinchwife.*  A Pox on't, the Jades wou'd jilt me, I could never keep a Whore to myself.

*Horner.*     So then you only marry'd to keep a Whore to your self; well, but let me tell you, Women, as you say, are like Souldiers made constant and loyal by good pay, rather than by Oaths and Covenants, therefore I'd advise my Friends to keep rather than marry.

[I (*WPW*, p. 271)]

He is more moral than Pinchwife, since he has a greater respect for the freedom of a woman's will, and he places greater confidence in women, believing that they respond to good treatment. Pinchwife's method is a mixture of force, fraud and bullying. The soundness of Horner's judgement is borne out in the world of the play by the relationship between Harcourt and Alithea. At a loss as to how to win Alithea, Harcourt has to turn to Horner for advice. In consequence, he adopts subterfuge akin to Horner's, disguising himself first as Sparkish's friend, then as a parson, thus gaining an opportunity to woo Alithea and time for her to realize that she wants him and to recognize the folly of her notions of honour. He also has confidence in her in the face of adverse appearances in Act V. Harcourt shares with Horner a low opinion of matrimony as an institution, but he is willing to accept institutionalized matrimony because he wants Alithea as a permanent partner:

Marrying you, is no more sign of his [Sparkish's] love, than bribing your Woman, that he may marry you, is a sign of his generosity: Marriage is rather a sign of interest, than love; and he that marries a fortune, covets a Mistress, not loves her: But if you take Marriage for a sign of love, take it from me immediately.

[II (*WPW*, p. 279)]

The other factor in Alithea's conversion to good sense is, of course, Lucy. She has a sturdy independence of judgement reminiscent of Foggy Nan's, and though she has acquired more of the polish of her mistress's fashionable world, she is as little taken in by its appearance. It is she who launches a diatribe at the beginning of Act IV against honour, 'a disease in the head, like the Megrim, or Falling-sickness, that alwayes hurries People away to do themselves mischief'; she highlights the idiocy of marrying for obligation without affection – 'Can there be a greater cheat, or wrong done to a Man, than to give him your person, without your heart?' – and finally delves down to discover Alithea's fundamental and quite selfish reason for marrying Sparkish – fear of being whisked out of town by a jealous husband. She then supports Harcourt's disguise by the subterfuge of the forged letter from Sparkish, thus clearing the way for the triumph of common sense, just as she rescues Horner at the end of the play, despite the interruption of Margery Pinchwife. This is partly the inherited device of the clever servant, so useful for disentangling plots, but it is also partly an ironic comment on the stupidities of so many of her social superiors. Men and women of sense were a small, discerning group to be found in any stratum of society and marked by their ability to distinguish between the surface of society and the human depth beneath.

The world of *The Country Wife* is thus, like that of *The Man of Mode*, one where nothing is what it seems. Etherege, however, accepts the difference with peaceful good humour, finding it entertaining. Wycherley's humour is much more savage; there is in *The Country Wife* and *The Plain Dealer* a sense of moral outrage at the stupidity that makes the world what it is, and his laughter is like lightning in a black night. Sir Fopling is happy in his folly, and even Bellinda is not too uncomfortable, but the same cannot be said of Wycherley's dupes; Pinchwife and Sir Jaspar have, moreover, a grotesque ugliness and clumsiness, as opposed to the feather elegance of Sir Fopling, and the basic vulgarity of Sparkish protrudes through his surface veneer like an outcrop of rock. Similarly, the arch-realist Horner suffers the ironic fate of almost having to cut Harcourt's throat for the sake of those appearances of honour that he despises, driven to this pass by the stupid honesty of a country simpleton.

Wycherley's harsh but very funny vision co-ordinates all the dramatic elements of *The Country Wife* superbly, so that the play is the most perfectly integrated of all the Restoration comedies. The brilliance of his technical skill is seen in the device of *double entendre*, the sustaining of discrete levels of significance in the dialogue so that various characters and the audience may take it in different senses. This he had begun to develop through long passages in *The Gentleman-Dancing-Master*, but in *The Country Wife* it articulates the core of meaning of the whole play. The climax in its use comes in the china scene (Act IV, scene ii). There is a crescendo from Sir Jaspar's bawling to his wife through the locked bedroom door –

*Sir Jaspar.*   Wife, he is coming into you the back way.
*Lady Fidget.*   Let him come, and welcome, which way he will.
     [IV (*WPW*, p. 327)]

– to her re-emergence, flushed and dishevelled, holding a china rol-wagon:

*Lady Fidget.*   I have been toyling and moyling, for the pretti'st piece of China, my Dear. [to her husband]
*Horner.*   Nay she has been too hard for me do what I cou'd.
*Squeamish.*   Oh Lord I'le have some China too, good Mr. *Horner*, don't think to give other people China, and me none, come in with me too.
*Horner.*   Upon my honour I have none left now.
*Squeamish.*   Nay, nay I have known you deny your China before now, but you shan't put me off so, come –
*Horner.*   This Lady [Lady Fidget] had the last there.
*Lady Fidget.*   Yes indeed Madam, to my certain knowledge he has no more left.
*Squeamish.*   O but it may be he may have some you could not find.
*Lady Fidget.*   What d'y think if he had had any left, I would not have had it too, for we women of quality never think we have China enough.

| Horner. | Do not take it ill, I cannot make China for you all, but I will have a rol-waggon for you too, another time. |
| Squeamish. | Thank you dear Toad. [To Horner *aside*] |
| Lady Fidget. | What do you mean by that promise? |
| Horner. | Alas she has an innocent, literal understanding. |

[*Apart to Lady* Fidget

[IV (*WPW*, p. 329)]

The rol-wagon, a phallus-shaped Chinese vase, is the visual centre
of the scene and, like Foggy Nan's basket of fruit, it has a surface
appropriateness (Chinese porcelain was collected by ladies of
fashion) and a symbolic significance. Around it the characters are
grouped on stage in a hierarchy of knowledge. Horner, who enters
just behind Lady Fidget, knows all; Lady Fidget and Mrs
Squeamish, both having experienced Horner's virility, are mutually
suspicious; further off are Old Lady Squeamish, Squeamish's
grandmother, and Sir Jaspar, Lady Fidget's husband, both of them
taking a piece of china to be merely a piece of china; and behind a
screen at the side of the stage is Quack, viewing the success of
Horner's scheme. The scene is, of course, so exaggerated as to be
almost farcical, though its intent is not. Quack, venting his
awareness of the farcical nature of events in such lines as 'This
indeed, I cou'd not have believ'd from him, nor any but my own
eyes' [IV (*WPW*, p. 327)], paradoxically ensures that the audience
will accept them and he acts as chorus, intermediary between
audience and scene.

The china scene is only one of the very many passages in the play
in which staging and dialogue prize apart the reality and the
enveloping social pretence. Single words like 'honour' acquire two
conflicting senses, as in Lady Fidget's remarks on discovering that
Horner is no eunuch:

But, poor Gentleman, cou'd you be so generous? so truly a Man of
honour, as for the sakes of us Women of honour, to cause your self to be
reported no Man? No Man! and to suffer your self the greatest shame that
cou'd fall upon a Man, that none might fall upon us Women by your
conversation.

[II (*WPW*, p. 289)]

(she had before referred to him as 'Brute! stinking mortify'd rotten
French Weather' — that is, 'wether'). The simultaneous presence of
two senses or more to the dialogue is paralleled by a stylish rep-
etition or juxtaposition in the development of the action: thus the
situation at the openings of Acts II and III is precisely parallel, as

the staging should be, the only change being the one in Margery Pinchwife herself: while Alithea's asides on the folly of Pinchwife's jealousy at the beginning of Act II are followed, after the arrival of Sparkish and Harcourt, by Pinchwife's asides on the folly of Sparkish's lack of jealousy. There is also a formal elegance in the way the dupes undo themselves step by step, and this contrived and formal element culminates in the dance of cuckolds that ends the play and is the final visual symbol of the contrast between the restrained formalities of social life and the realities beneath the surface. A sense of symmetrical form is a major part of the experience of the play and is largely responsible for making it a comedy. It presents a chaos which is at the same time exquisite order. In this way the play is not merely sardonic, but also liberating and refreshing. It has the spaciousness of true art, and the order of the play, greater than the social order that is being satirized, is large enough to accommodate the good sense of Lucy and Harcourt, the education of Alithea, the grossness of Sparkish, the hypocrisy of the fashionable ladies, the naivety of Margery Pinchwife and a Horner who would have understood Blake's line, 'The lust of the goat is the bounty of God.' Its exposure of social sham made it, in the opinion of Dryden, one of the most useful satires of the age. It is also the funniest play in English.

*The Man of Mode* and *The Country Wife* were very close in date (1676 and 1675 respectively), and they were the most acute dramatic expressions of the gap between the forms surrounding the relationship of the sexes and the real needs and desires of the individual. In the decades that followed, and especially after the Glorious Revolution of 1688, England became more sedate. There was a reintegration, particularly of the articulate elements in society, and open scepticism of conventional values began to be ferociously attacked. Collier continued the long-standing battle of the Puritans against the stage, that entrance porch to the abodes of hell, with his scurrilous outburst against playwrights who dared to be secular and pragmatic rather than religious and morally dogmatic, who depicted women who were unchaste and clergymen who were other than angels in black.[7] Meanwhile, just as some degree of compromise was exacted on the matter of the constitution to permit an accommodation of conflicting interests, so the first very small step was taken towards a modification of the institution of matrimony with the introduction of divorce by Act of Parliament in 1697, though the procedure was too long and costly, not to say unpleasant, to be of use to most people. The general shifts in attitude are reflected in later Restoration comedy.

*The Way of the World*, the greatest of all the Restoration comedies, appeared in 1700. Most of the earlier plays had featured bad marriages and hopeful, witty couples intending to do better, and had contrasted ruthless emotional individualism, possibly tempered by intelligent self-interest, with mendacious surface forms. The two levels remain distinct in *The Way of the World*, but with a difference. Neither heroes and heroines nor villains and villainesses are what they seem; all alike break the institutional codes, but this dissimulation is taken for granted as the way of the world. A *modus vivendi* has been arrived at and the institutions are not under serious attack; instead, the centre of interest is the subtle difference between the ways and reasons for breaking the rules in the case of the characters portrayed with approval or disapproval.

The difference slowly established between Fainall and Mirabell is slight but vitally important; they both manipulate others unscrupulously, but Mirabell has respect for the nature and interest of those he is manipulating. Fainall hates his wife, a woman with great good qualities, and is willing to 'rob her of all she's worth' for the sake of Mrs Marwood, of whom he is with reason jealous, and he is happy to defraud Millamant and ruin Lady Wishfort as well. All his relationships involve strain and suffering. Mirabell is no paragon but contrives to remain affectionate towards, and keep the affection and trust of people who might easily have hated him; the contrast between Mirabell and Fainall is deliberately highlighted when the violent quarrel between Fainall and Mrs Marwood in Act II, scene i, is followed immediately by the encounter between Mirabell and Mrs Fainall, who converse with poignant mutual understanding. The test case for the quality of Mirabell's emotional relationships is precisely Mrs Fainall, who, when a widow, had had an affair with Mirabell and been married off to Fainall when she suspected she was pregnant. She still has kindness enough for Mirabell to act as his accomplice in his campaign to win Millamant's hand and dowry. Fainall has been put upon, but Mirabell judges that Fainall wanted only financial support from Mrs Fainall's fortune, and Mirabell is right. Lady Wishfort, who makes herself ridiculous by her refusal to recognize her own situation in life, is exposed by Mirabell to a plot aimed at securing Millamant's dowry, as opposed to Fainall's plot that would have ended with her ruin and her daughter's. Finally, Mirabell has the worldly wisdom to use the institutions of his society well; the deed of trust, drawn up by his foresight, enables him to thwart Fainall, win Millamant and save Lady Wishfort, besides providing some hope of an accommodation between Fainall and his wife. This worldly wisdom and good will make him find a natural ally in Sir Wilfull, who has the same basic good will, and they distinguish him not only from Fainall, but also from Petulant and Witwoud, who produce strain by intruding themselves socially or putting others to the blush.

These distinctions are, however, left for a discerning audience to discover: as Harriett Hawkins points out, most plays give an audience a fuller knowledge of the dramatic situation than the characters themselves could have; *The Way of the World* does not.[8] This is the great excitement of the first act, the start of the long duel between Fainall and Mirabell, which opens with the exchange:

*Fainall.*    I'd no more play with a Man that slighted his ill Fortune, than I'd make love to a Woman who undervalu'd the loss of her Reputation.

*Mirabell.*    You have a Taste extreamly delicate, and are for refining on your Pleasures.

*Fainall.*    Prithee, why so reserv'd?
    [I, i, ll. 7 – 13 (*DCPC*, p. 395)]

Mirabell's reply is, of course, ironic and the note of censure is immediately picked up by Fainall. The audience senses the antagonism beneath the bland surface but does not know the reason for it, though it is already gaining insight into the characters of the two men. In the clash that follows Fainall presses suavely on the sore point of Mirabell's reception by Millamant the preceding evening, and then tries to extricate information concerning Mrs Marwood's suspected liking for Mirabell in order to allay his own jealousy. Mirabell parries with innuendoes concerning Fainall's unkindness to Mrs Fainall and affair with Marwood, and the falseness of Marwood's friendship for Mrs Fainall, while at the same time he pursues his real purpose of preparing for the launching of his servant Waitwell as Sir Roland. Hence his stress on the enmity between himself and Lady Wishfort, for the more firmly this enmity is established in the general opinion of the world, the less his plot will be suspected (his pretended agitation later in the act as Petulant speaks of the harm that may befall his fortunes by Sir Roland's arrival serves the same purpose). The audience has no previous knowledge of this background of intrigue and is left to surmise what it can from the oily surface and savage undercurrents of the dialogue. The clash ends in a discreet explosion as Fainall is forced to retreat: 'Fie, fie Friend, if you grow Censorious I must leave you' [I, i, ll. 99 – 100 (*DCPC*, p. 397)].

In the welter of family relationships and plot and counterplot which succeeds, the audience has the pleasure of picking its way delicately forward, following a clue here and an implication there – very much the way of the world, in fact. The play is an elite play, making no concessions whatever to stupidity or laziness, and an audience must be alert for all the innuendoes and undertones of the language (just as the actors must be alert and intelligent enough to bring them out) – a piece designed to be played by the aristocracy of the theatrical profession to an aristocracy of social intelligence (not rank) in the audience.

In the world of this play, where even the best have considerable limitations and weaknesses, as they do in life, the securing of happiness demands soundness of judgement. Love, if it is to be an enduring affection and not a transient liking, must be able to take in the practicalities of life and must rise above the dichotomy of passion and judgement. Precisely this is achieved in the proviso scene, where the playfulness allows a combination of both elements, and Mirabell and Millamant lightly discuss the practical arrangements which will enable them to reconcile their highly individual personal needs with the requirements of life together. There is great delicacy of feeling as each adjusts to the loss of freedom involved in marriage, and the conversation culminates in the humour of the exchange after Mrs Fainall's entrance:

| | |
|---|---|
| *Millamant.* | *Fainall,* what shall I do? shall I have him? I think I must have him. |
| *Mrs Fainall.* | Ay, ay, take him, take him, what shou'd you do? |
| *Millamant.* | Well then – I'll take my death I'm in a horrid fright – *Fainall,* I shall never say it – well – I think – I'll endure you. |
| *Mrs Fainall.* | Fy, fy, have him, have him, and tell him so in plain terms: For I am sure you have a mind to him. |
| *Millamant.* | Are you? I think I have – and the horrid Man looks as if he thought so too. |

[IV, i, ll. 284 – 94 (*DCPC*, p. 452)]

To Mrs Fainall, once Mirabell has left, her expression is more direct: 'I find I love him violently.'

The emotional delicacy of Congreve's work gives it a softness akin to that of his favourite, Terence. It is at once an aesthetic and a moral quality, as it was with Terence. The language frequently has a light, playful clarity which allows a phrase to be exaggerated yet

just, absurd yet elegant, and to flow with an easy rhythm that is full
of vitality. It can accommodate the grunts of Witwoud, the fluent
patois of Lady Wishfort, the restrained scintillation of Mirabell,
the cascade of light that flows from Millamant. It is this
delicacy and gentleness that makes almost all of Congreve's
characters in some degree sympathetic, and he learned from
Shakespeare the knack of producing an exaggerated caricature of
such vitality that it is humanly convincing. Lady Wishfort, a grossly
exaggerated old lady, nevertheless sums up poignantly a human
predicament that is not limited to her age or her sex, and she retains
a precarious dignity in the midst of the indignities that befall her.
At fortune's nadir she turns to Marwood for solace (it would be
Marwood, who is betraying her):

Well Friend, you are enough to reconcile me to the bad World, or else I
wou'd retire to Desarts and Solitudes; and feed harmless Sheep by *Groves*
and *Purling Streams*. Dear *Marwood*, let us leave the World, and retire by
our selves and be *Shepherdesses*.
        [V, i, ll. 131 – 5 (*DCPC*, p. 465)]

Ridiculous escapism, of course, and the sheep is not the greasy
animal of reality, but who has never harboured a similarly impossible fantasy? Sir Fopling was coldly cherished as an entertainment:
Lady Wishfort is portrayed with compassion.

It is the compassion of Congreve that makes him experience the
gap between social appearance and human reality in a different way
from his predecessors. Wycherley is enraged at the falseness of it
all, of the system foisted on human nature. For Congreve that
system is human nature, its expression and outcome, and cannot so
easily be foisted off.

While the falseness that is in all social systems cannot be abolished, it
may nevertheless be modified, and it was to this possibility that
Vanbrugh, an associate of Congreve and the final writer of the
Restoration school, and to a lesser extent Farquhar, turned their
attention. In *The Beaux' Stratagem* Farquhar makes much of the
miserable marriage between Mrs Sullen and her boorish husband,
but the element of rather over-ripe sentiment in the play becomes
sentimentality in the last act, when the fortune-hunter Aimwell, an
impoverished younger brother, unexpectedly comes into money
and a title and loses his qualms about marrying the heiress with
whom he has fallen in love, while the Sullens' ritual divorce is a
satisfying stage ceremony which ignores the exigencies of the real

world (the legal invalidity of such a divorce, with the consequent inability of the Squire to beget a legal heir, and the facing of Mrs Sullen with the legal choice between adultery and celibacy). Vanbrugh also takes up the unfortunate lot of younger brothers in *The Relapse*, young Tom Fashion plotting against his elder brother Lord Foppington (Colley Cibber's character, Sir Novelty Fashion, raised by Vanbrugh to the peerage). The title of the play refers to the relapse from virtue of Loveless, another character borrowed from Cibber, who had subjected his Loveless to a most improbable and sentimental reform of rakish ways in Act V of *Love's Last Shift*. In *The Relapse* the element of social realism and the reaction against the sentimental moralizings of Cibber are tempered by a delightfully farcical sense of fun.

In *The Provok'd Wife* there is a more serious portrayal of the misery of a marriage entered upon by both partners for the wrong reason, leaving unfaithfulness as a probability, since divorce was so difficult to obtain. The ending of the play is left open by the refusal to pretend that there was any satisfactory resolution, under contemporary law, to the jarring incompatibility of Sir John and Lady Brute. In his unfinished play *A Journey to London* Vanbrugh went further, showing the problems of a husband whose estate is being ruined by a wife addicted to gambling, and the financial and family repercussions of the folly of a country squire, who has embarrassed his estate and, in an ill-judged effort to recoup his losses, comes to London as a Member of Parliament, thus introducing his family to the vices of a sophisticated metropolis. Even the servants are outwitted by the vagabonds of the London streets, and all the incidents, from the wrecking of the coach down to the stealing of the goose pie, are of a type well authenticated in contemporary records. Vanbrugh provides his MP with a merchant uncle, who comments on the nephew's blunderings in the world of politics, and he intended to have had the gambling wife thrown out, presumably on a fixed annuity, before the play ended; but he came too late for this kind of criticism, which reflected badly on the very institutions of society. Morality conquered, and truth had to give way. The play was finished after Vanbrugh's death by Colley Cibber, who provided a sentimental reconciliation, and society was spared any painful self-examination. Vanbrugh's attempt to broaden the scope of the drama thus came to nothing: stimulation to reform was replaced by exhortation to conform, and what life remained in the drama was found mostly in burlesque and political satire.

Woman's bid for freedom, reflected in the strong-minded and financially independent heroines of Restoration comedy, had thus been only partially successful. Neither intellectual nor financial independence had been generally gained. Dorimant, as a young wit, could be dazzled by the intelligence with which Harriet had cast him in the role of Courtage; Horner could say, 'Methinks wit is more necessary than beauty, and I think no young Woman ugly that has it, and no handsome Woman agreable without it'; Restoration comedies as a whole could portray women as intelligent beings; but out in life it was not so straightforward. Prejudice dies hard. Halifax in his *Advice to a Daughter* commented at some length on the natural inferiority of woman's intelligence, and the Earl of Chesterfield, a descendant of his in the next century, was inclined to treat all women as fools. Perhaps many were; they were hardly educated to be anything else. Aphra Behn, the first woman writer to live by her pen (though her contemporaries unkindly imputed profitable sidelines as spy and whore), lamented her lack of a proper Latin education:

Till now, I curst my Birth, my Education,
And more the scanted Customes of the Nation:
Permitting not the Female Sex to tread,
The mighty Paths of Learned Heroes dead.
The God-like Virgil, and great Homers Verse,
Like Divine Mysteries are conceal'd from us.
　We are forbid all grateful Theams,
　No ravishing thoughts approach our Ear,
　The Fulsom Gingle of the times,
Is all we are allow'd to understand or hear.
　['To Mr. Creech on his Translation of Lucretius', ll. 25 – 34]

Yet it was an instance of the brief relative freedom of the late seventeenth century that Aphra Behn was a distinguished poet, novelist and playwright in her own right and under her own name. While the learned professions remained firmly closed to women, the introduction of actresses on the Restoration stage provided one additional outlet for feminine talent. Nevertheless, since the legal status of marriage remained much what it had been, the main gain for women was an increasing recognition of some freedom in their choice of husbands, a softening of the emotional relationships within the family and the development of fashionable life and the season in Bath and London; small gains perhaps, but not unimportant. While the blue-stocking hostesses of early eighteenth-century

London continued a rearguard campaign against masculine prejudice, it seems to have consolidated again in the following century.
It was only with the French Revolution and the Romantic movement that an articulate feminism developed, and it is only in our
century that it has bitten at all deeply into our society. As in
politics, so also in the context of woman's status, it has taken over
three hundred years for the most daring ideas of the seventeenth
century to begin to bear fruit.

# 15 Postscript: The flight of the butterflies

I do not like new notions, they breed caterpillars of the mind.

ANONYMOUS

In the two sections of this book I have dealt with the family-in-large of the state and state-in-little of the family. The family was, and still is, the basic unit of the state, but in the seventeenth century a correspondence between the two levels of organization was quite explicit. Tudor policy, attempting to consolidate royal power at the expense of the powerful kinship networks of the nobility, encouraged the patriarchal nuclear family; Filmer based his theory of the state on the paternalism of kings; Hobbes reduced the subject to a well kept slave and women and children to chattels; Milton consigned authority in family and state to the right reason of regenerate males; Locke asserted the primacy of Natural Law over power, whether royal or parental. Meanwhile, signs were emerging, slight but significant, of feminine rebellion against the male-dominated hierarchy of both family and state: there was unease at spiritual subordination among Puritan wives, a bid by Leveller women to make their political demands heard, defiance of family morality by the Ranters, and a pursuit of social pleasure and personal fulfilment by women in the developing London season. State and family were felt to be closely parallel because the dominant mode of both experience and imagination was still personal; a personal hierarchy ruled in the home and in the country and was generally accepted as ruling the operations of the external world and the affairs of the cosmos.

A human being, however, exists in depth on many different levels, from the external, where personality exists as part of a shifting continuum of interaction with others and is moulded by the group or culture, to a more interior level of individual identification as Mr X or Ms Y, a person having a particular sex and more stable, yet still changing, characteristics of preference and dislike, and beyond this to levels where pure individuation can be experienced free from external identification. Having depths which elude the net of circumstances on the surface of life, no one is ever entirely predictable: conversely, the surface personality exists in the social world, a world which was at this period being subjected to violent and unexpected upheavals.

Awareness of inner and outer flux is awareness of the need for stability; change demands the changeless. At the beginning of the seventeenth century the imagination of Shakespeare took a great leap inwards as he faced characters like Lear with the question 'Who am I?', and during the century the mind of Western European man reached inwards and outwards in search of the permanent basis of things. The outward movement gave rise to science and, until recently, a mechanistic interpretation of physical laws. The inward investigation led to scepticism of traditional standards, and religious and economic circumstances permitted an explosion of individualism. In practical life the result was a shift of emphasis, the individual no longer content to exist in terms of the group, the family or state, but insisting, or attempting to insist, that the group exist to serve the individual. Charles, the embodiment of the hierarchical state, was beheaded in the name of his people, and when opportunity arose sections of the populace claimed some measure of individual freedom; the Parliamentarian soldiery sought it as their 'birthright', and the more independent-minded of the wealthy young ladies of the Restoration also determined to claim as much of it as they could in the circumstances of their world. In religion too the demand grew louder for toleration, for plurality not conformity of worship.

Moves of this kind in the general mind of a nation cannot easily be undone. After the Revolution the panoply of Church and state was restored, but its nature had changed. Milton's Adam in the Garden of Eden questions the justice of the hierarchy in which he finds himself; while he absolves God of all blame, the questioning itself is significant. A distinction between social surface and the true nature of things beneath (corruption for the Jacobeans and hypocrisy to Wycherley) is blandly accepted as inevitable by Congreve and gives a delightful irony to Pope:

On her white Breast a sparkling *Cross* she wore,
Which Jews might kiss, and Infidels adore.
[*Rape of the Lock*, II, ll. 7 – 8]

Does this mean that religious symbols should not be used for sexual enticement? Or is it a recognition that the allure of sex is, in fact, more fundamental than man's intellectual construction of the supposed commands of the Almighty? And if the good advice in Canto V of *The Rape of the Lock* is intended without qualification, why is it given by Clarissa, the woman who handed the Baron the scissors for the severing of the fatal lock? Similarly, it is when Tom Jones is most busy swearing eternal fidelity to Sophia that he is most likely to retreat into a grove with Molly Seagrim. In the high Augustan culture there is always an awareness of the limitations of mental categories. And that culture also embraced strong contrasts. In some ways so rational, it entertained the polite Platonism of the third Earl of Shaftesbury, suitably dressed up for reception in society, and Pope's own circle included men like Dr Cheyne, with his great interest in mysticism.[1] While the moral wing, headed in literature by Addison, was stuffy, theirs was not the only voice to be heard by the intellectual elite. Bernard Mandeville could alarm and amuse by the idea, advanced in *The Fable of the Bees*, that a state was dependent on the individual vices and weaknesses of its citizens (a systematization of the kind of thinking behind Rochester's line, 'All men would be cowards if they durst'); and he even launched a shocking proposal to nationalize the brothels in the interests of health and hygiene.[2] Outside polite society the sects continued a semi-underground existence, and they had an intellectual elite of their own, while the mystical strands of thought were sustained by a national network of Behmenists, men and women who had at least some sympathy with the work of Boehme, or Behmen, as he was more usually called.

In the late Augustan period the façade of society became ever heavier and more pompous; Johnson is full of social deference and moral conservatism. Nevertheless, at the same time Romanticism was coming in. In the work of Blake the seventeenth century lives again, but its experience is transmuted by a century of development in the understanding of the human mind, by an increased social awareness within England and by the political explosiveness of the French Revolution. It is to Milton that Blake turns instinctively, rewriting the earlier poet's thought and work to draw out implications that Milton preferred to leave hidden.

It is no accident that Blake is popular today. We are the grandchildren of the seventeenth century. The revolutionary demands of the Parliamentarian soldiery seem such obvious good sense to us, but it is only in this century that they have been acceded to. Similarly, the seventeenth-century bid for women's freedom seems very mild by today's standards, but had it not been made, our standards would not be what they are. Hence the historical interest of the minor literature of the period: it shows us where we came from. Great literature is another matter, for that always rises beyond the restricted moral, political and social codes of the age that produced it. Nevertheless, even here an understanding of past codes and circumstances has its value, bringing clarity to the muted undertones a modern ear might miss.

# Notes and references

## Introduction

1 Edward Gibbon, *Decline and Fall of the Roman Empire* (1776 – 88) vol. 1, ch. 3.

2 See Norman N. Holland, *The First Modern Comedies: The Significance of Etherege, Wycherley and Congreve* (Harvard University Press 1959) especially chs. 7 and 8; and Paul C. Davies, 'Rochester and Boileau: a reconsideration', *Comparative Literature*, 21 (1969), pp. 348 – 55, and 'Rochester: Augustan and explorer', *Durham University Journal*, no. 30 (1969), pp. 59 – 64. While admitting Rochester to be subversive, Paul Davies nevertheless makes him out to be a traditionalist at heart, and the advocate of good sense, self-awareness, restraint and decorum. His interpretation of 'A Satyr against Reason and Mankind' seems to me particularly perverse. For my own view of Rochester see pp. 146 – 7 above.

3 Leszek Kolakowski, *Main Currents of Marxism: Its Rise, Growth, and Dissolution*, trans. P. S. Falla, vol. 1: *The Founders* (Oxford: Clarendon Press 1978), p. 155.

4 *ibid.*, pp. 311 – 12.

5 *ibid.*, p. 134.

6 Arthur Waley, *The Way and its Power: The Tao Tê Ching and its Place in Chinese Thought* (Mandala Books 1977; originally published 1934), pp. 44 – 5.

7 *ibid.*, pp. 57 – 8. In Plotinus universal mind, or, as MacKenna translated it, the 'Intellectual Principle', is the basis for the individual human mind, which is as it were an individualized ray of the central sun. Universal mind is self-sufficient, being the self-cognition of the One by the One – 'The Intellectual-Principle, its exercise of intellection, and the object of intellection all are identical' – and the individual mind can reassume this condition by reuniting with its own inherent source: see the Third Tractate of the Fifth Ennead, and for the MacKenna quotation see Plotinus, *The Enneads*, trans. Stephen MacKenna, rev. ed. (Faber 1969) pp. 386 – 7. A modern translation by A. H. Armstrong is currently appearing in the Loeb Classical Library.

8    For Wordsworth see Melvin Rader, *Wordsworth: A Philosophical Approach* (Oxford: Clarendon Press 1967). For Plotinus references see preceding note. For a sensible general investigation of this area of experience, see W. T. Stace, *Mysticism and Philosophy* (Macmillan 1961).

9    Kolakowski, *Main Currents of Marxism*, vol. 1, p. 375.

10   See Wolfgang Iser, *The Act of Reading: A Theory of Aesthetic Response* (Routledge and Kegan Paul 1978), and *The Implied Reader: Patterns of Communication in Prose Fiction from Bunyan to Beckett* (Johns Hopkins University Press 1974).

11   See Peter Mathias, *The Transformation of England: Essays in the Economic and Social History of England in the Eighteenth Century* (Methuen 1979). The first chapter, 'British industrialization: unique or not?' contains the following passage:

> When social, political, administrative, legal, cultural, even the psychological and motivational characteristics of a society are seen to be integral influences upon the processes of economic growth (not just autonomous or dependent variables to that process) then the 'uniqueness' (or the probability of the 'uniqueness') of each national experience is much enhanced. Even the term 'economic growth' has given place to a more diffuse entity called 'modernization' and the search for an agreed set of variables, let alone a theory of their inter-relationships, is becoming more, rather than less, problematical. [p. 11]

(It is amusing to note the 'even' in 'even the psychological and motivational characteristics of a society' – as if these were the last factors to be taken into account.) The whole essay is important and extremely stimulating.

## Chapter 1    Prologue: Jacobean and Caroline political trends

1    The best introduction to the changes that led to the Civil War is Lawrence Stone's *The Causes of the English Revolution, 1529 – 1642* (Routledge & Kegan Paul 1972). For the 'masterless men', see *HWTUD*, ch. 3. For the circumstances of the aristocracy, see Lawrence Stone, *The Crisis of the Aristocracy, 1558 – 1641*, abridged ed. (Oxford University Press 1967). The least painful way of getting some understanding of the economic trends is through John Burnett's *A History of the Cost of Living* (Penguin 1969).

## Chapter 2    Denham's 'Cooper's Hill' and the constitution: a royalist viewpoint

1    See Brendan Ohehir, *Expans'd Hieroglyphicks: A Critical Edition of Sir John Denham's 'Coopers Hill'* (Berkeley: University of California Press 1969). Quotations are from this edition and I have drawn heavily on the critical commentary it contains. I have also made use of Earl R. Wasserman, *The Subtler Language* (Baltimore: Johns Hopkins Press 1959).

2   See Robert A. Aubin, *Topographical Poetry in XVIII-Century England* (New York: The Modern Language Association of America 1936), pp. 3 – 11.

3   For the symbolic and ritual significance of such houses, see Mark Girouard, *Life in the English Country House* (Yale University Press 1978).

4   For a detailed analysis of the metrics of this passage, see Wasserman.

5   Marvell's 'Upon Appleton House' is the most interesting of the later estate poems with political overtones. For a discussion of its political significance, see Christopher Hill, *Puritanism and Revolution* (Mercury Books 1962), pp. 353 – 9. The whole section on Marvell is of considerable interest.

### Chapter 3   Marvell and the constitution: a Parliamentarian viewpoint

1   *The Rehearsal Transpros'd and The Rehearsal Transpros'd, The Second Part*, ed. D. I. B. Smith (Oxford: Clarendon Press 1971), p. 135, ll. 2 – 14.

### Chapter 4   Liberty and order: the wider spectrum

1   See introduction to Sir Robert Filmer, *Patriarcha and Other Political Works*, ed. P. Laslett (Blackwell 1949), pp. 22 – 6. Page references to *Patriarcha* are to this edition. See also *LWWL* and Part Two below.

2   For an engaging description of the life of the country, see *ECK*. For the family in seventeenth-century life, see Part Two below.

3   Page references are to *Leviathan*, ed. G. B. Macpherson (Penguin 1968).

4   For a clear discussion of these ideas, see W. T. Stace, *Mysticism and Philosophy* (Macmillan 1961).

5   Quoted in *CP*, p. xi. This contains material not in Woodhouse's selection; references to and quotations from it are prefixed by the letters *CP*. All other references to the Putney Debates are to A. S. P. Woodhouse (ed.), *Puritanism and Liberty: Being the Army Debates (1647 – 9) from the Clarke Manuscripts*, 2nd ed. (Dent 1975). Clarke's shorthand notes have been expanded by the editors, hence the large amount of material inserted in square brackets. All this is in the original editions except for the material prefixed by the abbreviation 'i.e.'.

6   I have in this instance preferred *CP* to the text as edited by Woodhouse, pp. 120 – 1. The editorial abbreviations in Woodhouse, in my view, misinterpret the speech: Rainborough is urging Ireton to think in a new way, not accepting a concession that Ireton has not made.

7   In this account I have drawn heavily on Locke, *Two Treatises of Government*, ed. P. Laslett, 2nd ed. (Cambridge University Press 1967). References are to this edition.

**Chapter 5    Milton: the political pamphlets and *Paradise Lost***

1   References are to *The Works of John Milton*, vol. 5: *The Tenure of Kings and Magistrates*, ed. W. Haller (New York: Columbia University Press 1932).

2   References are to *The Works of John Milton*, vol. 6: *The Readie & Easie Way to Establish a Free Commonwealth*, ed. W. Haller (New York: Columbia University Press 1932).

3   Book and line references are to the arrangement of the second edition of *Paradise Lost*, which is usually followed by modern editors. The text used (with one exception, on p. 94) is that of Helen Darbishire, *The Poetical Works of John Milton* (Oxford: Clarendon Press 1952).

4   William Law, *The Grounds and Reasons of Christian Regeneration*, 6th ed. (1762), pp. 46 – 7.

5   William Law, *A Demonstration of the Gross and Fundamental Errors of a late Book called, 'A Plain Account of the Nature and End of the Sacrament of the Lord's Supper'*, 3rd rev. ed. (1752), p. 184.

**Chapter 6    Dryden: *Absalom and Achitophel* and the Popish Plot**

1   The text used for the Dryden quotations is that of *The Poems of John Dryden*, ed. J. Kinsley (4 vols., Oxford: Clarendon Press 1958).

**Chapter 7    The satirical aftermath: Dryden, Oldham, Shadwell and Settle**

1   Jonathan Swift, *A Tale of a Tub 1710*, facsimile, Scolar Press (n.d.), pp. 165 – 6.

**Chapter 9    The inheritance from the Middle Ages**

1   Much of the information in this paragraph is drawn from David Herlihy, 'Life expectation for women in medieval society', in R. T. Morewedge (ed.), *The Role of Woman in the Middle Ages* (New York University 1975), pp. 1 – 22.

2   Much of the information in this and following paragraphs comes from Eileen Power, *Medieval Women*, ed. M. M. Postan (Cambridge University Press 1975).

3   For an account of Christine de Pisan, see Power, and Charity C. Willard, 'A fifteenth-century view of woman's role in medieval society', in Morewedge.

**Chapter 10    Propagation and contraception in the seventeenth century**

1   *LWWL*, p. 92.

2   Gregory King's figures are reproduced in *LWWL*, p. 108. For a discussion of ageing, see *LFLIL*, pp. 174 – 213. Infestation by parasites and general conditions of hygiene are mentioned in both *SFSM* and *TRDM*. For infantile mortality rates, see *LWWL*, pp. 130 – 4. They appear to have been markedly higher in London, as they were in the following century; *GLLEC* records burials of children under two as 74.5 per cent of christenings during the 1730s.

3  *LFLIL*, p. 184. See also *SFSM*, pp. 55, 60.

4  For remarriage, see *LWWL*, pp. 102 – 5. For the nuclear family, see also *LFLIL*, pp. 12 – 49; Edward Shorter, *The Making of the Modern Family* (Fontana 1977), pp. 38 – 9; and (together with household size) *LWWL*, pp. 66 – 73.

5  *TRDM*, pp. 189, 635. For the statistical evidence, see *LWWL*, p. 107.

6  George Sinclair, *Satan's Invisible World Discovered (1685)*, facsimile introduced by C. O. Parsons (Gainsville, Fla. 1969), p. 235.

7  I am indebted to Roger Thompson, *Unfit for Modest Ears* (Macmillan 1979), p. 26, for the information about *The School of Venus*. It apparently mentioned three methods of contraception, the other two being interrupted coition and unsimultaneous orgasm; the latter, obviously ineffectual, was presumably based on the older physiological theory that the woman, like the man, deposited seed at the time of orgasm.

8  For the bastardy rates, see *LFLIL*, pp. 102 – 59. For a critique of some of Laslett's interpretations of earlier society, see 'A one-class society?', in *HCC*, pp. 205 – 18. For Laslett's reply, see *LWWL*, especially pp. 34 – 40, 171 – 5, 306 (n. 178).

9  See 'The dark corners of the land', in *HCC*, pp. 3 – 47; *TRDM*, pp. 159 – 73; *GLLEC*, pp. 305 – 6 (on Fleet marriages); *HWTUD*, p. 311 ('Elizabethan Familists divorced, as they married, by simple declaration before the congregation') and ch. 15, *passim*.

10 Quoted from John Aubrey, *Brief Lives*, vol. 1 (Oxford 1898), pp. 205 – 6, in Arthur H. Nethercot, *Sir William D'Avenant*, rev. ed. (New York: Russell and Russell 1967), p. 92.

**Chapter 11  Love, sex and attitudes to women in the poetry**

1  See Edward Shorter, *The Making of the Modern Family* (Fontana 1977), especially pp. 71 – 2, and his 'Illegitimacy, sexual revolution, and social change in modern Europe', in T. K. Rabb and R. I. Rotberg (eds.), *The Family in History: Interdisciplinary Essays* (New York: Harper & Row 1973), pp. 48 – 84.

2  See Rachel Trickett, *The Honest Muse: A Study in Augustan Verse* (Oxford University Press 1967), for the movement in Augustan culture towards factual truth.

3  I do not accept the interpretation of this poem, or of Rochester's general thought, that is advocated by David M. Vieth, the editor of the standard edition of Rochester's poems. For an alternative interpretation and a critique of one of the readings in Vieth's text of this poem, see K. F. Paulson, 'The Reverend Edward Stillingfleet and the "Epilogue" to Rochester's *A Satyr against Reason and Mankind*', in *Philological Quarterly*, no. 50 (1971), pp. 657 – 63.

**Chapter 12    The theory and practice of Protestant marriage**

1  For details of what constituted a binding contract, see Gellert Spencer Alleman, *Matrimonial Law and the Materials of Restoration Comedy* (Privately published, Wallington, Pa. 1942), especially pp. 5 – 14. In this chapter I have drawn heavily on *SPF, SFSM* and *TRDM*, as well as on John Halkett, *Milton and the Idea of Matrimony* (Yale University Press 1970), and the classic articles, W. Haller and M. Haller, 'The Puritan art of love', *HLQ*, no. 5 (1941 – 2), pp. 235 – 78, and W. Haller, 'Hail Wedded Love', *ELH*, vol. 13, no. 2 (1946), pp. 79 – 97.

2  Quoted in *TRDM*, p. 53.

3  *SPF*, p. 10.

4  Quoted in *SPF*, p. 23.

5  Quoted in *SPF*, p. 39, from Jeremy Taylor, *Holy Living* (1650), ch. 2, sect. 3, 2.

6  Quoted in *SPF*, p. 36, from Jeremy Taylor, *The Marriage Ring*, in *Illustrations of the Liturgy and Rituals of the United Church of England and Ireland*, ed. J. Brogden (1842), vol. 3, p. 139.

7  Walter Hilton, *The Ladder of Perfection*, trans. L. Sherley-Price (Penguin 1957), p. 122. The editor seems embarrassed by this assertion of Hilton's, but Hilton certainly meant what he said.

8  Quoted in *SPF*, p. 75. The passage is also quoted in *SFSM*.

9  Isaac Watts, *Divine Songs in Easy Language for the Use of Children*, quoted and discussed in *SFSM*, pp. 252 – 3, where it is related to attitudes to death and the inculcation of the fear of damnation in the Puritan and evangelical traditions. Watts's volume, one of the best-sellers of the late eighteenth century, provoked the indignation of Blake, who satirized it in *Songs of Innocence*: see Kathleen Raine, *Blake and Tradition* (Routledge & Kegan Paul 1969), vol. 1, pp. 30 – 3.

10  Quoted in *HMER*, p. 142, from A. Powell, *John Aubrey and his Friends* (Heinemann 1963), p. 278. The passage is also quoted in *SFSM*, p. 168 (see also pp. 159 – 78).

11  The passages are quoted in *ECK*, pp. 44 and 120.

12  I have stated what I believe to be Stone's more settled opinion, expressed, for instance, on pp. 180 – 1 (where Shakespearian romantic comedy tends to be discounted), on pp. 101 – 2, p. 5 and during most of the earlier part of the book. In the summary on pp. 193 – 4 the emphasis seems to move more in favour of affection.

13  For an account of Leveller women, see Patricia Higgins, 'The reactions of women, with special reference to women petitioners', in B. Manning (ed.), *Politics, Religion and the English Civil War* (Edward Arnold 1973), pp. 179 – 222.

14  See Halkett, pp. 73 – 82, for this controversy.

15 Quoted in Norman Cohn, *The Pursuit of the Millennium*, rev. ed. (Paladin 1970), p. 291. The revised edition has an extremely useful appendix of excerpts from documents by and about the Ranters. They are also treated with sympathy in *HMER*.

**Chapter 13  Milton: from tracts on divorce to *Paradise Lost***

1 References are to *The Works of John Milton*, vol. 3: *The Doctrine and Discipline of Divorce*, eds. C. L. Powell and F. A. Patterson (New York: Columbia University Press 1931).
2 *Paradise Lost and the Seventeenth Century Reader* (Chatto & Windus 1947).
3 See *HMER*, p. 379.
4 In this discussion I am indebted to Marcia Landy, 'Kinship and the role of women in *Paradise Lost*', *Milton Studies*, no. 4 (1972), pp. 3 – 18, and to the rather wild but shrewd and very funny article by Jackie Disalvo, 'Blake encountering Milton: politics and the family in *Paradise Lost* and *The Four Zoas*', in J. A. Wittreich, Jr (ed.), *Milton and the Line of Vision* (Madison, Wis.: University of Wisconsin Press 1976), pp. 143 – 84.
5 *The Works of Meister Eckhart*, trans. C. de B. Evans, vol. 2 (Watkins 1931), pp. 8 – 9.

**Chapter 14  'Imparadist in One Anothers Arms' or 'The Ecclesiastical Mousetrap': marriage in Restoration comedy**

1 *LWWL*, pp. 84 – 92.
2 For the Restoration repertoire, see Gunnar Sorelius, *The Giant Race Before the Flood* (Uppsala: Almqvist & Wiksell 1966).
3 For the audience of the Jacobean private houses, see Alfred Harbage, *Shakespeare and the Rival Traditions* (New York: Macmillan 1952), especially pp. 47 – 57.
4 See Harold Love, 'The myth of the Restoration audience', in *Komos*, no. 1 (1967), together with a reply by A. S. Bear, 'Criticism and social change: the case of Restoration drama', in *Komos*, no. 2 (1969), and a further rejoinder by Harold Love, 'Bear's case laid open: or, a timely warning to literary sociologists', *ibid.*
5 See Don Cameron Allen, 'Richard Lovelace: "The Grasse-Hopper" ', in Don Cameron Allen, *Image and Meaning* (Baltimore: Johns Hopkins Press 1960), reprinted in W. R. Keast (ed.), *Seventeenth-Century English Poetry: Modern Essays in Criticism* (New York: Oxford University Press 1962), pp. 280 – 9.
6 Quoted by F. J. Fisher in 'The growth of London', in E. W. Ives (ed.), *The English Revolution, 1600 – 1660* (Edward Arnold 1968), p. 84.

7   Just as Jack and Peter often meet in *A Tale of a Tub*, so the more zealous non-jurors on the extreme right of the Church of England often shared something of the moral outlook of the Puritans on the extreme left. William Law, another zealous non-juror in his earlier years and a graduate of Emmanuel College, Cambridge (an institution with a strong Puritan tradition), also launched a tract against the stage, *The Absolute Unlawfulness of Stage Entertainments Fully Demonstrated*, in 1726. In later life Law softened under the influence of Boehme.

8   Harriett Hawkins, *Likenesses of Truth in Elizabethan and Restoration Drama* (Oxford:Clarendon Press 1972). This book contains, in my opinion, the best criticism to date on Restoration comedy: I am particularly indebted to the author for her comments on *The Way of the World*.

### Chapter 15   Postscript: the flight of the butterflies

1   I am indebted to Mr R. Eddy for information about the link between Dr Cheyne and Pope.

2   Bernard Mandeville, *The Fable of the Bees*, ed. Phillip Harth Penguin 1970). *A Modest Defence of Publick Stews (1724)*, Augustan Reprint Society, no. 162 (Los Angeles: University of California 1973).

# Suggestions for further reading

## Historical and sociological

Any selection is bound to be arbitrary, given the amount of distinguished work that is being published. Most of the following books have been chosen as major seminal studies, or as very clear accounts of certain areas of knowledge, or as readable accounts of particular major events of interest.

John Carswell, *The Descent on England* (Barrie and Rockliff 1969). An exciting account of the logistics and political background to William III's invasion.

Norman Cohn, *The Pursuit of the Millennium*, rev. ed. (Paladin 1970). Starts with the eleventh century and earlier background; ends with an appendix on the Ranters.

Alan Everitt, *The Community of Kent and the Great Rebellion, 1640 – 60* (Leicester University Press 1966). Full of human interest; gives a real sense of the impact of events on individual people at the time.

Christopher Hill, *The World Turned Upside Down* (Penguin 1975). A fascinating survey of the revolutionary Sects and those on the edge of official society.

E. W. Ives (ed.), *The English Revolution, 1600 – 1660* (Edward Arnold 1968). Different articles introduce most of the main topics of seventeenth-century historical research.

John Kenyon, *The Popish Plot* (Heinemann 1972). Full and interesting.

Peter Laslett, *The World We Have Lost*, rev. ed. (Methuen 1971). A very good introduction to the sociological history of the period.

Levin L. Schücking, *The Puritan Family: A Social Study from the Literary Sources*, rev. ed. (Routledge & Kegan Paul 1969). The revised edition originally came out in 1964 and the first edition in 1929; the work has, in very minor ways, dated, but the survey of the literature is still of great value.

Lawrence Stone, *The Causes of the English Revolution, 1529 – 1642* (Routledge & Kegan Paul 1972). An extremely clear survey of what is known on the subject, and of the continuing scholarly disputes on it.

Lawrence Stone, *The Family, Sex and Marriage in England, 1500 – 1800* (Weidenfeld and Nicolson 1977). A massive book, recording virtually all that is known on the subject as well as arguing for a particular interpretation of the facts.

Keith Thomas, *Religion and the Decline of Magic* (Weidenfeld and Nicolson 1971). A fascinating account of folk magic, witchcraft, astrology, and sturdy scepticism among the people, and the interaction with official religion.

**Literature**

Selection here is even more difficult than among the historical works. Writers like Milton have attracted a vast critical literature, some of which consists in excellent but specialized studies like F. T. Prince, *The Italian Element in Milton's Verse* (Oxford University Press 1954), or Christopher Ricks, *Milton's Grand Style* (Oxford University Press 1963), which are distant from the subject of this book; while others are more general but have a polemical edge to them, like the criticism of C. S. Lewis or the critical biography by Christopher Hill. Similarly, most of the criticism of Restoration comedy is based on false premises and therefore ingenious but invalid. The very short selection given below, therefore, contains works which link writers with the thought of the age or stimulating selections of articles, and only one of the books is a straightforward, single critical work.

Phillip Harth, *Contexts of Dryden's Thought* (University of Chicago Press 1968). Authoritative on the ideas, especially the religious ideas, in Dryden.

Harriett Hawkins, *Likenesses of Truth in Elizabethan and Restoration Drama* (Oxford: Clarendon Press 1972). Excellent sense of theatre; pragmatic investigation not dogmatic classification.

W. R. Keast (ed.), *Seventeenth Century English Poetry: Modern Essays in Criticism* (New York: Oxford University Press 1962). Wide range of articles.

Harold Love (ed.), *Restoration Literature: Critical Approaches* (Methuen 1972). Lively selection of articles.

William A. McClung, *The Country House in English Renaissance Poetry* (University of California Press 1977). Illustrated; contains information on the houses as well as the poems.

John M. Wallace, *Destiny his Choice: The Loyalism of Andrew Marvell* (Cambridge University Press 1968). Very perceptive linking with the thought in the political pamphlets of the time.

Anyone trying, for the first time, to unravel the complexities of Miltonic criticism might perhaps follow C. S. Lewis's *A Preface to Paradise Lost* (Oxford University Press 1942) with Christopher Hill's *Milton and the English Revolution* (Faber 1977).

# Index